Praise for *The Way o*

I have long dreamt of bottling Kerry's words so others could benefit from her marvelous mind and mentorship, just as Moriah and I have. I can now truly say, "Dream Realized!" *The Way of Becoming* is a beautiful work that does just that. Consider her insights "bottled" and ready for the drinking.
JOEL SMALLBONE, 4x Grammy Award Winning Artist, For KING + COUNTRY, Actor, Director, *Unsung Hero*

Kerry's ability to communicate through writing, speaking, and interacting with people from all walks of life is a generational gift to the world. Her boldness to live out her faith no matter the season or environment has been one of the greatest encouragements of the 20+ years I've known her. It gives me great joy knowing *The Way of Becoming* will impact people across the globe just as it has impacted me. Kerry is one of the strongest, most enduring humans I have ever known, and if I had even an ounce of her endurance, I would win every race on the planet."
SALLY MCRAE, Professional Ultra-Mountain Runner, Speaker, Podcaster, and Author, *Choose Strong*

It's rare to find an individual who combines spectacularly sharp intellect with a beautifully softened heart. Kerry is one of those rarities. *The Way of Becoming* is simply brilliant! Its brilliance stems not from Kerry's exceptional talent but from what God carried her through and revealed to her. The candid narrative, the divine teachings, and the profound tools of encouragement are a must-read for a generation stuck on their journey toward the Divine.
MARK STUART, 2x Grammy Award Winning Artist, Audio Adrenaline, Author, *Losing My Voice to Find It*

What Kerry created in *The Way of Becoming* is based on Scripture, yet it is outside any particular church denomination. She wants to give people what God has given her so they, too, can grow and get unstuck by applying these soul-care tools to their lives; I certainly have.
MELODEE DEVEVO, Singer and Violinist, Grammy Award Winner, Casting Crowns

Kerry has always been an engaging storyteller and a fantastic public speaker, but this book shows she is an equally great writer, which is rare. What sets Kerry apart most, however, is how her stories and insights consistently change people for the better.

DR. MARTY MAKARY, Surgeon, Public Policy Expert, and 3x *New York Times* Bestselling Author, *Unaccountable, The Price We Pay, Mama Maggie,* and *Blind Spots*

Kerry Hasenbalg is a spiritual pioneer in the contemporary world. Through her compelling testimony, *The Way of Becoming* reveals how each of us can communicate with our Creator—24/7—and that nothing is beyond His eternal care and powerful reach.

BENTLY T. ELLIOTT, Director of Speechwriting for President Ronald Reagan

Kerry has gone against the grain of culture to craft the art of soul-sorting for leaders. With the tools from *The Way of Becoming*, I can guide my career and colleagues with a sound mind and open heart. I'm so thankful her research is finally in sharable form so I can gift the gold in these pages to those I love most.

MORIAH SMALLBONE, MŌRIAH, Artist, Actress, and Producer

Kerry's writing is wonderful, and her heart so deep. Of course, they go together. Her analysis reveals the opportunity for a new life to take root—a contemplative life, a life of intentionally practicing the presence of God, which is indeed the beauty for ashes.

HYATT MOORE, Former CEO, Wycliffe Bible Translators, Fine Painter, and Author, *The Rear View Mirror*

Kerry's tools have helped me connect my faith with my background as a psychologist. Just one afternoon of using the tools during a personal crisis saved me hours of therapy. *The Way of Becoming* is a gift that can help transform you if you are ready to dive in and do the work.

DR. KATHY ZAKARIAN, Licensed Clinical Psychologist, 20+ years in college counseling.

When I heard Kerry speak at a women's retreat, God's presence was palpable. Kerry's unique voice weaves together her experiences of miracles and pain, telling God's timeless story and creating space for others to encounter God's presence. In a world of bookshelves filled with Christian self-help and intellectual depictions of who God is and what He wants, *The Way of Becoming* will wash over readers like cleansing water. It vibrates with tested authenticity and offers a simple, freeing framework for *how* to meet God in our broken places and build wholeness-growing lives.

LYDIA VOGT, Strategy and Execution Senior Lead, International Justice Mission

This beautiful and eminently practical book, *The Way of Becoming*, is a treasure. Kerry writes with the urgency, sensitivity, and clarity of a heart undone by the deep things of God. She's a true friend of Jesus, and her words speak of a lifetime spent cultivating His presence and walking in His love and wisdom.

AKHTAR SHAH AND SARAH BELCHER, The Foundry, Kingdom Embassy, UK

I am so grateful that Kerry published her book, *The Way of Becoming*, a profound guide for navigating life's darkest valleys. Each page echoes the assurance that God's presence is woven into every trial, and His promises remain unshaken. With raw honesty and vulnerability, Kerry invites us into her personal journey. Her words inspire, equip, and embolden others to rise with renewed faith and purpose. Even in Kerry's darkest times, she was a light in my life, always willing to lend a hand to those in need.

JEANNE CELESTINE LAKIN, Human Rights Advocate and Author of *A Voice in the Darkness: A Memoire of a Rwandan Genocide Survivor*

One of the biggest gifts is the gift of Kerry, and her ability to speak life into leaders. She has an anointing to understand deep biblical and theological truths and communicate them in a way that unites people to build a common mission and vision.

BRITTANY DUNN, COO, Safe House Project and coauthor, *Eradicating Human Trafficking*

Kerry weaves a tapestry of the transcendent faithfulness of our Abba Father in the ordinary sufferings and joys of life, inviting the reader to make prayer a continual conversation.

PRESTON ATKINSON, Senior Pastor, Sunbury Bible Church

The Way of Becoming is about pursuing God. That pursuit molds and shapes us as we lean into Him and His Word. It reminds us that God is interested in every aspect of our lives. All we must do is invite Him in, and He will join us on our life's journey. This book enriched my soul.

SHAREN FORD, PhD, Director, Foster Care and Adoption, Focus on the Family

After sitting under Kerry's teaching at two retreats, I wondered, "How could the table be set for such a feast on God's Word? How can I have this every day?" As I began to read *The Way of Becoming*, I started in the chapter called "Imagine," and straightaway, that same feast of spirit and wonder rose before my eyes, and the Lord filled my heart with joy and gratitude. The sanctified imagination is a life raft when life is swirling, a tool in parenting, a refuge in the storm—we can be assured that His plans are beyond what we could ask or imagine. So, we imagine daringly and beautifully and enjoy Jesus in every season.

MANDII ERWIN, mother of three and wife to Andy Erwin, Kingdom Story Company

As a relational therapist, I engage in the unresolved hurts people bring into my office. The tools in *The Way of Becoming* are compatible with any age, intellect, denomination, ethnicity, and spiritual maturity, offering daily practices to bring people into God's design for wholeness, purpose, and freedom in Christ.

LORI SANNER, LPC, Marriage and Family Counselor

Kerry puts words and testimony to the beliefs we hold on to but don't know how to access. She gives us a road map out of despair and into tremendous hope.

DR. ERICA MCELROY, ER Physician, Founder, Hava Foundation and Casa Materna Atitlán

No matter who we are or what we have become, we all have areas of our lives in the process of becoming. Having had the chance to glean from Kerry's soul-care teachings, we were inspired, both personally and in our marriage, to press deeper into Jesus and advocacy for the vulnerable.

LEXI AND J.T. REALMUTO, All-Star Catcher, Major League Baseball

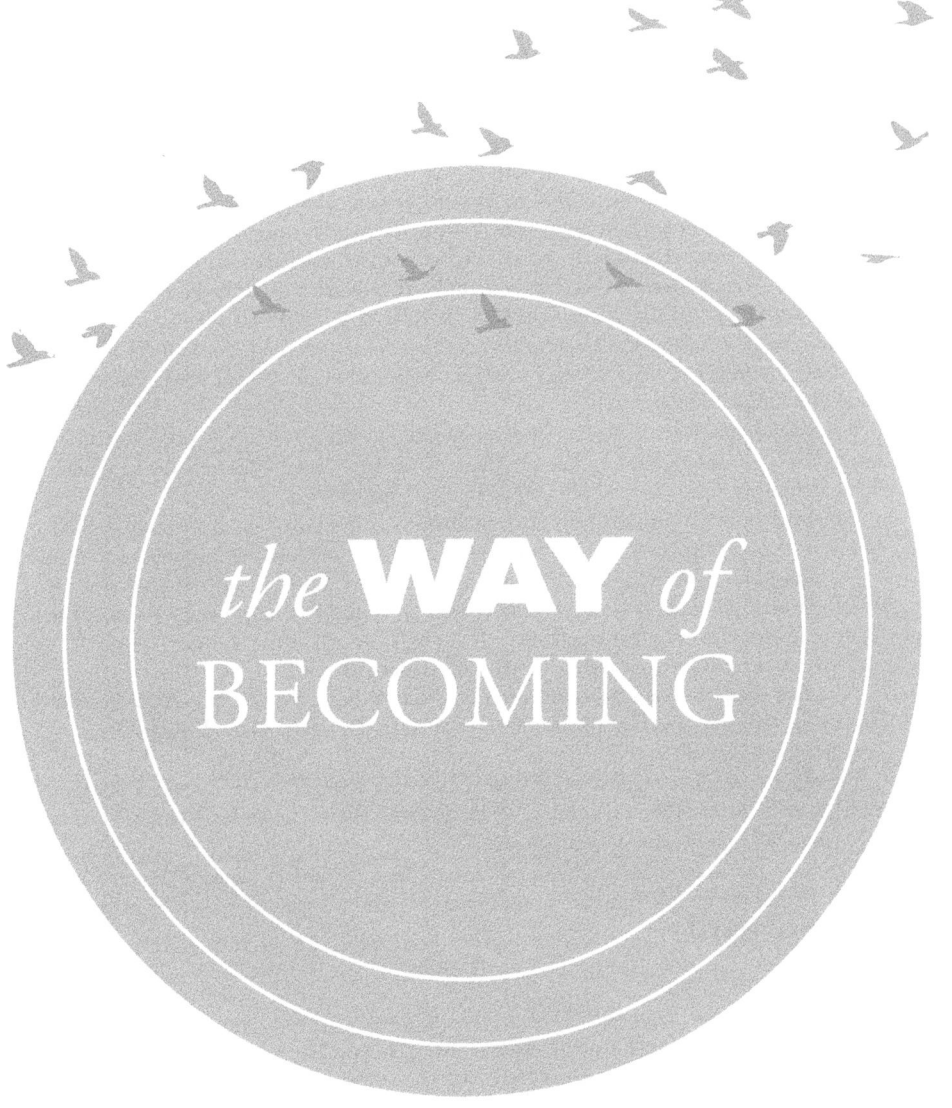

the **WAY** of BECOMING

12 PRACTICES FOR A THRIVING SOUL

KERRY HASENBALG

© 2025 by
KERRY HASENBALG

All rights reserved. No part of this publication may be reproduced, distributed, or transmitted in any form or by any means, including photocopying, recording, or other electronic or mechanical methods, without the prior written permission of the publisher, except in the case of brief quotations embodied in critical reviews and certain other commercial uses permitted by copyright law. For permission requisitions, write to the publisher, addressed "Attention: Permissions Coordinator," at the address below or email permission@thebecomingacademy.com.

All Scripture quotations, unless otherwise indicated, are taken from the Holy Bible, New International Version®, NIV®. Copyright ©1973, 1978, 1984, 2011 by Biblica, Inc.™ Used by permission of Zondervan. All rights reserved worldwide. www.zondervan.com The "NIV" and "New International Version" are trademarks registered in the United States Patent and Trademark Office by Biblica, Inc.™

Scripture quotations marked (NLT) are taken from the *Holy Bible*, New Living Translation, copyright ©1996, 2004, 2015 by Tyndale House Foundation. Used by permission of Tyndale House Publishers, Carol Stream, Illinois 60188. All rights reserved.

Scripture quotations marked (ESV) are from the ESV® Bible (The Holy Bible, English Standard Version®), © 2001 by Crossway, a publishing ministry of Good News Publishers. Used by permission. All rights reserved. The ESV text may not be quoted in any publication made available to the public by a Creative Commons license. The ESV may not be translated in whole or in part into any other language.

Scripture marked (KJV) is taken from the King James Version.

Scripture cited The Message taken from *The Message*, copyright © 1993, 2002, 2018 by Eugene H. Peterson. Used by permission of NavPress. All rights reserved. Represented by Tyndale House Publishers.

Scripture quotations marked (NASB) taken from the (NASB®) New American Standard Bible®, Copyright © 1960, 1971, 1977, 1995, 2020 by The Lockman Foundation. Used by permission. All rights reserved. lockman.org

Scripture quotations marked (ISV) are taken from the International Standard Version, Copyright© 1995-2014 by ISV Foundation. All rights reserved internationally. Used by permission of Davidson Press, LLC.

Cover design: Mark Ford
Interior design: Brandi Davis
Cover and interior art: Samantha Frolich, Georgine Patt, and Logan Stephens
Author photo credit: Annika Hasenbalg and Maya Hasenbalg

First printing edition: 2025

Hardcover ISBN: 978-1-7365469-4-9
Paperback ISBN: 978-1-7365469-5-6

Blue House Books
PO Box 205
Riverside, PA 17868

Printed in the United States of America

info@thebecomingacademy.com
www.kerryhasenbalg.com

For the glory of our heavenly Father and His Son, Jesus, who is *The Way*, and in recognition of the eternal lives of Billy Marks and Isabella Hasenbalg, I dedicate this work to all who embark upon *The Way of Becoming*. May you discover your *unique* story in the *all* story of God.

DIVINE DIALOGUE
Reconciliation with God

Believe
Remember
Ask
Imagine

DIVINE EXCHANGE
Reconciliation within

Trust
Redeem
Stand
Praise

DIVINE CORRESPONDENCE
Reconciliation with Others

Anoint
Create
Assemble
Abide

CONTENTS

Foreword — 11
Introduction — 13

PART 1: DIVINE DIALOGUE

1. Believe: *Confident Beliefs and Struggles of Unbelief* — 19
2. Remember: *God Encounters and Stones of Help* — 37
3. Ask: *Questions and Requests* — 59
4. Imagine: *Visions and Promises* — 83

PART 2: DIVINE EXCHANGE

5. Trust: *Broken and Incomplete Parts* — 111
6. Redeem: *Fears and Sins* — 133
7. Stand: *Storms and Trials* — 155
8. Praise: *High Notes and Low Notes* — 175

PART 3: DIVINE CORRESPONDENCE

9. Anoint: *Gifts and Healing* — 197
10. Create: *Work and Worship* — 221
11. Assemble: *Integrating Parts and People* — 245
12. Abide: *Sacred Rhythms and Cycles of Grace* — 267

The Art of Practicing — 295
Afterword — 305
Acknowledgments — 307
Notes — 309

FOREWORD

Where do I begin talking about perhaps the kindest and most loving friend and Jesus follower I have ever known? I'm so glad you are reading this book, as you will get to experience this wonderful woman and the powerful teaching of BECOMING for yourself . . .

I first met Kerry and her husband, Scott, over the phone in 2018, and they have been a source of wisdom and encouragement ever since. I met Kerry in person soon after at the Kingdom Bound music festival, where I invited her to join me in prayer before I took the stage for my set. She became an instant soul sister.

The first time I was able to experience some of the practices from *The Way of Becoming* was during a private retreat in 2019 when we spent a few days with the Hasenbalgs at Smith Mountain Lake. My husband and I had some soul-searching questions that we wanted to "hang on the line" before God (you'll understand this reference soon!). We wanted to be mentored by Kerry and Scott and to seek God's wisdom together, especially regarding whether or not we should try for another baby after multiple miscarriages. God spoke powerfully through our time with them, and two years later, our little son, River, was born. We can't imagine life without him, and his presence is a daily reminder of the blessing that came, in part because of their faith-filled advice! Kerry and Scott have been a tremendous blessing, and the BECOMING principles have been used over and over again in our lives.

Another natural point of connection I have with Kerry is how she sees profound messages from God, speaking to His children who have ears to hear, all through creation. I perceive God's faithfulness when I look at the moon and hear a call to trust Him when I see birds flying. I've had many experiences and soft words spoken to my heart like this in my journey with Jesus. Kerry also hears God speaking through countless aspects of nature, and she teaches others how to do the same.

With each BECOMING retreat I attended, I experienced God speaking to me in fresh ways through the deep biblical truth you are about to encounter. I am thrilled that the practices and tools I have experienced in workshops and soul-care sessions with Kerry are now embodied in this book, *The Way of Becoming*, so everyone can benefit from her wisdom and guidance anytime, no matter where they are on their journey.

Ultimately, Kerry believes in the power of our stories and that our callings come out of the gifts we've been given and saying yes to Jesus when He crosses our path. Whether it's across the street with a neighbor, among the poor, with your child, or somewhere across the sea, our mission field is ever before us. This book is an invitation to live out our faith more authentically by asking our questions and seeking God for answers, to hear and see Him more clearly, and to build a solid relationship with Jesus so that we not only survive life's storms but so that our souls can thrive on that other side of them.

I highly recommend *The Way of Becoming* to all because I know this friend and soul sister of mine. I know your life will be blessed by the truth you read within these pages and by experiencing the heart and story of a great woman of God.

Together with you in the journey of BECOMING,
your sister in Christ,

REBECCA ST. JAMES
Recording artist and author

INTRODUCTION

When a series of overlapping "hurricanes" hit my family, and some of the worst things I could ever imagine happening began unfolding in my life, I became desperate for tools to mend my broken heart and find my way back to wholeness.

As our lives fell apart, well-intentioned people tried to comfort and encourage us, using words like *hope, trust, believe,* and *pray.* But those words rang hollow in the chasm of our pain, and I questioned whether we would ever flourish again. My need to know *how to* put these lofty ideals of faith into practice became vital as the possibility of perpetual ruin was hitting too close to home.

I cried out to God with all the strength I had left and asked Him many questions. In response, the Spirit began to reveal to me, piece by piece, a series of twelve "tools" that would create a scaffolding for rebuilding my belief system and renewing my faith. As I applied these tools to my life, I was led moment by moment out of the darkness and despair and into greater light and hope. I slowly rediscovered the life and power that can only flow into us when we walk in daily communion with our Maker.

Josephus, the most notable of Jewish historians, said that Moses led the children of Israel through *their* wilderness times by raising their minds upward to *contemplate* God and His creation of the world in order to show that God comprised perfect virtue and that people ought to strive after the participate of it.¹ That was the way through the wilderness then, and it is still the way for us today. That is, with the addition of one critical thing, today, because of Jesus, we can access the power of God's Spirit from the inside out. "This is what the LORD says: 'Stand at the crossroads and look; ask for the ancient paths, ask where the good way is, and walk in it, and you will find rest for your souls." (Jeremiah 6:16).

THE WAY OF BECOMING is a collection of stories bathed in Scripture and written as an invitation and a guide to lead you farther along the ancient paths of the Christian faith, to take you from despair and deprivation to hope and abundance. Its twelve faith practices will show you *how* to experience a deeper, more intimate relationship with God and recognize His empowering presence in *your* story.

The purpose of sharing my stories is not so you will become a spectator in my life but an explorer in your own. Along the way, I will show you where God's divine storyline intersected with mine and the practical tools I used to access His grace in the areas of my greatest need. Using these tools will make God's Word come alive in your reality just as it has come alive in mine. I encourage you to search for parallel truths in your experiences and consider their connections to God's promises. You will learn how to apply each faith practice to your trying circumstances, your soul's condition, and the complexities of your relationships.

On a practical note, you will find that the stories in each chapter are not ordered chronologically. God's ways of teaching are not linear in the way we might think—sometimes He shows us things cyclically, and other times, it is only in retrospect that His handwriting within our life's stories takes on new light and clarity. Each chapter's stories are organized according to the tool being illustrated. Timing and sequence are less relevant than the underlying principles contained in the tools. The book is divided into three parts, Divine Dialogue, Divine Exchange, and Divine Correspondence, each addressing different aspects of spiritual reconciliation: with God, within oneself, and with other people, and are based on the ministries of the Father, Son, and Holy Spirit.

Introduction

As you walk in *The Way of Becoming* and invite the Spirit's gap-filling grace into your broken places, you will become acquainted with various aspects of God's character. Through this process, you will become transformed by each divine attribute according to His Name as *Yahweh*, the Becoming One, the One Who causes you to become.[2]

BECOMING more like the Lord in virtue and wholeness is not something that happens all at once; instead, it is a progressive matter, taking place as we seek and encounter God's presence in the context of our *neediness of the now*. Perhaps you need to find your way back to wholeness after being broken or fight fear because what you feared most has come to pass. Maybe you seek to silence the voices that steal your inner peace or long to hear God speak, but in the silence, you wonder if God still speaks at all. I assure you that the Lord has seen you in your places of need. He has not forgotten you, and He has much He wants to speak. I invite you to make space in your life to enter deeply into the Divine Dialogue and continue to walk along the ancient paths.

As an active participant in this faith exploration, you will experience movement that will take you from being transfixed by fear to BECOMING transformed by grace. You will go from wondering to discovering, needing to believing, hoping to receiving, imagining to creating, and on to greater flourishing. At the end of each chapter, there is a section called *YOUR BECOMING STORY*, inviting you to practice each tool in the context of your life. Through these relational practices, you will be guided in BECOMING all God uniquely created and redeemed you to be. I pray your experience will be one of greater believing, belonging, and BECOMING in Christ as you travel along *THE WAY*.

"As all of us reflect the glory of the Lord with unveiled faces, we are becoming more like Him with ever-increasing glory by the Lord's Spirit" (2 Corinthians 3:18 ISV).

PART 1

DIVINE DIALOGUE

1

BELIEVE

Confident Beliefs and Struggles of Unbelief

In 2004, I was transitioning out of my job in Washington, DC, where I worked with members of Congress from both sides of the political aisle to improve systems affecting orphans and vulnerable children. At the time, I was helping select finalists for the Congressional Foster Youth Internship Program. We created this program so talented young adults who had grown up in foster care could serve as congressional interns on Capitol Hill, expanding their own horizons and sharing their lived experiences with lawmakers to help inform policy. After combing through dozens of applications for the program, I was overcome by the story of a young man named Adier.

GOD SEES THE INVISIBLE

Adier had come to the US as one of the survivors of the Sudanese Genocide—part of a group of young refugees known as the "Lost Boys"—and had spent the remainder of his childhood in foster care. His written account of his life was profound and compelling; he was a great communicator with the heart to make a difference. Once my team and I had a chance to affirm his selection, I phoned to tell him the good news.

I was confused, however, by Adier's lackluster response to my congratulatory call. His application indicated a sincere desire to receive this competitive congressional internship. I knew this experience could be life-changing for him, but he did not seem excited.

"You don't seem pleased," I said. "May I ask why?"

"I'm sorry," he replied and then explained how, after many years of hoping and searching for his birth parents in Africa, he had just learned that his father was still alive and living across the Sudanese border in Uganda. All he could think about now was finding a way to reunite with the father whom he had long feared dead. I understood his predicament and offered Adier more time to consider the internship. As I hung up, I prayed for God to make a way for Adier to reunite with his family *and* still participate in this rare internship opportunity.

A few weeks later, I was invited to help organize a trip to Uganda with Scott for the founders of Show Hope, Christian music artist Steven Curtis Chapman, and his wife, Mary Beth. Scott was Show Hope's executive director, and the purpose of the trip was to minister to families in that region, where tens of thousands of children had been kidnapped and forced to become child soldiers. Our goal was to help communicate the needs and struggles of these children to those who could help alleviate their suffering. I had led two congressional trips to that same area only a year earlier, so I was familiar with the setting and players necessary to make the trip successful on the ground.

Before I agreed to organize and help lead the trip, I sought to secure separate funding and permission to take Adier with us so he could reunite with his father. These needs were met miraculously and with incredible speed. Before we had even stepped foot on African soil, I was dreaming with God about what it might look like for a parent to reunite with their lost child after mourning their death.

God indeed blessed me with the privilege of witnessing the reunion of Adier and his father, who had been separated for over a decade. It remains one of the most moving things I have ever seen. As soon as Adier's father saw him, he raised his hands high in the air and proclaimed in Arabic for all to hear: "Only God sees what's invisible, but today, the Lord has granted me the grace to see the invisible—my son alive!" I was thankful my bilingual friend, Vicky Bentley, was standing beside me so she could translate the father's words. He embraced his son, his own resurrected hope now standing before him. Beyond a doubt, I believed that God had done this miracle; I had been an eyewitness to the glory of this father's fulfilled hope in the resurrection of his lost child.

Yet, all too soon, this would become the very miracle I would need to believe could be done for me one day.

"LORD, I BELIEVE; HELP MY UNBELIEF."

When we began planning this trip to Uganda, we didn't know that I would be pregnant with my second child when the trip took place. I was approximately fifteen weeks along when we arrived on Ugandan soil. I am not sure I will ever know whether or not I should have gone on that trip, but I went. Within only a few days of beholding the miracle of the reunification of Adier and his father, I fell ill and remained so even after we arrived back in the States. The illness I contracted in Africa made me violently sick and caused my water to break too soon. By the time I got home, the miscarrying process was already underway.

> I struggled to understand and reconcile these things with what I already believed about God.

I found my soul torn between two different kinds of belief. Because of what I had witnessed with Adier and his father, I believed God could restore and resurrect what was lost. But now, I also longed to believe He would do this someday for the little girl I was losing. I knew the Lord had sustained Adier all those years and had even used the painful separation to bring about another kind of good in his life. Now, I longed to believe God could use my painful separation from my daughter for good in my life. I wanted to believe that God would comfort me in my sorrow, heal my broken heart, and help me know she was safe with Him. Was I to blame? Would I heal? I struggled to understand and reconcile these things with what I already believed about God.

In the gospel of Mark, I found Scriptures addressing my heart's most pressing question: *How much faith do I need to access God's power in my current pain?* The reunion of Adier and his father served as a seed of hope for me—the hope of wholeness and a potential future reunion in glory. In Mark, chapter 9, we find two stories, set side by side, which speak to the incredible tension between what we have come to believe already about God and what we still struggle to believe amid our brokenness and pain.

A Father and a Son

Both stories are about a father and a son. One depicts a parent and child enjoying their longed-for wholeness and glorious destiny. The other tells the story of a parent and child in profound brokenness, desperately longing for God's help and healing. In the first story, we see Jesus, who, having just been transfigured on the high mount by His heavenly Father, is glowing with light, and His clothes have become dazzling white. His heavenly Father declares, "This is my Son, whom I love. Listen to him!" (Mark 9:7). Next, we meet another father and son in the valley below that mountain. Out of desperation, this father sought the healing of his mute son.

The juxtaposition of these two narratives invites us to consider the relationship between them. The heavenly Father on the mountaintop is calling to all who would listen to hear the words of His Son, Jesus, while the father in the valley is deeply suffering because no one, not even he, can hear his own son speak any words at all. One represents the joy that comes from being made complete in the presence of God and raised to the redemptive mountaintops of life. In contrast, the other describes the deep sorrow and desperation felt in the valleys of life's brokenness.

The boy's father came to Jesus' disciples for help because of what he had heard about Jesus. But the father's hope suffered a crushing blow when the disciples could not heal his mute son. We all know how it feels to seek something that does not come to pass. However, when Jesus descended the mountain, and the father of the mute boy saw the Lord with his own eyes, hope rose in him again. The glory-filled presence of Jesus caused this hurting father to believe what could be possible. But surely the question remained in his heart: *Will Jesus do this for me?* The father mustered enough faith to humbly ask Jesus, "If you can do anything, take pity on us and help us" (Mark 9:22).

This father, who believed Jesus *could* do anything, wanted to know if Jesus *would* do this impossible thing for him and his son, so he asked for it by faith. It is precisely in the asking where faith is found. The King James Bible defines faith in Hebrews 11:1, saying, "Now, faith is the substance of things hoped for and the evidence of things not yet seen."

Next, Jesus responds to the father of the mute boy, "What do you mean, 'If I can'?" Jesus asked. "Anything is possible if a person believes" (Mark 9:23 NLT). Here, we see Jesus, the Son of God, issuing one of those lofty religious promises that people often use to encourage someone suffering. But through the response of the boy's father, we find a simple yet profound way to access the extraordinary power of God's grace. He said, "I do believe; help me overcome my unbelief" (Mark 9:24). In these words, we find the answer to what our hearts most need to know: *the way to go about believing so that the impossible becomes possible for us.* From this father, I learned that in my own valley of despair, I, too, must begin the healing process with a heart willing to admit, "Lord, I do believe; help my unbelief."

Much of life is lived in the tension between the marred and the beautiful, the broken and whole, the good and evil, the truth and lies. In these liminal spaces, understanding how to apply faith is vital if we are to emerge on the other side of trials with a sound mind, stable emotions, and the capacity to do good.

Regardless of our struggles believing, we are meant to step out in the kind of honest faith that the mute boy's father expressed as he sought his son's healing. Our faith cannot be based on something dishonest or pretend. God knows our hearts and whether or not our words match what is in them. We don't need to claim that all our beliefs are confident or deny that our hopes have been repeatedly deferred.

Keep Seeking

Proverbs 13:12 reminds us why it is crucial to keep seeking the Lord, even while we struggle to hope and believe: "Hope deferred makes the heart sick, but a longing fulfilled is a tree of life." God longs for us to seek Him diligently and share our hearts authentically because, in time, newness in life is promised to come. Our hearts may say, "Lord, I believe some things, but I am struggling to believe other things; help me overcome my unbelief." Or perhaps, "I can believe these things for another person, but I struggle to believe that they could be true for me; Lord help me believe them for myself."

Just like a garden has a variety of plants, each at a different stage of growth, our souls have beliefs all at various stages of their development. Some of our beliefs have grown strong and proven sustainable no matter how intense the storm is. In contrast, others are still small or weak, perhaps only in their vulnerable seedling form. Every word of God's truth is like a new seed we must receive for ourselves. It must become planted in our hearts so it can grow over time as we diligently seek His provision for its maturing. Earnestly seeking more of God causes our beliefs to go from seedlings to maturity. In our difficult seasons, the promise of Hebrews 11:6 beckons: "Without faith, it is impossible to please God, because anyone who comes to him must believe that he exists and rewards those who earnestly seek him."

Psalm 105:4 encourages us to "look to the Lord and his strength; seek his face always" because there is always more for those who continue to seek His presence. The very nature of belief is progressive and is intended to be built up, one experience at a time, throughout our lives. We will always need to overcome areas of unbelief because of the variety of our struggles and the layered nature of our backgrounds. Thankfully, God's nature is infinite, and His grace can complete and integrate every belief within us as we continue to seek after Him. It is by expressing our struggles of unbelief and applying the tools of faith that our belief systems become formed and firm and our souls can experience freedom from fear no matter what we are facing. Thus, in hope and by faith, we named the little girl we lost Malaya Grace, meaning "freedom in the presence of God."

Although this experience marked the beginning of a longer journey of tribulation, God would also use these years to reveal twelve tools of faith to me that would carry me through all of my trials and bring me increasing freedom in the presence of God. These tools have helped answer my heart's most profound questions, replace lies I believed with truth, and allow me to become more of who I was created and redeemed to be. Each tool has been like a key, opening a different door to the Lord's empowering presence. They have helped me more fully understand what Jesus promised in Matthew 16:19, when He said, "I will give you the keys of the kingdom of heaven; whatever you bind on earth will be bound in heaven, and whatever you loose on earth will be loosed in heaven."

THE JOURNEY

I wish I could say that after that heartache and loss, we were set back on our feet to resume life as usual. Instead, my husband, Scott, and I experienced a series of consecutive trials that rolled over us like overlapping hurricanes. We would start to recover, only to get knocked down again. This challenging season had left us feeling unbecoming, unsafe in relationships, and unusable in ministry. The biblical concepts of faith and belief I had long held close suddenly felt obscure and far off instead of real and practical. Spiritual words meant to encourage us seemed almost patronizing as we worried our current condition might become our forever.

We struggled to trust people and God, particularly in the harder-hit areas of our lives. To cope, we tried to close off the messier, more vulnerable parts to make them less open to public viewing and judgment. It worked for a time. But as the brokenness grew with each consecutive storm, it became increasingly difficult to keep the wounded parts separated from the more beautiful parts. The bad began to bleed into the good.

After losing our daughter, Malaya Grace, I would become pregnant six more times over twelve years, but I would lose three more of those babies. Over those same years, my husband traveled about half the time with Show Hope. One year, he traveled to more than ninety cities as part of two Christian music concert tours. I was bearing most of the weight of managing our household while dipping in and out of my own unseen periods of grief. Mostly, I tried to pull myself up by my bootstraps for the sake of our children, whom I was homeschooling or nursing.

Both Proverbs 8:29 and Job 38:10–11 express how God sets the boundaries in His creation. They say that He places limits on the ocean's waters so as not to overstep His command. Just as the Lord says to the sea, "This far you may come and no farther," God also sets up boundary markers for His children so we will not wander too far and cause harm to ourselves or others. God had brought Scott and me to a complete stop, saying, "This far you may come, and no farther!"

Although what happened next was not the most painful of trials, it was the exclamation point or final straw. I had struggled with ice-pick headaches for years, so I went to the doctor for some medical tests. Although they could not determine the precise cause of my headaches, the MRIs revealed something completely unexpected: the presence of two tumors on the meninges of my brain. This news brought Scott and me to the end of our self-sufficiency and feeble attempts to manage all our brokenness, as these overlapping storms had touched practically every part of our lives.

It would take time to understand how to walk step by step through each of the challenges. But it was squarely in that season, marked by uncertainty, that I would learn how to access God's reassuring and strengthening presence. I clung to God's promise in Isaiah 41:10: "Do not fear, for I am with you; do not be dismayed, for I am your God. I will strengthen you and help you; I will uphold you with my righteous right hand." Seasons of suffering are precisely when we need to hold on to hope the most and when the things of faith need to become tangible enough to grasp in the darkness. Engaging with God by faith would enable me to keep walking even when my human knees felt ready to buckle.

THE VISION

Despite these sufferings, God graciously gave us four wonderful children to raise. Each has been a constant reminder of the goodness of God and the blessings that exist alongside the hard parts of life. As a mother of four, I rarely had time alone. I can hardly remember going to the bathroom when my children were young without one of them following me. But now and again, when I stumbled upon a rare instance of solitude, I would use one of these miracle moments to contemplate deeper things. On one of these quiet occasions, God gave me a vision while looking out the back windows of my house at my half-acre plot of land.

As I gazed at our backyard, I suddenly seemed to be looking upon a field of broken glass fragments and pottery shards scattered across my yard, blanketing some sections of it entirely. These pieces were all different colors, shapes, and sizes. Some of the pieces looked very sharp. Others appeared smooth, more like sea glass. But the sheer amount of them was clearly hindering anything from growing up from the ground underneath. This vision profoundly affected me and helped me understand why I felt so stuck.

Broken Glass

As I considered the vision of broken glass pieces strewn upon my land, my soul's "inner librarian" brought a Bible verse to mind. It was one I had memorized years earlier, found in 1 Corinthians 3:9: "We are co-workers in God's service; you are God's field, God's building." The irony of this verse, considered alongside that vision, caused my soul to respond to God: *Well, if I am Your building and Your field, Lord, then You should know there's a hole in Your house and Your garden's covered in broken glass.*

For years, I had thought of my house as representative of my life and my garden as the place where my creative endeavors grow. Essentially, my house is the "being" of my life, and my garden is the "doing." Even though I didn't fully understand the significance of the broken pieces, this vision somehow brought me comfort, knowing there was a mutual understanding between God and me about my life's current condition.

The words "co-workers with God" in that verse made me realize that the Lord wasn't shaming me or blaming me for my life's messiness, nor was He asking me to do this recovery work alone. Instead, He was inviting me to collaborate with His Spirit to clear, rebuild, and tend the land of my soul. I wasn't yet sure how this work would be done. But I sensed it would not be some kind of hostile takeover, such as when human "helpers" come in and haphazardly begin discarding our things because they're unaware of their importance to us. This hard work of becoming realigned and healed would be done with the only One who intimately knew everything about me and my story.

I wasn't sure how the debris would be collected, removed, or remade, but I sensed it would require time and work. I already knew some pieces had come from my own broken heart, others from unfulfilled hopes, and some from shattered dreams. But other parts had not come directly out of my life at all; instead, they were broken pieces from other people's stories that had found their way into mine. And some were not actually broken but rather just incomplete, unresolved parts of my story that I could not bring to completion on my own. One thing was sure; all this fragmentation had been pushed aside for a long time by the more urgent things demanding center stage. The time had come to clear away the broken pieces. They were now infringing on other healthier parts of my life. Becoming aware of my need for help and admitting it to God would prove the first step on my journey toward healing.

A Masterpiece

A soul can carry a lot of brokenness for a great deal of time. But carrying brokenness has its consequences. The broken fragments covering the soil of our lives will eventually crowd out the light, impede the water's flow, and stop the nutrients necessary for beautiful things to grow. My vision had shown me that parts of my world and the land of my soul had become dry, desolate, and covered in sharp shards of glass. "What had gotten broken? Could it be fixed? What beauty could ever come from such a mess?" These are the things I wondered about. Time with God would soon reveal that He had brought us to a complete stop to invite us on a transcendent journey out of brokenness and on to abundance in Him.

> Extraordinary beauty can come from many broken pieces—even the most painful parts of our story.

I asked questions like, "What can become of all this mess? Where do we begin this work? What is my part, and what is Yours, Lord?" In response, the Holy Spirit brought Romans 8:28 straight to mind: "And we know that all things work together for good to them that love God, to them who are the called according to his purpose" (KJV). This Scripture inspired thoughts of God as a Master Mosaicist who can rework broken pieces into masterpieces. And that led my mind to recollect the magnificent mosaics I had seen in the glorious cathedrals of Russia while I was living there. St. Isaac's Cathedral in St. Petersburg is filled with magnificent works of art made of millions of pieces of tessellated glass covering the floors, walls, and ceilings, retelling the biblical narrative of God's great redemption through Jesus Christ. These images, which I had seen before the time of my great undoing, were comforting to me now. They reminded me that extraordinary beauty could come from many broken pieces—even the most painful parts of my story.

For the first time, this truth encouraged me not to fear the darkest parts of my story and what they meant about His purposes for my life. I had long been afraid to face the shame associated with my story's brokenness and its unfinished parts. I had spent years trying to silence a cruel internal dialogue that lied to me about my worth, undermined my faith, and hindered my ability to move forward in freedom. But somehow, this Divine Dialogue between God and me, where I would question, and He would answer with Scriptures and pictures, helped me understand that I was seen, heard, and loved by the only One who could make me whole.

The Lord wants all His children to know that it is by His love that we are seen and invited to rise out of our broken states to become whole and flourish again. When God reveals our needy state, He is not seeking to shame us. He will not pass by the cry of His child's heart. Instead, He desires to set up a meeting in the garden of our lives, inviting us to join Him in a collaborative project that will lead to the thriving of our souls. I know this because I experienced it.

SISTERS

There was much work to be done on the house of my soul and in the garden of my life, but God had already given me a picture of how this work could begin. For years, I had witnessed my mother and her identical twin sister,

Georgie, working together in one another's gardens. The sisters are both exceptional gardeners, just like their mother before them. Ironically, my Nana and aunt were both named Georgine, which means gardener. In John 15:1, Jesus uses this same name to refer to His heavenly Father as the Master Gardener of human souls, *Georgios*,[1] saying, "I am the true vine, and my father is the gardener."

The twins' way of working together in the gardens would significantly inform the journey I was about to undertake with God, beginning with understanding their sisterly way of communicating.

"Your garden's overcrowded," one would say.

"You should never have planted this here; it's far too invasive," the other might say.

Their way of speaking to one another had always seemed blunt and even harsh to me, that is, until my recent dialogue with God concerning the state of my soul's house and garden. When the Lord showed me the mess of my life, I suddenly began to appreciate the straightforwardness of my mom and aunt. God's direct correction had not made me feel ashamed, as I would have assumed, but rather seen and known by Him in my needy state. The sisters were not trying to be cruel but instead to help one another make their houses and gardens become all they could be. I know this because each sister would follow up her corrective words with the actions of rolling up her sleeves, putting her hands into the dirt of her sister's garden, and staying until the job was done.

Proverbs 7:4, which says, "Say to wisdom, 'You are my sister,'" became living words as I considered the twins' interactions. Because I did not have a sister, though I always longed to, I had only ever viewed an intimate and honest sisterly relationship from afar. But in this, I turned to the wisdom of God, realizing that it was this sisterly aspect of the Spirit I needed most to work alongside me in the messy garden of my life. The way wisdom is always referred to in Scripture in the female form helped me understand that God is not only my Father but also that His wisdom is my Sister and Friend. It was not the strong, fatherly figure who protects and defends me that my soul needed most now, but a sister willing to get into the clean-up work with me. I also hoped that Wisdom would prove to be a collaborative, creative partner, willing to give suggestions and hear my hopes for my house and my dreams for my garden.

I told Wisdom I was willing and imagined her replying, "Kerry Georgine, let's get to work." (Yes, Georgine, meaning gardener, was also *my* given middle name.)

Just because we intuitively believe God can do anything does not mean we have come to experience Him in everything. We may have experienced God as our Healer but long to know Him as our Defender. We may have come to know Him as Wisdom, but we long to know Him as Friend, Father, or Protector.

Many of our beliefs, as well as our struggles, are based on our experiences in human relationships. For example, because my earthly father was always quick to welcome me into his law office and treated me like one of his most important clients, I did not struggle so much with the idea of God being a Father willing to make time for His children. Still, I longed to know the Lord as Healer and Comforter in my pain.

Because of the uniqueness of our individual experiences and the specific needs we express in our prayers, we all develop different beliefs at different times. The Lord continually seeks to reveal new aspects of His character through how He operates in each of our lives. As He reveals aspects of His character to us, these traits become manifest in us and, in time, express themselves through us.

A WRITTEN NOTE

No matter our age or how long we have walked with the Lord, there will always be obstacles to overcome and confident beliefs to be formed. I learned this truth most profoundly through the life of my 93-year-old Russian teacher, Olga. During the last few years of her life, she carried a little piece of paper with her that said, "Lord, I believe, help my unbelief."

My mother had written down this verse for Olga to help her overcome her struggles that came out of decades of living under Soviet atheistic programming and from experiencing her children's deaths at the hands of Nazi soldiers. After the deaths of her children, Olga and her husband were imprisoned in German work camps until the end of World War II. When Olga came to the United States as a refugee under the 1945 Truman Directive after the war, she grew in her belief in the existence and love of God because of the people who befriended her in her new homeland. How Christians lived and loved resonated with her.

Nevertheless, many of her new beliefs had not had time to become fully integrated, that is, held in both her heart and mind. How could they have been, since many of her hopes could never be realized this side of heaven due to the absence of her people, her homeland, and the passing of so much time? The prayer my mother wrote for Olga was an incredible comfort to her, giving her permission to be honest about her pain and her questions. Olga asked to be buried with that prayer, signifying that until the day of her death, she would continue to become more faithful and formed in her belief system.

A Simple Prayer

Undoubtedly, her faith was authentic and precious to God. This simple prayer, "Lord, I believe, help my unbelief," is the ideal starting point for forming every new belief, not just for Olga but for all of us, not just once but every time we find ourselves stuck in the tensions of life. There is too much pressure to claim we already confidently believe all the things we have not yet experienced. The faith of a child is a beautiful thing, and, in a spiritual sense, it's the goal. But as life throws us curveballs and our beliefs take some hits, we must seek ongoing reconciliation in our embattled belief systems.

> We all long to see God's grace become manifest in the context of our needs and answers to our prayers.

One kind of belief comes through beholding glory in the story of another, as the father of the mute boy beheld the glory upon Jesus, and just as I beheld the glory of God in the reunion of Adier and his father. However, a different kind of belief comes through experiencing it in our own lives, as the father did when Jesus healed his mute son. We all long to see God's grace become manifest in the context of our needs and answers to our prayers. Having unbelief does not make someone a nonbeliever, but rather, a believer still on a transformational journey toward wholeness and perfection in Christ. Every soul requires room to question, as the father of the mute boy did. The very act of questioning and requesting help from God is itself faith because it is the evidence of hope's flicker remaining. Remember, faith is the evidence of hope. Like the mute boy's father said, "If You can . . . will You?"

TRUSTING BELIEF AND THE MERCY SEAT

We all have gaps in our belief systems. We all believe some things based on our experiences, but other things only because we have been told they are true or because we have seen them in the lives of others. It is not that these are not true beliefs; they are simply ones that have not yet become fully integrated in our minds, hearts, and wills through study, personal experience, and actions of faith.

This way of developing confident beliefs reminds me of an interaction I had with my brother, Tommy. We had just bought two hammock chairs and hung them from beams on our porch. Tommy had seen my kids swinging in them and even commented on how comfortable they looked. I encouraged him to give one a try. "That wouldn't hold me," he answered. I reassured him that the installation instructions indicated a weight limit of 500 pounds, so it would certainly hold him. He believed me enough to try it. Nevertheless, he eased himself gingerly into the chair, keeping his feet planted firmly, without swinging, because he did not yet confidently believe in its ability to hold him. The chair held. His confidence grew. And his belief in the chair's integrity became more firmly established. Now, nearly every time Tommy comes to our porch, he chooses the hammock and swings freely.

This is how our belief systems progress, how our trust grows in everything, including our beliefs in the things of God. Watching Tommy learn to trust the reliability of the hammock chair taught me how natural it can be to learn to trust the "mercy seat of Christ." Faith formation requires experiencing the Lord's mercy, believing it will hold our weight, and taking time to rest in His love when our souls are weary.

YOUR BECOMING STORY: BELIEVE

The formation of every new belief involves its own transcendent journey that begins with recognizing your need and concludes with a more confident and formed belief. To begin each journey, you must consider your "neediness of the now" and be willing to admit to the Lord your struggles of unbelief.

This exercise consists of two parts. First, use the list below, which speaks to character aspects of God's Name, and consider what aspects of His character you have personally experienced and, therefore, more confidently believe.

Next, consider the different aspects of His character that you long to believe based on your current area of struggle. In what areas of life are you struggling to overcome unbelief based on your fears, uncertainties, losses, brokenness, or unfulfilled hopes? What is your "neediness of the now"?

The fill-in-the-bank statements below can help you as you proceed with this exercise.

"Lord, I believe You are _____ because I have experienced this divine aspect of your Name in my life when _____.

Now, Lord, I long to believe You can become _____ _____ in the area of my current need, that is, [insert here your "neediness of the now"] _____."

- ☐ Heavenly Father
- ☐ The One Who Sees
- ☐ The Living God
- ☐ Everlasting God
- ☐ Wisdom
- ☐ My Helper
- ☐ My Shepherd
- ☐ The One Who Loves
- ☐ Defender
- ☐ Restorer
- ☐ Recompense
- ☐ Transcendent One

BELIEVE

- ☐ King of Nations
- ☐ My Rock
- ☐ The First and the Last
- ☐ Truth in Love
- ☐ Provider
- ☐ God of my Praise
- ☐ King of Kings
- ☐ All Sufficiency
- ☐ Great Physician
- ☐ Living Word
- ☐ Assembler/ Integrator
- ☐ The One Who Lifts my Head
- ☐ Redeemer
- ☐ The Lord in the Midst
- ☐ Launderer's Soap
- ☐ Forgiving God
- ☐ God with us
- ☐ Mighty Creator
- ☐ Father to the Fatherless
- ☐ Spirit
- ☐ Friend
- ☐ Healer
- ☐ God Outside of Time
- ☐ The One Who Hears
- ☐ Dwelling Place
- ☐ The Only Wise God
- ☐ Creator
- ☐ Life Breath
- ☐ The Way
- ☐ My Rescuer
- ☐ The Lord of Peace
- ☐ The Lord my Guide
- ☐ My Righteousness
- ☐ Comforter
- ☐ My Exceeding Joy

As more of your stories come to mind, consider returning to this page to check more boxes, indicating the new things God has revealed about Himself through your experiences.

"Need to Believe"

In hurting, we need.
In needing, we long.
In longing, we seek.
In seeking, we find.
In finding, we realize.
In realizing, we remember.
In remembering, we ask.
In asking, we receive.
In receiving, we know.
In knowing, we trust.
In trusting, we stand.
In standing, we imagine.
In imagining, we see.
In seeing, we redeem.

In redeeming, we heal.
In healing, we praise.
In praising, we hear.
In hearing, we anoint.
In anointing, we share.
In sharing, we assemble.
In assembling, we belong.
In belonging, we love.
In loving, we create.
In creating, we become.
In becoming, we rejoice.
In rejoicing, we abide.
In abiding, we believe.

2

REMEMBER

God Encounters and Stones of Help

"Do this in remembrance of me," said the pastor from the pulpit. With my eyes closed, cup and cracker in hand, and preparing to take Communion as sanctimoniously as possible, my heart suddenly staged a rebellion against the whole remembrance process. It wasn't that I didn't want to honor the Lord's sacrifice; it was that my mind would no longer ignore my heart's most pressing questions: *How can I remember something I never saw? How am I supposed to recall what I've never witnessed? I wasn't there when You wept before Your arrest in the garden of Gethsemane, Lord, or when Your body was nailed to the cross at Calvary.*

Despite all the times I had tried to imagine the physical sufferings of Christ, I could no longer continue the mental gymnastics required to do so now that my life had fallen to pieces. Grief has a way of leading us to confront things we could not have before the time of testing. In the hollow emptiness of my own loss, I broke my silence and voiced my wrestling to the Lord, hoping for relief in the asking. A bit of relief did come, but so did something I did not expect — He answered back!

"Remember *Me* in *your* story" was what the Holy Spirit spoke to me.

My story? How can the Lord's story be found in mine? I wondered.

At that moment, the iron gate that had long separated my human narrative from God's flew wide open. Memories from events in my life began rushing in, reminding me of where God had intervened. Each memory, curated by the Holy Spirit, had begun in difficulty but resolved by grace, and each required me to take steps of faith.

CHINA: MY STONE OF REMEMBRANCE

One of the scenes that flickered most brightly as I remembered God in my story was a memory from Capitol Hill. After serving eighteen years in Congress, Senator Mary Landrieu gathered a group of women for a private luncheon to celebrate the work we had done together for vulnerable children. One of the women present posed a question, asking, "What is the greatest thing that ever happened to you in your time as a US senator?"

Senator Landrieu mused: "The greatest thing that ever happened to me as a Senator . . ."

She paused then, looked at me, and continued. "Actually, it happened to *you*, Kerry, when we were in China together, meeting with the Chinese president!"

> I recalled the awe we had shared as we witnessed God reveal His glory.

Instantly, I knew the moment she was referring to, and I recalled the awe we had shared as we witnessed God's glory revealed. The senator recounted the miraculous mountain-top experience to the ladies at the luncheon. While the summit of that mountaintop had been spectacular, I quietly thought back to the *full* experience—the backstory—including the long and challenging crawl up the mountain's steep and rocky incline, which I had ascended on my proverbial hands and knees . . . exhausted, sick, fearful, tearful, and prayerful. Had it not been for the countless interventions of God keeping me from quitting, this meeting with the Chinese president would not have happened, or at the very least, I would not have been present for it.

The Answer Was Yes

To adequately explain what happened in China, it is important to have a little background on how I came to organize a congressional delegation in the first place. I am an enthusiast-generalist who lives in the moment, says yes too quickly, and is curious about everything. I also grew up in a household where we were prohibited from quitting the things we started. The problem with this combination is that I would say yes to too many things and then remain in them for far too long.

This tendency led me to rack up twelve years of private Russian lessons and ten years of piano lessons. I earned a social diploma in music from the National Piano Auditions despite my inability to play anything by ear. Even though my years of Russian language study led to my choice of double majors in college and the beginning of my work in nonprofits, I did not have much use for either skill after coming to work in DC. After all those years of study, both skills felt lost to me, having no outlet or need to use them.

In 2001, while serving in my second year as a staff fellow for the Congressional Coalition on Adoption (CCA), a bipartisan caucus of the US Congress, I wrote a proposal recommending the creation of a nonprofit entity that could do some of the "grunt work" for the Caucus and handle the advocacy aspect of the work. The four congressional co-chairs of CCA, Senators Landrieu and Craig, and Congressmen Bliley and Oberstar, accepted the invitation to meet with me for a private luncheon in the Senate dining room where we would discuss my proposal. All four members agreed to create the entity as long as I agreed to be its executive director. Ironically, after sharing the proposal with them, I had intended to resign to start a family. But when Congressman Oberstar stipulated my leadership of the entity as a requirement for his agreement, the enthusiast in me quickly accepted.

It was only after I got to my car that I was confronted with reality. I cried the rest of my long commute home as I realized what I had just committed to. The work of building a new nonprofit that supports a congressional caucus would entail crazy hours, be high pressure, and require raising hundreds of thousands of dollars, which I had no idea how to do.

When I walked through the door of my townhouse, still teary, I was met by my mother and her dear friend Barb Walzer. After hearing what happened, Barb offered to be our first donor. She shared that her mother had been an orphan who had grown up in an orphanage. She wanted to provide the seed money for this endeavor to honor her late mother and support me. Barb and her offering would prove a critical piece in the masterful work God was inviting us to create with Him.

But no sooner had we set up desks in our basement and purchased phones and computers second-hand than China had announced a new quota limiting international adoptions. Those salvaged phones began ringing off the hook with calls from families and civil servants working to unite children and parents.

Because of its "one-child policy," leading to a surplus of "unwanted" children (often those with disabilities or "undesirable" traits), China had become the nation where the largest number of orphans were being adopted internationally. Due to this newly imposed adoption quota, thousands of US families found themselves stuck in the international adoption process. I began to field phone calls from adoption groups asking if CCAI, our newly formed organization, would organize a congressional delegation to China. Chinese officials had made it clear that they would only speak with government officials qualified to engage in international affairs, such as representatives of the US Congress or State Department. But our meager budget made such a trip impossible.

Dave Malutinok, a prominent leader in adoption advocacy, called to add his voice to those wanting a congressional delegation on adoption to travel to China. I told him it was impossible, adding wistfully before we hung up, "Maybe if we had a plane to fly there." Dave called back within a day, saying that his friend Valdur Koha, also an adoptive parent, had offered his plane, capable of flying to China, for this trip. Despite my fears and insufficiencies, I could see this was undoubtedly a display of providence by heaven's Way-Maker. If God was putting this trip together like a puzzle, He had just placed another critical piece. Though much more work was needed, this encouraged me enough to keep walking by faith.

Facing Obstacles

McLane Layton, Legislative Counsel for Senator Don Nickles, was one of the Senate staffers invited on the trip. Even though McLane was an adoptive parent and deeply involved in adoption policy, her primary interest in joining this delegation was driven by another human rights issue unrelated to our agenda. Specifically, the US State Department's Human Rights division had informed her of the recent arrest of a Hong Kong businessman, Li Guangquiang, accused of smuggling 16,000 Chinese-language Bibles into Southern China.[1] Guangquiang had been imprisoned and was facing a death sentence. Another pastor in China who had been holding secret home church meetings had also been arrested and sentenced to death. At first, I questioned whether adding these tragic but unrelated human rights cases to our agenda would cause confusion and perhaps undermine our trip's focus. But, in time, we would see that it was God who caused this issue to rise in importance in the minds of some of our delegates and eventually stand alongside the more known parts of our agenda.

From the moment I agreed to the trip, there would be opposition and trouble. More than once, the words of Jesus came to mind: "In this world you will have trouble. But take heart! I have overcome the world" (John 16:22). The Lord would indeed provide a way to overcome every obstacle and accomplish His will, but it would not be without its many challenges. My mother reminded me to claim the promises in Scripture. I claimed John 42:22, "I know that you can do all things; no purpose of yours can be thwarted."

On one occasion, while on Capitol Hill buying gifts for the Chinese dignitaries at the Senate gift shop, I ran into Kathleen Strottman, a colleague with whom I worked closely and who would be staffing Senator Landrieu on the trip. She asked why I wasn't already in the meeting about our trip to China. I didn't know anything about a meeting. She said it was news to her, too, but that we both better get there ASAP, particularly me, since I was the trip's leader.

When I walked into the meeting, those already seated looked shocked that I had come. I soon discovered they were there to undermine me, even replace me as the trip's leader. There were Chinese businessmen present whom I did not know, making accusations that I had an alternative agenda. Their accusations did not land because the senator already knew my character. Although this was the first time I would witness God confound the agendas of those seeking to seize control of the trip for their own selfish gain, it would not be the last. "The LORD, your God, who is going before you, will fight for you" (Deuteronomy 1:30). The warfare continued and kept me on my knees, crying out in tears and praying to God nearly every night leading up to the trip and throughout our stay in China.

When I agreed to the trip, the lack of resources and competing agendas would not be the only hurdles to overcome. I would soon realize I was several months pregnant with our first child and would be five months along by the time the trip happened. I was so focused and overworked that, early on, I attributed my pregnancy symptoms to the stress of building a new organization while also planning a full-fledged international congressional delegation that would determine the fate of thousands of orphans.

Working out of my townhouse basement, I had only one other staff member, Wendy Cosby, a former colleague in adoption work, and one part-time volunteer, Lynnette Cole. After being crowned Miss USA 2000, Lynnette came to volunteer with our organization based on her commitment to advocate for adoption as an adoptee herself. We were small and few, and I was pregnant, scared, and weary. But God was with us.

The trip took place in January 2002. Wendy stayed back to run CCAI by herself, and Lynnette would travel with me and the rest of the delegation to China as the only other CCAI staff representative. Brian Luwis, one of our trip's participants, was so concerned about my pregnant condition because I was still sick daily that he insisted on sponsoring Scott to join us on the trip to support me.

We had secured meetings with ministry-level Chinese officials through the US and Chinese embassies. We had also requested a meeting with President Jiang Zemin, China's supreme leader. We understood, however, that getting a meeting with Zemin was a long shot. His ministry officials told us that he had never had a formal meeting on adoption. Miraculously, several days into our trip, we were informed that we had been granted a meeting with Zemin that would be held at the presidential palace.

Before departing for the meeting, Congresswoman Anne Northup asked me if there were any agenda items that Senator Landrieu would not be addressing with the president. It is the protocol for senators to speak before congresspeople. I reminded her of the human rights cases pertaining to the imprisoned Christians, adding that these cases were not included in the senator's official meeting agenda. Our fifteen-member delegation was introduced to President Zemin and the other Chinese officials when we entered the meeting.

As soon as we were seated, Zemin asked a question in Chinese that was translated into English. "Tell me, what is the difference between a pretzel and a biscuit?" His question seemed odd to me, but apparently, it was prompted by a very recent choking incident that happened to our president, George W. Bush. Next, President Zemin and Senator Landrieu began discussing their shared connection in mayoral leadership. Before becoming president, Zemin had been the mayor of Shanghai, and Landrieu's father, Moon Landrieu, had been the mayor of New Orleans during the 1970s. Well past the fifteen minutes slated for the meeting, I began to worry that we might not get to the agenda's main point after the discussions about pretzels and mayorship. Eventually, the issue of adoption was raised. The two leaders spoke joyfully, now dialoguing directly in English, about how Chinese children, adopted over many years by American families, had come to serve as China's most excellent ambassadors to America.

When the congresswoman was called on, she spoke briefly on adoption. Then, she respectfully transitioned to the issue of the imprisoned Christians, asking for their sentencing to be reconsidered. Despite his discomfort with the topic, Zemin agreed reluctantly to discuss this because of how much he said he was enjoying our delegation. As the meeting seemed to be concluding, President Zemin stood up, stepped in front of our entire group, and asked if anyone else had something to share.

As I looked around, it dawned on me that over half of our delegation were women. President Zemin gestured to Lynnette Cole to speak, even though the former Miss USA had not indicated she wanted to share anything. Lynnette gracefully stood, introduced herself as an adoptee, and then thanked the President for his role in bringing orphans and families together. Zemin smiled, showing his pleasure with her spoken words. The power in her poised presence and the president's response to her statement made me feel I was witnessing an "Esther moment." But it would not be the only Esther moment before our time at the palace concluded, which was already well past an hour.

Are You Kidding Me?

After an official picture was taken, President Zemin offered to give us a personal tour of the palace, specifically to see where the room in which the infamous founder of the People's Republic of China, Chairman Mao Zedong, had last lived and worked. He led us into a giant hall with a grand piano in its center and asked if anyone could play it. At first, no one spoke up to answer his question, and I was pretty sure we didn't have any pianists in our delegation. But then my mother's dear friend Barb Walzer, a board member of CCAI at the time, spoke up from the back of the group, announcing confidently, "Kerry plays the piano!"

NOOOO! I thought. *She did not just say that!* Barb had not heard me play a single note in over ten years. But before I could say anything, my husband, Scott, who had *never* ever heard me play a single note, said, "Yeah, don't you play?"

WHAAAT IS happening to me? This has to be a nightmare! I thought.

When Zemin realized they were talking about me, he turned to me and said, "Yes, you will play!" When the Supreme Communist Leader of the largest people group on earth says, "You will play," YOU PLAY! My heart began racing, and full panic set in as I sat at the piano with Chairman Zemin standing right beside me.

Oh, Lord, help me! I silently begged. And in one miraculous instant, the Lord placed before my eyes a sheet of music from one of the last sonatas I ever performed when I played for the National Piano Auditions twelve years earlier. It appeared in a vision propped up before my spiritual eyes as if sitting on top of the piano, readied for me to play. Was the Spirit bringing me back to a distant memory of the times I spent hours in front of this very page, or was it actually there in the unseen realms set before my spiritual eyes? I will never know for sure, but I could see it.

God knew I didn't play by ear but could read the notes. I played the first two pages. When I came to the bottom of the second page, the page did not turn in my vision. So, I played a strong G octave twice as if this was intended to be the end of the piece. The astonished look on the senator's face was priceless. In the three years we had already worked together, I never once mentioned I could play the piano. She later told me she feared I might play something like chopsticks and embarrass her.

Zemin spoke first in English, saying, "That is one of my favorite pieces."

Senator Landrieu responded enthusiastically, "And our little Kerry speaks Russian too."

Once again, I was speechless. *Why would she say that?* I wondered, seeing as we were in China and not Russia. But it turns out that God had compelled her to say it. The moment after she spoke these words, the president of China turned to me and began speaking to me directly in Russian. Yes, Russian! I couldn't believe it. Nevertheless, since we were the only two people in the room who spoke Russian, I found myself having a private conversation with the supreme leader of China.

Now, speaking together in Russian, I thanked him for being so gracious with his time. He said it was his pleasure and that he was pleased with the meeting. I thanked him for making it possible for orphans to find families and couples to adopt. I acknowledged his position as the one with the power to continue extending this mercy and then thanked him for considering mercy for those who had broken their religious laws.

It was clear that he was pleased to talk in Russian with me as well. And as we would come to find out later, aspects of his own life were being assembled through this meeting, too. Zemin himself had been adopted by his uncle, Jiang Shangqing.[2] God knew that part of his story, but at the time, we did not. My private conversation in Russian with the president would serve as the finale to this extraordinary and providential meeting.

As we departed, Senator Landrieu, now walking beside me, asked jubilantly, "How did *you* do this, Kerry?! How?"

My response to her question was much stronger than when I usually spoke to a congressional member, based on my utter surprise. "What!? How did *I* do this? I didn't do this! I couldn't do this! I'm as shocked as you are! GOD DID THIS! Look at me; I am five months pregnant. I prepared for this trip on my knees in tears and prayers. No human being could have done this! God did this."

> This was about God's goodness and His plans coming to pass in His time and in His way.

What we had asked and imagined for orphans, prospective adoptive parents, and prisoners would come to pass. But God had done exceedingly more than we could have ever asked or imagined. This would reveal itself over time in so many ways. Many incomplete and lost fragments in my life story had suddenly been shown to me as a beautiful mosaic by the Master Assembler of human stories. I experienced God as Strength in my weakness and Provider in my neediness. My Lord was indeed the Supreme Leader over all the earth and the King of all kings.

And even though this was an extraordinary moment for everyone present in that palace room, it also felt like an intimate moment between Jesus and me. Although some people treated me as insignificant and replaceable, God wanted me to know I had been chosen for this noble purpose. I felt embraced by the Lover of my soul, even kissed by heaven in front of many witnesses. This was about God's goodness, faithfulness, love, and glory being revealed, His involvement in the happenings of people and nations, and His way of answering the prayers of many.

> Surely his salvation is near those who fear him, that his glory may dwell in our land. Love and faithfulness meet together; righteousness and peace kiss each other. Faithfulness springs forth from the earth, and righteousness looks down from heaven. (Psalm 85:9–11)

Upon our return to the guest residence that evening, Senator Landrieu noticed that the television in the lobby, which was set on the state-sponsored news channel, was reporting on our visit with the Chinese president. She called us over, pointed to the TV, and said, "Do you see this? God did that!"

REMEMBER

The Master Mosaicist

As I was flying back on the commercial plane with some of the other staff members, thinking about all that had transpired and knowing it was a miracle orchestrated by God, a stewardess came by and offered me a copy of the *Rénmín Ribào*, the daily newspaper of the Central Committee of the Communist Party. On its cover was a picture of our delegation with the Chinese president. It made me chuckle as I thought about our makeshift office in the basement of my townhouse with our two meager desks and our salvaged phones. God wanted me to know that He was not only the God of that miracle moment but the God of every moment that led up to it.

Shortly after returning to the US, McLane told us that while watching CNN one night, a headline ran across the bottom of her TV screen that read, "Bible Smuggler in China released from prison, pastor's death sentence converted to life."[3] Our organization, CCAI, followed up on this trip by hosting some of the same Chinese officials from the China Center for Adoption, the Ministry of Civil Affairs, and the Ministry of Foreign Affairs on their next visit to the States. The delegates confirmed for us the release of the two Christian prisoners and the lifting of the adoption quota, which resulted in thousands more Chinese orphans being adopted into families around the globe. They also said that our meeting with Zemin had been the second-longest he'd had with foreign delegates up to that point in his twelve years as president, only surpassed by his meeting with Arnold Schwarzenegger. I couldn't tell if that was a joke, but their smiles showed appreciation for its length and fruitfulness.

Before they flew out of DC, one of them asked on their delegation's behalf if they could meet the child who had been in his mother's womb when she played the piano for their supreme leader, referring to our son, Cole, as the "chosen baby." So, I brought Cole to Dulles Airport to see them off. As Cole grew up, this became his favorite part of this miraculous but true story.

Who knows the mind of Christ? Who could have fathomed all that God would do? His faithfulness as a Father to the fatherless, as the One who sets the captives free, and the One who answers the cries of the needy was now undeniable. He had also revealed Himself as a Master Mosaicist who takes all the incomplete and fragmented parts of our lives and turns them into something of magnificent beauty for His glory and because of His love.

REVIEWING YOUR B-ROLL

Many would retell the amazing happenings of that day with the Chinese president, but God would be faithful in reminding me that He was the power and wisdom behind it all, that He was and still is the Miracle Worker. One of the first reminders came when I was making final preparations for our Congressional Angels in Adoption Gala in Washington, DC. This event is where members of Congress recognize people from their states for their excellent work in child welfare. For this particular year, one of Hollywood's A-list actors had agreed to participate in honoring our national award recipient. Though we had hoped he would come in person, as most presenters had done in the past, he could not. We were, however, still pleased he had agreed to participate by sending a video to show at the gala—that is, until we watched the video he sent. The actor was distracted, clearly disinterested—not even looking at the camera. He was getting his coffee and asking the other people in the room if he even had time to record something for an event he had never heard of before.

Naturally, his disinterest and disregard were offensive. I contacted his publicist to explain why we could not use the recording. She was mortified. "Oh no!" she exclaimed. "We must have accidentally sent you the B-Roll film instead of the final, edited cut." Without revealing my true thoughts, I told her it wasn't too late to swap it out for another one if she could send a better version.

When I hung up the phone, however, I decided I would never support this actor again and certainly would not watch another one of his movies. But no sooner had I written him off in my heart than I heard a strong word of rebuke from the Spirit, asking me, "What about *your* B-Roll, Kerry?"

Wow! My judgment was stopped dead in its tracks, and my pride was silenced as God began replaying some choice parts of the unedited feed of my life. I began viewing up close and personal how I was not better than this actor, nor better than anyone else, for that matter. My faults, failures, flailings—in short, my humanness—was on full display in my B-Roll film. I saw how God had kept me from being ashamed many times by His mercy, how the good I had done had always involved His grace, and how Jesus had been the true hero of my unedited story.

When we wrongly attribute the gifts and experiences that God has entrusted to us as having come from ourselves, it becomes "natural" to compare our strengths to the weaknesses we perceive in others. "Who makes you different from anyone else? What do you have that you did not receive? And if you did receive it, why do you boast as though you did not?" (1 Corinthians 4:7). I was wrong to judge this actor's weaknesses against my strengths, especially as I actively denied the part that grace had played. Colossians 3:13 reminds us, "Bear with each other and forgive one another if any of you has a grievance against someone. Forgive as the Lord forgave you."

In fact, Scripture shows that it is actually dangerous to compare ourselves to the foibles of others because it sets us up for an inevitable fall. Matthew 23:12 reminds us, "For those who exalt themselves will be humbled, and those who humble themselves will be exalted." Prideful misremembering not only blocks the grace that we need for future success but also activates a harmful boomerang effect of judgment. "Do not judge, or you too will be judged. For in the same way you judge others, you will be judged, and with the measure you use, it will be measured to you" (Matthew 7:1–2).

> Who among us does not long for others to make allowance for our faults and view us through a merciful lens and with a gracious heart?

Of course, it is a natural tendency to take credit for the good in our lives as having come from us apart from God. This is why we must actively look for ways to tell "the full story" and give credit to God for our A-Roll blessings. B-Roll connects God's power to our weakness, and in this remembrance process, we become partakers of His glorious nature. B-Roll is also a wonderfully efficient tool for protecting our relationships from harmful judgment. Proper remembering has a way of righting many of our relationships with God and others.

The newly edited version of the actor's congratulatory video arrived just in time for the event. In viewing it, we could see more of the beauty of his character through the caring words he spoke. I decided I would still see his movies. Who among us does not long for others to make allowance for our faults and view us through a merciful lens and with a gracious heart? The good news is that the spiritual boomerang effect applies not only to judgment but also to mercy. "Blessed are the merciful, for they will be shown mercy" (Matthew 5:7). If we want people to make allowances for our faults, we should be wise enough to store up mercy in advance by granting it to others. The tool of B-Roll helps us do this so we can join with the wise in saying, "There, but for the grace of God, go I."

THE ISRAELITES REMEMBER THEIR B-ROLL

Moses taught B-Roll, too. He knew that if the children of Israel could REMEMBER their desert journeys accurately, they would be ensured success in the land of the promise. After forty years in the wilderness and preparing to cross over the Jordan River, the Israelites would hear one final message from their leader. This message was centered entirely around the importance of remembering the whole way they had walked. Moses knew that if they forgot God and foolishly returned to their self-sufficient and idolatrous ways, they would not win their future battles, receive the blessings intended, or access the provision meant for them.

They had seen much of God's power and faithfulness during their desert journeys and learned many aspects of His character through personal experiences. And now, what would be most vital for their future was to REMEMBER what they had come to BELIEVE confidently through their past experiences. These beliefs would need to be intentionally remembered to give them courage and remind them to access the proper Source of their rescue.

Remember how the LORD your God led you all the way in the wilderness these forty years to humble and test you to know what was in your heart, whether or not you would keep his commands. He humbled you, causing you to hunger and then feeding you with manna, which neither you nor your ancestors had known, to teach you that man does not live on bread alone but on every word that comes from the mouth of the LORD. Your clothes did not wear out, and your feet did not swell during these forty years. (Deuteronomy 8:2–4)

SOUL AMNESIA

God wants us to clearly see His patterns with humanity so that we will know how to enter into each new leg of our journeys empowered by His grace. Proper remembrance is the way to access His grace when we are in trouble again. It is also key to our success in the good lands where abundance is promised. It causes us to see Him as the rightful hero of our redemptive stories and to place our confidence in Him again.

Remembering God keeps our souls safe; forgetting Him puts us in danger. Humans, by nature, suffer from soul amnesia. The word forget means to lose the power of recalling what was once held, had become, or was produced. Forgetting is not only the opposite of remembering; it is the opposite of begetting, meaning to birth, build, or bring forth from oneself.[4] When we forget, we lose our grip on what we once held dear and undermine our ability to live productively.

Picking up where we left off in Deuteronomy, Moses continues warning the children of Israel about this universal reality, saying,

> "When you have eaten and are satisfied, praise the LORD your God for the good land he has given you. Be careful that you do not forget the LORD your God, failing to observe his commands, his laws and his decrees that I am giving you this day. Otherwise, when you eat and are satisfied, when you build fine houses and settle down, and when your herds and flocks grow large and your silver and gold increase and all you have is multiplied, then your heart will become

proud and you will forget the LORD your God, who brought you out of Egypt, out of the land of slavery. He led you through the vast and dreadful wilderness, that thirsty and waterless land, with its venomous snakes and scorpions. He brought you water out of hard rock. He gave you manna to eat in the wilderness, something your ancestors had never known, to humble and test you so that in the end it might go well with you. You may say to yourself, 'My power and the strength of my hands have produced this wealth for me.' But remember the LORD your God, for it is he who gives you the ability to produce wealth, and so confirms his covenant, which he swore to your ancestors, as it is today." (Deuteronomy 8:10–18)

Holy remembrance is critical to countering misplaced pride, human forgetfulness, and despair. But how do we do this? As in all things, we need to look to God's Word for the answers.

In Joshua chapter 4, after the whole nation had finished crossing the Jordan, the Lord instructed Joshua to set up a monument using twelve stones taken out from the center of the Jordan River. God specifically wanted one man appointed from each tribe to choose a rock and do the work of setting it up as a reminder to tell the story of this miracle to their children and their people forever. "In the future, when your children ask you, 'What do these stones mean?' tell them that the flow of the Jordan was cut off before the ark of the covenant of the LORD. When it crossed the Jordan, the waters of the Jordan were cut off. These stones are to be a memorial to the people of Israel forever" (Joshua 4:6–7).

Israel received a lecture on remembrance on the front side of the Jordan River from Moses and another on the back side of the river from Joshua. Here, God gives specific instructions on making their memories tangible and visible so they would have something to remind their wandering eyes and hearts that it was God who had brought them this far.

We must not just read about these holy remembrances and the act of setting up stones of help in the Bible text; we must do it ourselves. Just as our physical bodies require exercise, our souls also need the practical and repeated exercise of our faith to strengthen our belief systems. Just as each Israelite leader had to choose, carry, and set up a stone themselves as a sign of their personal responsibility to REMEMBER God in their lived experiences and pass down these stories to their children, we must do the same, for our soul's sake and for the sake of those who will come after us. China has become a significant stone of remembrance for me and an encouragement to my children to set up their own.

> Our stones of remembrance are the solid places on which we can stand firm when we find ourselves in the tensions of life.

God requires each of us to mine the precious stones of remembrance out of our own stories. The Bible refers to these memory stones as *ebenezers*, meaning "stones of help." The Word says that "Samuel took a stone and set it up between Mizpah and Shen. He named it Ebenezer, saying, 'Thus far the LORD has helped us'" (1 Samuel 7:12). *Shen* means "the place of breaking." But Mizpah means "A high place" and implies the place from which we stand watch, and stand confident in God's rescue. Our stones of remembrance are the solid places we can stand upon when we find ourselves in the tensions of life, weary, in the shadows, or buffeted by the wind. Our stones of remembrance are meant to stand somewhere between the place of our breaking and the mountain places where we will finally experience relief and become confident that redemption is near. These stones bid us to come and rest and REMEMBER to hold on to hope. This is how we begin to overcome our struggles of unbelief and take the next step of faith. We stand upon our stones and look to God, trusting Him to lead us the rest of the way. We are all called to do this sacred act of remembering and storytelling.

> Only be careful and watch yourselves closely so that you do not forget the things your eyes have seen or let them fade from your heart as long as you live. Teach them to your children and their children after them. (Deuteronomy 4:9)

Tell it to your children, and let your children tell it to their children, and their children to the next generation. (Joel 1:2–3)

PEBBLES OF REMEMBRANCE

Scott and I knew that teaching our children to remain connected to God's grace through holy remembrance was essential. But trying to figure out how to convey this to children who have lived so few years of life was more challenging. Randomly or perhaps divinely, Scott asked a question that perfectly kicked off this teaching at dinner one night. "How has God loved you in the last twenty-four hours?" he asked.

Even though the question was intended to steer our dinner conversation toward gratitude, it had the profound additional effect of opening our minds to small ways of remembering God in our stories. Our kids loved this exercise and went on to ask for it each evening that week and again the next. Over time, it became our regular Hasenbalg dinner practice. Each day, they would testify of God's love through a different friend or family member, success in a school assignment, a kind word spoken to them, or something they felt good about doing for another person. It could be as big as an award in a sporting event or as small as seeing a hummingbird visit our feeder. But every day, every person could find at least one way God had loved them in the last twenty-four hours.

This practice gently taught our children that stones of remembrance don't have to be giant ones that emerge from miraculous events like China. All of us, even the youngest child, can mine our stories to find the goodness and redemption of God. Through this simple family rhythm, we began tasting and seeing the morsels of God's goodness in the lives of one another every day. We began to see how, even on the "bad days," God never fails to pursue us with His love. He is, in fact, profoundly active in the small and ordinary parts of our everyday lives. The more we look for Him in our stories, the more we will realize this and receive the power that remembrance can provide.

Over time, we realized that our "Hasenbalg dinner practice" was helping keep our children looking to the Lord as their primary source of blessing rather than fixing their eyes on people or things to meet their needs. This way of remembering would keep their hearts and relationships safer from the snares of idolatry. The day will surely come when our children will have their own giant stones of remembrance, representing the miraculous savings of God that they will witness with their own eyes. In the meantime, this practice is laying for them a kind of pebbled path that leads them back into the empowering presence of God so that they might feel the embrace of His love whenever they are struggling with unbelief.

SETTING UP STONES

Recalling our lived experiences reveals much about God's faithful character, but it also helps us see how God's grace and our faith engage in a kind of Divine Dialogue. The Lord's grace, that is, His empowering presence, met me in my need and weakness every time I cried out or reached out my hand for His help. This was evidenced many times throughout my trip to China. By rewatching the movements of His grace and my small steps of faith in the narrative that played out, I saw how God had made a way for me every time there seemed to be no way.

In practicing holy remembrance, we are making a choice of faith over fear. And it is through faith that we come to experience more of Christ's life in us, empowering us to do the things we are called to do. We should all consider how the Lord has intervened in our life stories and ask the Spirit to guide us in this reflective process. Perhaps His grace came through another person, an answered prayer, a Scripture verse, something in nature, or through an inner whisper. Remembering what we have already BECOME and how God's transforming grace has already become manifest in our lives helps compel us to look to the Lord as our source for our future BECOMING. Some people find it helpful to write their "remembrances" in a journal, keep them in a memory box, or collect stones and assign names to them. The assigned names may be

> Holy remembrance is essential to living an abundant life.

places where we experienced God's faithfulness, the people or things used as vessels of His grace, or the specific attributes of His divine character revealed through them.

Holy remembrance is essential to living an abundant life. Once we have tasted and seen the glory and goodness of God, we want it to continue. For this to happen, we must REMEMBER how His grace came to us when we were small in our own eyes, aware of our neediness, open-handed, and hungry for the flow of His grace. Once we have identified our need, remembering God in our story is the ideal next step on the journey up and out of brokenness. When we find ourselves between the place of breaking and the destination of hope, we ought to REMEMBER our stones and stand upon them as a solid foundation to rest and from which we can take our next steps of faith.

It bears mentioning that when we engage in this kind of reflective process, we will also find troubling places still in need of God's intervention. Do not despair of these, nor abandon setting up stones of remembrance. God does not ask us to pretend that these hard places don't exist. Instead, He is asking us to set them aside to be addressed using other faith practices, like ASK, TRUST, and REDEEM, which we will find much easier to engage in once we have identified a few stones of help first. Having become strengthened in faith, we will be compelled to look to the Spirit again to ask and entrust to Him the things that are currently undone or unbecoming in our lives. Identifying our stones and sharing our testimonies will restore hope in the same God who saved us before and can do it again in whatever we are facing. "The LORD your God, who is going before you, will fight for you, as he did for you in Egypt, before your very eyes, and in the wilderness. There you saw how the LORD your God carried you, as a father carries his son, all the way you went until you reached this place" (Deuteronomy 1:30).

REMEMBER

YOUR BECOMING STORY: REMEMBER

Based on your life experiences, what has your heart already come to believe about God's character? Consult the names of God from the end of the BELIEVE chapter to dive further into how the Lord has revealed aspects of His love and character to you personally.

By taking time to REMEMBER where God has shown up in your life already and made Himself known to you as real, you will be inspired to turn to Him again in your *neediness of the now*. What matters most is not *how* you choose to REMEMBER but *that* you choose to REMEMBER. Once you have named a stone of remembrance, consider sharing your testimony of the Lord's faithfulness with someone who needs encouragement.

Naming Stones

Remember a time when . . .

- you saw no way through, and God made a way.
- you needed direction, and God revealed the way.
- you were sick or wounded, and God healed you.
- you were broken, and God restored you.
- you were alone, and God brought a companion.
- you questioned in prayer, and God answered you.
- You couldn't sense God's presence, but He made His presence known.
- your sin led you astray, but God brought you back and covered your shame.
- you were confused, and God brought clarity.

- your relationship was broken, and God restored it.
- you were too weary to go on, and God gave you the strength to endure.
- you asked for a blessing, and you were blessed.
- you needed discernment, and God provided wisdom.
- you were attacked by forces of darkness, but the Lord protected you.
- you were wrongly accused, and God proved your innocence.
- you were poor and needy, and God met your needs.
- you were grieving, and God comforted you and, in time, filled you with joy.
- you were sure of defeat, but God brought victory.
- you saw no end in sight to the raging storms, and God calmed the storm and provided light.
- you couldn't find your purpose, and God brought a need for you to fulfill.
- you were sinned against, and God gave you the power to forgive.
- you sinned against someone else, and God gave them the grace to forgive you.

3

ASK

Questions and Requests

"The Jesus-kid" was a name I got called growing up. It was said jokingly, but I was the neighborhood "goodie-goodie." Even after we all reached adulthood, when my brother got annoyed with me, he jabbed at me by saying, "But you're JESUS' SISTER," as if choosing rightly came easier to me. I wish I had been quick-witted enough to say, "If I'm Jesus' sister, that would make you Jesus' brother!" Instead, I went into my default mode of "turning the other cheek," but this only reinforced the "Jesus-kid" stamp. Labels have a strange way of sticking. They also come with their own unique set of expectations. This one was no exception. *Be the first to forgive, the last to disobey, always willing to serve, and unwavering in faith.* That's what I felt was expected of me.

I'M HUMAN TOO!

Even if I had wanted to hide my faith, it would not have been easy. My mother was the lead volunteer in our community's Christian youth ministry. The club meetings were announced every week over the high school loudspeaker: "Campus Life tonight at Bobby and Kerry Marks's house." Unbeknownst to me at the time, the "Jesus-kid" stamp set me up for expectations that I did not question my beliefs, that I should have a "red phone" running directly to the ear of God, and that somehow, I was immune to the human condition because of my faith.

I will never forget crying out to one of my long-time friends, saying, "I am made of flesh and blood just like everyone else. Why do people expect more of me when I am only human, too?" She responded tenderly but honestly, "Kerry, we don't want to know these things about you. We all want to believe you are stronger than the rest of us."

> I longed for the freedom to be layered, to be human.

False perceptions based on human comparison can bring a great deal of confusion. They lead to false expectations and false beliefs. They also limit our BECOMING journeys unless we have the proper tools to overcome them. The pressure to know what we have not yet learned, believe what we have not yet experienced, or pretend we have unshakable faith because of family heritage is a lot to bear. Like anyone else, I needed safe places to ASK my questions and wrestle over real-life issues without worrying it would lead to personal or religious shaming. I longed for the freedom to be layered, to be human.

When I became a parent, I learned just how easy it is to place unrealistic expectations on our children without making allowances for their shortcomings. Cole, the firstborn of our children, was a near-model citizen in our home from age two to thirteen. But he and I went through a rough patch when he entered his teen years. It was short, but it was real. I would ask him to help with chores around the house, and although he would do the required things, he did so while demonstrating passive annoyance. I would address his poor attitude, but unfortunately, sometimes I did so in a way that gestured to the whole of him. During one of these tense mother-son dances, I spoke firmly to him, saying, "Cole, why would you do that?"

In a sorrowful tone, Cole replied, "Because I'm human."

Wow! His words hit me like a two-by-four. And I am pretty sure that this two-by-four was the plank talked about in Scripture, which I now needed to take out of my own blind eye so I could see my son more clearly.

"How can you say to your brother, 'Let me take the speck out of your eye,' while there is still a plank in your own eye? You hypocrite, first, take the plank out of your own eye, and then you will see clearly to remove the speck from your brother's eye." (Matthew 7:4–5)

Cole was not only just as human as everyone else, but he was smack dab in the middle of the years of increased questioning, wrestling with his own will, and learning to discern things on his own. I was grateful for the Spirit's correction so that I could reengage with my teenage son in a better way.

When I was about Cole's age, I, too, wrestled with questions of my own about life, relationships, and the larger world. The contradictions between what I had been taught about God and what I perceived in myself and in the world around me had started piling up. Despite the inner conflict, I was afraid that by asking my questions, I would invite judgment or jeopardize relationships I cherished, particularly my relationship with God. I feared I might undermine the beliefs of others or, worse, harm the Lord's reputation. The few times I did share my struggles affirmed these fears. It seemed that either the wobbliness of my faith was celebrated by those who wanted to feel better about theirs, or my struggles of unbelief served to confirm the doubts they had about God. Once, I was told, "If *you* are not sure it's all true, and you're *you*, why should *I* believe?" So, I learned to hide my questions about faith and my struggles with unbelief. At least, I did so for as long as I could.

Eventually, however, my soul had mounted so many unspoken arguments against the goodness of God that it felt like cracks were forming between my soul and God's Spirit. The sense of inner hypocrisy in my belief system started to steal my joy and peace. I needed to find a safe landing place for my questions, a safe place to dump the clutter in my soul and begin to sort things out. *But with whom could I share openly? Whose faith would not be harmed by my doubt and struggles of unbelief? Who had questioned God themselves and come out on the other side with their belief system intact? And who would not judge the whole of my faith based on my inquiries?*

THE WAY OF BECOMING

SPIRITUAL CLOTHESLINE

The answer was my Mema, my father's mother. Mema was the one person I knew who had survived the worst kind of suffering. She had lost her two-year-old son, Billy, in a drowning accident in the river beside her house. I wondered how she had not become bitter, insane, or permanently distrustful of God after suffering the death of her child. I decided her faith must run deep because a shallow belief system could not have survived such a tragic loss. If the death of her child did not take away her faith, then my questions wouldn't either. Mema became my safe harbor.

She certainly had her quirks. Mema was a "collector" of all things. She accumulated stuff and had difficulty letting go of anything. But this made her even more approachable to me. Her habit of collecting also made sense to me. Not only had she suffered the tragic loss of her young son, but she had been raised without a father. Her dad left when she was only ten years old, and she had no further contact with him while growing up. Later, she found out that not only had her father remarried, but that he had also had another daughter and given her the *same name* as my Mema. My Mema was Beverley Ellen, and her half-sister, Beverley Elaine. I suppose if I had lost as much as she had, I would have held on to what remained with a tighter grip too.

> I suppose if I had lost as much as she had, I would have held on to what remained with a tighter grip too.

On one of the days that I was helping Mema sort some of her collections, I launched into my questions about God and the contradictions I was perceiving in the world. "Mema, what about the starving children in Africa?" I asked. "Does God feed them?"

Mema didn't even attempt to provide answers to my questions. Instead, she advised me to go directly to the One who had all the answers. "Hang your questions on the line," she said. "And just leave them there for God to answer in His time." She told me this would involve *intentionally asking* and *expectantly waiting* on my part.

I decided to open the door to my heart a little wider and release some more questions about God's character, the world, and His work in it. But when I did, the words poured forth like they were bursting from an overstuffed closet that had accidentally been unlocked.

"What about the poor children in India? How do they learn about Jesus? What do they need to believe? Does God provide for them?"

There was relief in just speaking these things out loud. I asked her many spiritual questions that day. And though she would give me a sense of how God had ministered to her regarding similar things, she mainly expressed the importance of my communicating directly with the Lord, asking and trusting Him to respond to me in His perfect time. Her words seemed reasonable and wise. Sitting there amid my grandmother's stuff, I decided to add my messiness and vulnerability to her piles of things. Together, we sorted her stuff and mine.

Even though I don't remember all she said that day, I remember how her words made me feel and the impressions they left on my heart. The confidence I saw in her eyes let me know God could handle my questions. The love and respect with which she spoke showed me she was not disappointed with me for asking them. Her clarity and brevity revealed that this was how *she* had dealt with *her* big questions. It was a well-worn pathway that had already proven itself to her. And the conviction with which she shared implied it was of the utmost importance that I entrust these things to God as soon as possible. It was time to stop ignoring my questions and hiding them away. The burden I had falsely taken on, to be the one with all the "God answers," was replaced with the lighter yoke that now beckoned me to ASK all of my God questions. Had I not hung my questions on the line, I might have missed the answers when they came, as well as the gift of seeing God's miraculous hand in them.

WILL YOU FEED MY PEOPLE?

In 1993, during one of my college semesters abroad, I had the opportunity to go on a tenting safari to the Maasai Mara of Kenya. On one of the evenings back at the camp, a few other college students came to hang out in our tent and began telling ghost stories. There was no electricity, and we had just seen lions and rhinos earlier that day. So, the ungated campsite was frightening enough without adding scary stories. I picked up my journal and quietly slipped from the tent.

Nearby, there was a burning campfire encircled by logs. I took a seat and began writing in my journal. Without realizing it, I had also started quietly singing "Alleluia." My singing was interrupted by a man's voice with a thick African accent, speaking to me from across the fire and out of the darkness. It startled me. I hadn't noticed anyone. The voice said, "I know your God is real."

As the figure stepped closer to the flame, I began making out his face, frame, and dress. With his earlobes stretched low, beaded necklaces around his neck, a *shuka* cloth around his tall, thin torso, and a towering staff in his hand, I understood him to be a warrior from the Maasai tribe. "Come," he said, "I want to tell you a story." He motioned for me to move with him to a better-lighted area where we could sit and talk.

The Maasai's Story

As we sat together on the picnic bench, he began by saying, "This is my story. When I was twelve years old, the people in my tribe were starving. My father was the chief of our tribe, and I was the eldest son of my father's first wife." He explained that the eldest son of the chief's first wife was responsible for ensuring that the entire tribe had enough food to eat when the leader was away. It had thus become his duty at the tender age of twelve to provide food for his people. So, he took the only gun in his village and walked out onto the savanna to hunt game. Walking away from the village, he looked into the sky and cried, "Are You going to let my people starve? Won't You feed my people?"

Right as he had sent these questions heavenward, a herd of impalas came running past as if out of nowhere. He pursued them, knowing he was not fast enough to catch them. Eventually, the herd ran behind a group of trees and out of sight. Nevertheless, he continued running along the same way they had gone. As he came around the brush, he saw they had all gone, except for a solitary impala, now lying at his feet and looking up at him as if in willing submission. He was utterly amazed, realizing intuitively that this was the divine provision he had sought. He used his foot to press against the animal to see if it would run away. It did not. Instead, it remained at his feet, staring up into his eyes. This Maasai tribesman explained to me how the power of his disbelief began to overtake his thoughts, which led him to declare in his heart, "This can't be true. The animal must be lame or bad for eating."

He told me that as soon as he formed those thoughts, "The creature stood to its feet and ran away." Even though his own unbelief had let this temporary provision slip through his fingers, this young man realized for the first time that he had gained long-term provision for his soul and, ultimately, for his tribe. It would prove to be a kind of supply that does not run out, with ongoing access to the Heavenly Provider.

In search of his father, the chief, he set out on a journey to the city of Nairobi. Eventually, he found his father drinking with some companions in a tavern. He went up to him and declared, "God is real, Father! God is real!"

At that, this Maasai tribesman sitting beside me stopped speaking and removed a brass pendant necklace hanging on a black leather string around his neck. It was in the shape of the African continent. As he held it in his hand, he said, "I give you this to remember." Then, he placed it in the palm of my hand and said, "You can see my name engraved here on the back. I am Gideon."

Gideon's Story

His name was Gideon. He bore the same name as Gideon of the Bible, and his story affirmed many of the lessons taught in the Bible story. In both stories, God had answered the desperate pleas of hungry people by appointing and equipping one of the least among them to become their vessel of rescue. In the book of Judges, the angel of the Lord came to Gideon, who was hiding from his enemies, and addressed him as a "mighty warrior." The angel of the Lord had called Gideon to become the salvation of his people. As the youngest person in his family and part of the smallest tribe, the tribe of Manasseh, Gideon did not feel he could live up to this new label of "mighty warrior." Both Gideon of the tribe of Manasseh and this Gideon of the Maasai tribe were fearful, doubting themselves and doubting God, and therefore, struggling to live into their callings. Still, both overcame their fears by asking God directly. God proved His faithfulness through hearing and responding to their cries and questions.

As I reflected on these stories in the context of my own story, I was fascinated by how Gideon had asked his questions in a similar way to how Mema had instructed me to ASK mine. According to Scripture, Gideon, too, had placed his questions before God like someone putting clothes on a clothesline. He used lamb's wool to ASK his questions of God. And God answered every one of them tangibly and visibly.

> Gideon said to God, "If you will save Israel by my hand as you have promised—look, I will place a wool fleece on the threshing floor. If there is dew only on the fleece and all the ground is dry, then I will know that you will save Israel by my hand, as you said." And that is what happened. Gideon rose early the next day; he squeezed the fleece and wrung out the dew—a bowlful of water. Then Gideon said to God, "Do not be angry with me. Let me make just one more request. Allow me one more test with the fleece, but this time make the fleece dry and let the ground be covered with dew." That night God did so. Only the fleece was dry; all the ground was covered with dew. (Judges 6:36–40)

Not only did each of the two Gideon stories affirm the other, but they also taught me much about God's character and patterns of engagement with people. I was coming to see how the Lord turns fearful people into courageous vessels by His grace. He invites us to dialogue with Him, ask questions, and receive what is needed to live into our new callings by faith. "The one who calls you is faithful, and he will do it" (1 Thessalonians 5:24).

I also saw a connection between the fleece that Gideon used to overcome his unbelief and the new spiritual "clothes" he was being called to wear. God had already named him a "mighty warrior," but he still needed to "put on" these spiritual clothes through belief. The woolen cloth symbolized the spiritual vestments he would wear to become a vessel of hope for his people.

Did I realize the connections between the two Gideon stories when I heard them? No, I did not, not then. Did I make the mental connection between the questions I had hung on my prayer line about the starving children of Africa and Gideon the Maasai's story of being a starving African child? No, I did not, not then! Did I connect my spiritual clothesline to the fleece coverings laid down by Gideon of the Bible as he made his requests to God? No, I did not, not then. I just received his story as I did the brass necklace that was placed into the palm of my hand—with awe and wonder. I was, however, becoming more acquainted with a big God who cares for those who are small.

"God Sent You to See"

At the safari's conclusion, our group returned to the port city of Mombasa. Here, we would board our university ship and continue our Semester at Sea. We would sail across the Indian Ocean *en route* to Madras, India. But before boarding, I went to see what the local merchants had laid on blankets to sell to the boarding passengers. As I was walking along the pier, I felt a hand on my shoulder. It was an African woman selling wooden giraffes. She began praying in a tongue unknown to me. She finished in English, saying, "It is God who sends you to show you His world." I knew the Holy Spirit was speaking yet again through a human vessel. I thanked her, purchased a giraffe, and boarded the ship.

After fourteen days at sea, we reached Madras, later known as Chennai. We disembarked, and I boarded a bus bound for an overnight visit to an "untouchables village." The program description indicated it was for students interested in getting firsthand knowledge of the culture and economics of extreme poverty. When I read this, the words seemed to jump off the page, compelling me to choose this program over all the other offerings, including an excursion to the Taj Mahal.

On the drive to the village, we stopped by a nonprofit center to hear a lecture from local leaders on the culture of poverty. They spoke about a deeply entrenched hierarchy of human valuing supported by the Hindu belief system of reincarnation, called the caste system. This belief system teaches that each soul receives what it deserves based on the good works performed in a soul's past life. Each soul iteration had the potential to do enough good to earn its way to a higher caste in its next life cycle. *Very convenient for the rich and powerful*, I thought. The remote village we would be visiting was populated by those considered lower than the lowest caste. We were encouraged to use the term *Dalit* instead of untouchables, as it was considered less degrading.

> The broken and small of this world can serve as gatekeepers into new experiences with Christ.

Little did I know, but hidden in this tiny word of Dalit were countless mysteries of the kingdom of God that my soul would discover bit by bit, beginning with this village and continuing over the next three decades. Dalit in the Sanskrit vernacular means poor and oppressed, but classically, it means divided, fragmented, scattered, or broken to pieces. In Hebrew, this same word refers to the poor and the weak, as well as a door or entryway. God would soon use my experiences in this Indian village to draw me deeper into understanding the interwoven nature of Dalit's spiritual meaning and how the broken and small of this world can serve as gatekeepers into new experiences with Christ.

Within the first hour of our visit to the village, I was utterly overwhelmed by the abject poverty. It was beyond my imagination. The villagers' homes were small circular structures made of mud and straw. Inside the first hut was a thin-framed woman sitting on a straw mat. Just outside, I noticed a single village cow. Its emaciated state made me wonder how this creature could provide any help to the villagers. In the corner of the second dwelling that we entered was a cooking fire with smoldering embers, and next to it was a dead animal. Hope rose in me for a moment, thinking this family had food to eat. Upon looking closer, however, I was horrified to realize it was a bat carcass, a source of sustenance, which seemed to epitomize the poverty of the Dalit people.

After exiting, I began wandering in disbelief. I recall thinking *it should be a requirement for anyone who wields power in a wealthy nation to see what my eyes are seeing now*. My heart ached. *Where is God in all of this?*

Tearfully, I stepped away from the group and sat on a rock in front of a tree. At some point, I quietly started to sing "Alleluia." I suppose this was my way of soothing my soul. I recall singing because a little girl who had come close to listen captured my attention. Her shirt was a tattered beige, which I am sure had once been white. She was dirty, but she was beautiful. She could not have been more than five years old. She shimmied herself closer to me on the rock, stretched out her hand, and traced the cross hanging around my neck with her tiny finger. I had forgotten it was even there until she touched it. Then, she pulled down the collar band of her torn shirt and showed me that she, too, had a cross hanging around her neck. Hers was made of reed and fastened by a thin piece of twine. Somehow, that simple act of tracing my cross and revealing her own communicated our shared hope. She held my hand, and we sat together in silence for a while.

At that moment, I was taken back to the time with my Mema when she had encouraged me, saying, "Hang your questions on the line and wait for God to answer in His time." Like a strong wind, the words of my questions came rushing back to me. "What about the starving children in Africa . . . and the poor children in India?" These were the very things I had asked of God and hung on my spiritual clothesline. *Poor! Starving! Africa! India!* How had God done this? What in the world!? How had He caused these exact questions to be addressed in living color and in the context of my own life now unfolding before me? Were these things already going to happen, or had my questions caused them to come into being? Hadn't the questions been my own random, freefalling inquiries? Either way, it seemed the doors of heaven had broken open for me. The Dalit people had taken my hand and led me across a threshold, going from the land of questioning to the land of knowing, at least in part.

Doorkeepers to the Treasures of His Kingdom

The words of the Mombasa merchant echoed within me. "It is God who sends you. He wants to show you His world." I was getting a spiritual education far beyond the university curricula during my Semester at Sea, affirming how alive God is in His world and my story. I could no longer think of the poor as a problem to be solved but as doorkeepers to the treasures of God's kingdom. Ironically, in Hebrew, the language of my ancestors, the dalet is drawn as both a hanging tent door and a man bent over in humility. This symbol affirms the connection between the necessity of humility and our regular entrance through the door into the very presence of God. By asking, and now Him answering me this way, the Dalit people served as the doorkeepers into God's promised kingdom riches.

This gift of asking, seeking, and even knocking on the doors of heaven helped me get unstuck from languishing places and caused every facet of my walk with Jesus to benefit. The more I engaged in this Divine Dialogue, where I would hang my ASKS on the line, the more God seemed to respond to me in a living way. God's responses came through various means. Sometimes, they came by the illumination of certain words in Scripture, sometimes by the spoken words or actions of others, and sometimes through nature's parables. My belief system seemed to be transitioning from a black-and-white type-faced rendition to a living, technicolor glory show of God.

BECOMING INVESTMENTS

I will never know what my Mema pictured in her mind when she encouraged me to "hang my questions on the line." She passed away before I thought to ask her. But I do recall what I envisioned that day in her presence. I pictured an outdoor washing line with colorful garments hanging on it. Each piece represented an aspect of God's truth that I was struggling to embrace fully. Over the years, I submitted many different things to this spiritual clothesline. Some were fragmented parts that symbolized stuff in my story that needed healing, and some were places where my understanding of God's ways and character was incomplete. Some were areas of my relationship with Him that had been soiled by sin and needed cleansing. Many were spiritual hand-me-downs that had come to me from the belief systems of others and were simply too big for me to wear comfortably without alteration or required more time for me to grow into them. Some were hopes, others were wounds, and many were just everyday curiosities or objects of my wonderment that I had put up on this drying line in the form of my questions. But all were things that needed the breath of God to blow over them so that, in time, they could be ready for me to wear in a becoming fashion. Fittingly, the word "breath" in Hebrew is also the same word as wind and Spirit—*ruach*. The breath of His Word provides the drying winds necessary for ASKS to come down from the line ready to wear.

No matter what questions I hung on my spiritual clothesline, each represented an investment into God's kingdom economy. And even though the word "investment" is mainly used in the context of a secular financial economy, there exists a divine economy in which we can invest by faith. Over time, every investment into God's economy proves worthy and wise. Our goal must be to receive dividends of God's grace, according to His name as *Yahweh*, the BECOMING One, the One who causes us to BECOME.

Making Investments

Like other investments, spiritual ones require waiting before returns can be realized. In a human economy, we must first demonstrate a commitment by sowing into an endeavor before we can expect to reap any gains. So it is with the divine economy. Prayer is one of the key currencies that allows us to participate in this economy and become more prosperous by faith. To those who do not invest in this way, Jesus says, "You have not because you ask not." But to those who ask, Jesus promises, "I will do whatever you ask in my name, so that the Father may be glorified in the Son. You may ask me for anything in my name, and I will do it" (John 14:13–14). Investing in the eternal kingdom of God is the most solid investment anyone can make.

The word investment literally means "in the clothes of." We see this word used in the phrase priestly vestments, referring to the clothing worn by holy men of the church. This seemed marvelous to me when I considered the spiritual practice of the clothesline. We hang our questions on the line like spiritual clothes that we are not ready to wear comfortably yet. But when our ASKS are answered, these newly integrated beliefs become like custom-fit clothes we can now comfortably wear, displaying the beauty of God's love and testifying to His character based on our lived experiences.

Trying to impart our belief systems to others, like our children or grandchildren, is akin to giving them our hand-me-down clothes. Some may fit well, and other pieces must be adjusted or set aside until the receivers have time to grow into them. Though we cannot hand others our complete belief system and see it all miraculously integrated into the fibers of another's soul, we can provide them with tools for their own spiritual exploration and faith formation. "Start children off on the way they should go, and even when they are old they will not turn from it" (Proverbs 22:6).

Parents can lay a strong foundation of faith by sharing the good news of Christ, teaching the Scriptures, and passing down their own stories of the Lord's faithfulness. But a foundation does not a whole house make. According to the Scriptures, God has no grandchildren; He only has children. Each person must grow up into a self-sufficient maturity in their own faith walk (Galatians 6:6). It is vital for our children to possess the tools and knowledge necessary to circumvent obstacles and to get unstuck when they get snagged, need help, or find themselves alone. The faith practice of ASK is one of the spiritual competencies we should give our children.

> Few things are more life-affirming, soul-empowering, and faith-edifying than when God responds to the specific things we have asked.

The physical visual of a clothesline provides an incredibly effective way to do this and an efficient way to invest in the kingdom of God. It is simple enough for a child to understand and provides an active means for engaging in a relationship with the living God. Through this practice, even a child can understand the Divine Dialogue and mindfully experience God, hearing and answering them directly. Few things are more life-affirming, soul-empowering, and faith-edifying than when God responds to the specific things we have asked. Each time this happens, we receive not only the fulfillment of the thing we sought but also a new seed that can grow into a life-giving plant of belief, revealing yet another aspect of God's character that is BECOMING manifest in us. The Bible says, "Hope deferred makes the heart sick, but a longing fulfilled is a tree of life" (Proverbs 13:12).

When our children got to the ages where they began asking more and more questions of faith, Scott and I would not only share what we knew from the Scriptures and our own experiences, but we would also teach them how to invite God to weigh in directly with their young hearts and minds. I strung up lines made of twine above their beds, clipped clothespins upon them, and gave them each a notepad on which to write their ASKS. My children loved that we were using notepapers in the shape of clothes made for paper dolls to hang their ASKS on the line. As Cole got older, he kept a personal ASK journal. Scott and I also began keeping a marriage and family ASK journal, taking turns speaking and scribing our prayers. However, we instituted one rule for the use of our Marriage ASK Journal. We could not counsel each other over what we had written; we could only take them to God together and let Him be our Counselor and Provider.

A CHILD'S PRAYER

When she was around ten, Maya asked me if she could have a horse. I answered bluntly, "Nope, we won't be getting a horse. Our neighborhood ordinances don't even allow chickens or above-ground pools; they definitely won't allow horses."

"Okay, Mom," she said solemnly.

As she walked away in silence, a wash of conviction came over me. *What if God had a different plan for our daughter, something I couldn't imagine?* But I did my best to quell this inner notion by using my rational mind to affirm that such a big thing as a horse was entirely out of reach, both practically and financially.

Maya had taken English riding lessons since she was six. She had fallen in love with all things equestrian from the moment she first fed a carrot to our friend's horse when she was just two. Her closest friend and riding buddy, Ingrid, was soon getting a horse and a barn on her family's property. Thinking about this reminded me of my daughter's tender heart and the importance of not playing God in her life. I felt convicted that I did not know what her future held any more than I knew mine. I knew we did not have the means to get Maya a horse, but it wasn't right for me to assume God would never work a horse into her life story in some way someday.

I went and found Maya in her bedroom and told her, "I'm sorry, honey. Just because I don't see how getting a horse could be possible, at least not any time soon, I'm not God, and God can do anything. Maybe you will marry someone with horses one day, or you might even have the means to buy one for yourself." Sadly, that was as far as my limited mind could imagine. Still, I reminded Maya to use her spiritual clothesline to hang her ASKS and wait for God to answer in His time and in His way. She went right to writing her ASKS on paper dresses and clipping them with clothespins on the string above her bed.

Providentially or ironically, not more than a week passed before my aunt Brenda reached out to ask if I knew anyone who could care for her daughter Hanna's horse while she was finishing her final years of college. She indicated it would not be more than a two- or three-year commitment.

What in the world? I was dumbfounded. The mental oscillations started immediately as I tried to talk myself out of believing this was God's divine provision for Maya. But as I was tossing these things over in my mind, trying to dismiss the apparent providence, I glanced up, and there, propped up against Scott's computer, was the only picture we had of Maya sitting on cousin Hanna's horse. The photo was taken two years earlier, and I hadn't noticed it in all that time, sitting on Scott's desk.

Treasures Poured Out

None of this made any sense to me, except that God must be deciding to grant Maya's ASK for a horse. The vessel God had chosen to answer her prayer was my aunt Brenda, Mema's youngest child. Brenda was the child God gave Mema after her son Billy had tragically died. God has such a miraculous way of weaving together the threads of human lives both inside and outside of time.

I was further humbled when I learned sometime later that Maya had *not*, in fact, explicitly asked God to give her a horse. Instead, she asked God to keep her from being jealous of her friend, who was getting a barn and a horse. She had written on her little paper dress that she did not want to harm her friendship by becoming jealous, so she asked God to keep her from sin, keep her friendship healthy, and provide whatever was in her best interest.

Jealousy is far too often the great ruin of once-loving relationships. It is responsible for wrongful injuries to countless souls throughout all of human existence, even the crucifixion of Jesus. The Bible has a lot to say on this topic. "What causes fights and quarrels among you? Don't they come from your desires that battle within you? You desire but do not have. . . . You covet, but you cannot get what you want, so you quarrel and fight. You do not have because you do not ask God" (James 4:2–3). The most essential thing to remember is that asking God is the antidote for combatting jealousy.

Living on these pedestrian planes of life with a pizza-pie mentality rather than on the celestial planes with a wise and generous spirit reveals how little we know about the kingdom of heaven. There are limitless resources in God's economy, treasures ready to be poured forth, awaiting anyone who would ASK and seek Him diligently. "You make known to me the path of life; you will fill me with joy in your presence, with eternal pleasures at your right hand" (Psalm 16:11). Asking God directly to meet our needs, heal our pains, quell our anxieties, and empower our endeavors is the way back into a healthy relationship with the Spirit and others.

> The one thing I love more than having God's presence come alive in my story is having it come alive in my children's.

God answered my daughter Maya's ask and protected her treasured friendship. He provided a beautiful chestnut mare for her to ride over the next three years while Hanna finished college. But Maya's heavenly Father did not just give her any old horse, but the granddaughter of Triple Crown winner Seattle Slew. The horse was named Christmas Wish and arrived just before Christmas. The one thing I love more than having God's presence come alive in my story is having it come alive in my children's. Through this experience, the truth of Ephesians 3:20 began to reside deeply in the soul of my daughter. God can "do immeasurably more than all we ask or imagine, according to his power that is at work within us."

The "immeasurably more" refers to the returns on investment by faith using the pathways of ASK and IMAGINE. God indeed did more than Maya had asked and more than I had imagined. He not only made it practically and financially feasible for the horse to be with us for those three years, but He prepared my daughter's heart when it was time for this horse to go.

After that experience, Maya became consistent in using her prayer line to ASK, seek, and knock. She strung up a second clothesline in her bedroom and began helping her two little sisters, who shared her room, write their ASKS before bedtime. Leah liked dictating hers to Maya, and Annika preferred drawing them as pictures. Maya would take the little paper dresses down from the line once they had been answered and then place them in a large box filled with all of God's replies. The responses to their ASKS provided tangible proof that God had heard and seen them and that, in His time, He would answer their prayers and supply all their needs. We often refer to these answered ASKS as "closed circles" or completed Cycles of Grace.

Each closed circle becomes a newly integrated belief in the souls of those who asked them in prayer. They are like vested stocks, making us richer in faith and belief. They represent things that are no longer just hopes in the truth of the written Word but instead, words of truth that have come alive in us and as beliefs to which we can now fully testify.

Even though most of our children's answered questions were not something as grand as a horse, each closed-circle experience became a newly integrated belief, teaching them something more about God's love, faithfulness, and power. These stories based on their lived experiences become stones of remembrance that continue to build their houses of faith, in which they can dwell more securely even through the storms of life.

CLOSED CIRCLE

It has been five years since Maya got her "Christmas Wish" and thirty years since my first encounter with the Dalit of India and Africa. Even now, no matter what new belief comes down from my spiritual clothesline as a spiritual garment ready to wear, I find my heart declaring as if, for the first time, *God is real!* Through every encounter, He becomes real to me in a new way in the context of my life story.

Even in light of these miracles and the many more encounters that followed, I still tended to doubt whether my prayers were altering the course of my life's events or if I was simply participating in God's already firmly laid plans. After meditating on this idea, I finally asked God; and He was faithful to answer me yet again.

A New Thing

The year was 1996, and I was about to board a flight from the East Coast back to California, where I was living, studying, and working at the time. I read an excerpt in my daily devotional, *My Utmost for His Highest,* written by Oswald Chambers, that talked about not relying on the glory of our past experiences but instead looking to God to do a new thing today.[1] Just as one of my mother's mentors said, "It is not in the victories of the past that we have Jesus; it is in the neediness of the now."[2]

I had already experienced many glorious interventions of God. I had witnessed thousands of people transformed through a Billy Graham Crusade in Moscow a few years before this. But my days as a missionary in Russia were now in the past, and it was time to wake up to His divine interventions—or at least the possibility of them—in my current reality. Right there at the airport gate, I asked the Lord to do something special on my upcoming flight. I figured it would require my willingness to share the message of God's love with whoever would be seated next to me. So mentally, I began to gear up for what this would cost me and the reality that I might not get my book read on the plane.

I boarded, took my assigned seat at the window, and started reading my *Pilgrim's Progress* book. A man came and sat in the middle seat next to me and began eating the Reuben sandwich he had brought with him on the flight. For me, as a vegetarian at the time, the meat and sauerkraut smells were a bit much, so I resumed reading, hoping God would not take me up on my offer to have a conversation with my meat-eating neighbor in the middle seat. Though feeling a little guilty before God, I turned toward the window to read.

What if this man doesn't know God loves Him? The thought niggled as I considered what I had asked and promised God. *And here I am, turning away because I don't like corned beef? How shallow am I?* Guilt started setting in until I glanced over and noticed that this man had pulled out a Bible to read. *Phew!* I was off the hook and free to enjoy my book. So, I did just that—until Mr. Reuben Sandwich started talking to me.

"That's a good book," he remarked.

I responded, "Well, that's *the* good book!" gesturing to the Bible on his tray table and feeling clever.

He asked me why I was heading to California. He seemed kind and genuinely interested.

So I engaged, but now more happily. I shared that I was a teacher at a Christian high school. He asked me the school's name.

"Calvary Chapel High School," I responded.

"That's interesting," he said. "I attend a Calvary Chapel in Baltimore, Maryland."

"Really?" I said and then proceeded to blurt out some words before I even had a chance to process them, asking, "You aren't Rick Plantholt, are you?"

With a face revealing his utter shock, he replied, "Yes, I am! How did you know?"

There's noooo way! I thought as I sat there, just as stunned as he was.

I explained that I genuinely did not know who he was, but that when I was a missionary living in Russia, I asked God if I could meet "this Rick Plantholt guy" one day.

"I asked that because your name was printed on some teaching tapes lent to me by another missionary living in my dorm, who went by 'Anne with an e.'"

A sign of recognition came over his face, acknowledging he knew her, which emboldened me to continue.

"I would listen to these cassettes on my Walkman during my runs around

Moscow. Your words got me through some really hard days there. But I also felt guilty for asking to meet you because I realized I was giving you credit instead of God for comforting me. So, I thanked God for your ministry and then forgot all about it—until right now. When you said that you went to Calvary Chapel of Baltimore, I suddenly pictured the words written on the cassette tapes: Rick Plantholt, Calvary Chapel Baltimore."

Then, I explained to him how this was not the *only* reason I asked his name and why I suspected God might be up to something. I shared about the devotional I read by Oswald Chambers, which encouraged me to ASK God to show up in a new way *today* and not rely only on His miracles from the past.

"And so, I did just that."

I could see by the look on his face that he was just as in awe of the weaving hand of God as I was.

"Wait!" he said. "Tell me again when you prayed for God to do something new?"

"Just as I was getting on this plane," I answered.

"Wow! Now that explains it!" he said with a kind of happy relief. "And right before I got on this flight, I was called up to the counter and given a new seat assignment." Then, he pointed to a woman sitting a few rows behind him and asked me, "You see that beautiful woman sitting back there?" He waved to her, she waved back, and we all smiled at one another. "That's my wife, and that aisle seat was supposed to be mine."

God had not only answered a hope I expressed long ago to meet this pastor who had ministered to me while I was living in Russia, but He also answered two other particular and current ASKS of mine: to experience His hand in my life *today* and to know if prayer really can change things. I had now learned, unforgettably, that prayer actually does *change* things and that God is actively involved in my life *today*!

> When we know God is near, we possess a kind of peace that enables us to endure.

Asking God by faith and receiving His empowering presence by grace as He answers is the great secret to enduring the many struggles we face in this human life. When we know God is near and involved in our lives because He has made His presence known, we possess a kind of peace that enables us to endure. Sometimes, we receive specifically what we ASK for, and sometimes, we receive something even better for our souls. Either way, when we ASK God directly for help, we become more familiar with His ways, and we experience His presence draw near to us.

Intentional Steps

Faith is about taking intentional steps toward our source of hope, which is the great revealer of what we truly worship. When we're anxious, an excellent first step of faith is simply looking to God and asking in prayer. Philippians 4:6–7 affirms this, saying, "Do not be anxious about anything, but in every situation, by prayer and petition, with thanksgiving, present your requests to God. And the peace of God, which transcends all understanding, will guard your hearts and minds in Christ Jesus."

Sometimes, we think we are asking God when, actually, we are not. Discussing prayer requests with our neighbor is not asking God. Ruminating in our minds and worrying in our hearts is not asking God. Sharing our hearts and our pain with other people is not asking God. Talking about our needs, blogging, or posting on social media is not asking God. Though it is powerful to have others pray for us, Jesus' words in Matthew 18:19 remind us that intercessory prayer is most powerful when those praying for us are doing so in agreement with what we have already asked of God directly ourselves. "Again, truly I tell you that if two of you on earth agree about anything they ask for, it will be done for them by my Father in heaven." And this is why we are to begin by petitioning God directly for our needs and desires.

According to Hebrews 11:6, God rewards those who believe He exists and diligently seek Him. When we are not confident in God's existence, we should begin there, asking Him to show us that He is alive and to reveal Himself in a way we can receive and understand. With a quiet heart, we simply need to ASK. What is there to lose by humbling ourselves to call out to heaven? We can ASK God to show Himself in a way that is undeniable to us and involved in the context of our stories. He longs to show His love. He wants us to ASK Him, to express our needs, our unmet desires, hopes, and the things we question in our lives and in the world. We can come to Him with the contradictions we perceive between the Scriptures and our experiences and even the things we simply wonder about.

The Word of God promises that "Everyone who asks receives; and the one who seeks finds; and to the one who knocks, the door will be opened" (Matthew 7:8). Using the acronym A.S.K. can make it easier to remember the words ASK, seek, and knock. Even though asking God about literally anything is easy, I have been surprised to find that *most people simply do not do it*. This is why we do not see many miracles today. It is particularly true in wealthier nations where we have forgotten the importance of a humble and poor spirit before God and, therefore, miss the doorway to becoming rich in faith.

Our needs, desires, and questions can serve as glorious invitations to ASK, seek, and knock on heaven's door. Whether we use an ASK journal, hang up our spiritual questions on a physical clothesline, as my family likes to do, or simply speak requests in prayer to God. Using ASK as a faith practice is a beautiful way to develop our BECOMING stories. The Lord promises to do far more than we could even ASK or IMAGINE (Eph. 3:20).

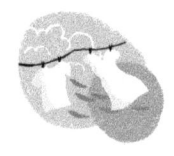

YOUR BECOMING STORY: ASK

Consider hanging a clothesline in your home or keeping an ASK journal to express your soul's questions and concerns that need to be "hung on the line" for God to answer in His time. Your questions do not need to fester, cause you to get stuck, or remain unanswered simply because they have gone unasked.

Make your requests known to God, asking for His help, wisdom, direction, and deliverance. It is important to *be as specific as you can* with your ASKS. Don't limit Him; He is the Almighty God, your Maker, the One who loves you indescribably.

"This is the confidence we have in approaching God: that if we ask anything according to his will, he hears us. And if we know that he hears us—whatever we ask—we know that we have what we asked of him" (1 John 5:14–15).

"Cycles of Grace"

Past traumas become triggers, presenting in anger,
But really, they're fears in disguise.
Wounds become weapons in our self-protection,
And harm the ones standing close by.
Let's name all our fears and entrust them to God,
To end the down-spirals and strife.
Actions of faith begin cycles of grace,
And bring healing and newness to life.
A soul that abides will soon start to rise,
Being filled with love, peace, joy, and power.
There's little more needful to meet our hearts' cries
Than hope in our most trying hour.[3]

4

IMAGINE

Visions and Promises

As a little girl, I vividly recall holding Jesus' hand to ascend the long wooden staircase through the darkness on my way to bed. Even though my physical eyes could not see Him, the eyes of my heart were thoroughly convinced He was there. I hugged the banister as I walked to give plenty of room for Jesus to walk beside me. This confidence in His presence compelled me to reach out my trembling hand to clasp His strong, invisible one. Did I imagine this? Quite possibly. But even if I did, imagining something does not mean it isn't real. It may simply mean it is being seen by the eyes of the heart rather than our physical eyes.

REGARDING THE UNSEEN

God encourages His children, when facing times of darkness, to fix their eyes not on what is seen, but on what is unseen, since what is seen is temporary, but what is unseen is eternal (2 Corinthians 4:18). Without the use of the human imagination, how would it be possible to look at what is unseen or understand what is eternal? The only way to see the unseen is by forming mental images of that which is being perceived by the heart, mind, or spirit. Just because something is first seen by the eyes of the heart does not mean that it is untrue or merely fantastical. In truth, the unseen things may be more "real" from heaven's perspective than what can be seen.

God has always interacted with humanity by making the unseen realm of the Spirit visible through images in creation. The apostle Paul reminded the first-century Christians that He had imprinted His invisible attributes into His creation. "For since the creation of the world, God's invisible qualities—his eternal power and divine nature—have been clearly seen, being understood from what has been made, so that people are without excuse" (Romans 1:20).

Sacred Imagination

We are also intended to live by faith, which involves making what is unseen become apparent through the actions we choose. "Now faith is the substance of things hoped for and the evidence of things unseen" (Hebrews 11:1 KJV). Do not miss the importance of this biblical definition of faith! It calls faith evidence and substance. Faith is made of "stuff." Making hope manifest in the physical realm is the very essence of faith. This biblical definition of faith underscores how integral the imagination is to its practice. If hope is the bridge linking the seen realm to the unseen realm, then using our imaginations by faith is what allows us to walk over that bridge.

The sacred imagination serves as a tool for the believer's journey from sentiments of hope to actions of faith. "And without faith it is impossible to please God" (Hebrews 11:6). By faith, we ASK God our questions, and by faith, we understand His answers. This is the essence of the Divine Dialogue spoken between our faith and His grace. Engaging in the Divine Dialogue involves the faith practices of ASK and IMAGINE.

Using our sanctified imagination as a faith practice teaches us to hear God's voice more clearly, perceive His guiding hand more readily, and receive His provision more fully. The Lord often uses the things in His creation to answer our questions and provide for our needs. Therefore, knowing *how* to receive these seeds of wisdom by reading the many canvases of God on earth is critical to our spiritual development and our soul's transformation. But to begin this journey of new life and growth, we must start with a willingness to return to a childlike sense of wonder so we can perceive and receive the good gifts from His Spirit, given to us in seed form.

As a child walking alone to bed in the darkness, I was afraid and longed for a comforting presence. God responded to my heart's cry and came to my side. My response to reach out my hand was an act of faith that pleased God and brought me into His very presence and kingdom of light. "Truly, I tell you, unless you change and become like children, you will never enter the kingdom of heaven" (Matthew 18:3). Perhaps God's great call requiring adults to become like children is an invitation to see as children more naturally see, with the eyes of their hearts. Our Lord urges us to use our childlike faith to see what is unseen, especially when facing trials.

> Our Lord urges us to use our childlike faith to see what is unseen, especially when facing trials.

Because trials have a way of adding up the longer we journey here on earth, it is precisely in our adulthoods that we need to use our imaginations the most. Having spiritual vision and making connections to God's written Word is critical in helping us persevere by faith, especially when we are facing life's more challenging terrain. Proverbs 29:18 emphasizes the great importance of vision, "Where there is no vision, the people perish" (KJV).

SUFFERING AND THE SACRED IMAGINATION

As I sat alone in my car outside the Nashville airport with an aching heart, waiting for Scott to return from a business trip only a few weeks after our most painful loss, the full-term stillbirth of one of our daughters. Tears clouded my eyes as I cried out, "Lord, it's all so wrong! I can't even picture where my baby lives. It's all too painful for me."

"Lord, Help Me See!"

In that season, waves of grief and confusion had become commonplace. But on this day and in this place, I was overcome by an acute awareness that it was my own lack of imagination that now robbed me of any real sense of the heavenly realm. The lack of even having an adequate picture of my baby's new home and surroundings felt unbearable. For nine months, my body had kept her warm, safe, well-fed, and lovingly embraced. All the earthly comforts of our home, which had been meticulously and lovingly prepared for her arrival, were, in an instant, rendered useless by her tragic passing. The glaring absence of our daughter's tender frame from the wooden cradle that sat in our living room—an heirloom passed down to me by my great-grandparents—brought tremendous sorrow. Yet, the most unbearable part was that her new home was utterly unknown to me.

Suddenly, I found my most pressing need was to grasp the promise of resurrection and the eternal realm. I would not want any of my children to stay the night at a house I had not visited or with people I had not met. But now, I was facing the fact that my daughter had permanently gone to live in a place that I could not even IMAGINE. Cries rose into my throat, tears began to roll down my cheeks, and I called out, "Lord God, help me. You must help me! Help me picture where my daughter lives. Have mercy on me and help me see!"

Then, like a ray of heavenly hope shooting through the clouds, a whisper from within spoke to my battered soul, gently inviting me to open my eyes. Through a watery gaze and a dirty car window, I noticed that the colors of the scene before me had grown several times brighter. The sky was now a magnificent shade of light blue, with only a few transparent clouds hanging in it. It was as if a luscious green landscape with trees scattered about had been rolled out like a carpet before me. In the distance, rays of sunlight shone down on the earth like inter-dimensional pathways connecting this world to the next. Literally and figuratively, my heart began to follow the sunbeam up to its source.

At that exact moment, my soul knew very well that the Author of this world was posing a question to my bereft soul: "Do you have the faith to trust Me, as the Author of this world, to prepare a suitable home for your daughter in the next?" The Lord was using this work of art that He had created, set before my tear-drenched eyes, to invite me to IMAGINE what He could do in the world to come.

"Can You Trust Me?"

As if to reinforce this message, the Holy Spirit brought a stream of Scripture verses to my mind that I had collected over many years of walking with Jesus and studying His Word. It felt as though by asking my questions, my inner spirit had gone to work, searching the archives of my soul—where God's Word had been written on my heart—like some inner librarian, helping me find answers to confirm whether the experience could be substantiated as truth.

> What no eye has seen, what no ear has heard, and what no human mind has conceived—the things God has prepared for those who love him—these are the things God has revealed to us by his Spirit. The Spirit searches all things, even the deep things of God. (1 Corinthians 2:9–11)

When all else seemed to have failed, God's Spirit searched what had already been deposited in the storehouse of my soul and used these truths to minister a healing balm of encouragement to my broken heart. It felt like my open heart was saying, "Look! Kerry, Look! It says it right here. The Bible tells you that this is true, and so it is indeed God's Spirit speaking to you!"

Then, another verse surfaced. "Now to him who is able to do immeasurable more than all we ask or imagine, according to his power that is at work within us" (Ephesians 3:20). If the Word told me that God could do more than all I could even ASK or IMAGINE, I figured, then I might as well start by asking and imagining! In Scripture, Jesus promises, "You may ask me for anything in my name, and I will do it" (John 14:14). Often, He does it by answering our ASKS using the things in His creation. But often, we miss His answers. It is difficult to perceive God's responses when our spiritual senses have grown dull or because we have forgotten their importance altogether. Engaging in any Divine Dialogue requires speaking to God by faith and mindfully listening for the Holy Spirit to answer. We perceive His responses to our ASKS through our sanctified imaginations. Even if the answers come through Scripture reading, it still requires the use of our spiritual senses to discern the applied meaning of the Spirit's timely responses.

If using my imagination is as far as my mind can go to get close to my children now living in heaven, my heart compelled me to do so. I had learned to ASK God many questions up to that point about theology, the suffering of the poor, and what steps I should take next in fulfilling my calling. However, I had not sought answers to other complex and severe questions about personal suffering, life, and death. My heart was now listening intently to hear the heart of the Father. And He was faithful to respond and reveal these things because He wanted me to know that where my daughter resides is more beautiful than anything I've ever seen in this life. Being reminded of the many beautiful things, even in this broken world, and feeling personally invited to envision something even more than what is found in it caused a new hope to rise in me and minister comfort to my aching soul. Through this experience of imagining heaven, based on the track record of earth's Creator, a whole new living library seemed to open up to me through the messages in God's creation.

> My heart was now listening intently to hear the heart of the Father.

THE DIVINE NATURE

Later that same year, I took a trip with our five-year-old son, Cole, and our two-year-old daughter, Maya, to visit the Georgia Aquarium in Atlanta. It was my first significant outing after our daughter's stillbirth. I had crossed into what seemed to be some new stage of healing, where I was able to handle more public environments and no longer given to random episodes of crying. I was, however, only half present in mind and heart, while my soul remained shrouded in a thick layer of secret grief.

Walking through the aquarium with my children, I found myself staring into the various tanks but caring little about what they contained. Of course, I pretended to care for my children's sake. But as we walked along, the unwelcome houseguest of grief began rapping at the door of my heart again, and I could feel a deep swell start to rise within me. *Here it comes again,* I thought. The sadness and questioning had become strangely familiar, returning unannounced and stirring up the angrier parts within me.

The internal argument I had been trying to suppress began to win out. *Where were You, Lord, when my babies died? And where are You now? You're far away, completely uninvolved in my reality. Is this supposed to be love?* As soon as I vocalized my heart's inner wrestling, the Spirit responded immediately to my questions, encouraging me to return to the saltwater tank I had just passed.

He Is Still Here!

It is strange to think things you would have never said to yourself. But at such moments, I had learned to obey these internal notions just in case they were indeed directives from the Lord. So I did. I returned to the tank I had just passed by and looked in.

I couldn't find even a single creature. *Empty!? How ironic,* I thought, almost mockingly, *that God would choose to tell me to look in the one tank devoid of life. Yep, just like God—absent.*

But then, my Lord spoke to me again: "Look closer. I'm there."

I could not deny that it was the Spirit speaking because, once again, I would never have said these things to myself. Out of my soul's desperation, I indulged the voice within and took another look in the tank. Much to my surprise, as if looking at one of those hidden picture puzzles, this time, I could make out tiny seahorse-like creatures that looked so much like the vegetation to which they clung that they had been completely hidden from me at first.

"Leafy Sea Dragons" were the words on the label next to the tank. The longer I gazed, the more of them I saw . . . so well hidden among the actual leafy seaweed as to be almost invisible.

Can you see Me now? came the Spirit's inner voice. I realized at this moment that the Lord of all creation wanted me to know that although I was having a difficult time perceiving Him, He was still there! He was right there with me in my loss, merely hidden from my limited physical view—just like the Leafy Sea Dragon.

As my mind observed the amazing camouflage that marks these creatures, my heart understood that God had used them to reveal to me that He is where He says He is, even when my physical eyes cannot perceive His presence. I was learning a new aspect of the Maker's divine nature as *the God who conceals and reveals Himself in the things He has made.*

The descriptive name of God as *Yahweh Olam* or *El Olam* found in the Bible (Genesis 21:33; Psalms 90:1–2 and 102:25–27; 1 Peter 1:13–2:3; and Jeremiah 31:3–6) incorporates several Hebrew concepts:[1] *El Olam*, meaning the God of the Universe; *le olam*, meaning from everlasting to everlasting; *ni olam*, meaning hidden or concealed; and *ha olam*, denoting the whole created world.[2] Therefore, *Yahweh Olam* expresses one of the grandest of all God's names: *the God of the universe, who is from everlasting to everlasting and who has cleverly hidden Himself in the world He created.* This understanding of His character helps us know how to find Him, see Him, hear Him, touch Him, and even become more like Him as we interact with His created world. We must look closer and deeper, trusting He is where He says He is.

For far too long, I had missed the beautiful invitation offered in Romans 1:20 to receive the messages of God hidden throughout His creation and to understand them by the wisdom of the Holy Spirit who dwells in me. I believe all such messages can be confirmed by the written Word. Just as the Lord's Spirit sanctifies our hearts so we can love more purely, it also heals, enlightens, and purifies our minds so we will see more clearly with the eyes of faith. Through this gift of the human imagination and the renewing of our minds by the washing of the waters of the Word of God, we become able to see, hear, and understand God's messages given to us (Ephesians 5:26). When we are in the darkness, the Spirit's words bring comfort to our hearts and light to our paths.

Look Up, Look Out

Before these experiences, I had been quite bothered by the biblical discourse between God and His faithful servant, Job. But as I began to encounter God in His creation, my negative perceptions about God's dealings with Job began to soften. When Job came to the Lord for answers regarding the tragic loss of all ten of his children, all his possessions, and even his health, it had seemed to me, based on the Lord's responses, that He was sidestepping Job's earnest questions. God even appeared to change the subject and brag about all He had created. He replied to Job with rhetorical questions like, "Can you bring forth the constellations in their seasons . . . send lightning bolts on their way . . ., or [provide] food for the raven when its young cry out to God?" (Job 38:32, 35, 41). God was contending with Job at what appeared to be the most inappropriate time, even as poor Job sat upon a pile of dung, cutting open his sores using broken pottery shards and grieving the loss of all his children, his possessions, and the respect of his fellows.

Lord, did You even hear what your faithful servant said? I asked as I reread Job's story. *Did You even take notice of his broken heart and shattered life? Isn't the better answer to tell Job how sorry You are and that he doesn't deserve this suffering? And shouldn't You address his questions directly?*

But now that the Creator of all things had answered me in my sorrow from out of His creation, I was beginning to understand that in His love, God had been inviting Job to look out, to look up, and to see the wonders of His love, His perfect plan, and His glory in creation. The Lord wanted Job to know that nothing is beyond His eternal care or powerful reach. Even amid trials, the Lord wanted His faithful and beloved son Job to see His divine hand in the things of earth and envision, or IMAGINE, all that had been prepared for him and his children.

> Even amid trials, the Lord wanted His beloved son Job to IMAGINE all that had been prepared for him.

My heart went on to pray the Scriptures: *Yes, it is You, alone, Lord, who laid the foundations of the earth. You provide food for the ravens and send ravens to provide food for those who seek You. You wrote the laws of heaven and can do all things. You loved us enough to give Your only Son to die for us so that we could live eternally in heaven with You and all our loved ones. I do trust You, Lord, to do as I have asked: to care for my children who are with You, to replace my ashes with beauty, and to heal my broken heart.*

THE WAY OF BECOMING

DIVINE SENSES

During Jesus' earthly ministry, He taught exclusively in parables through things in the creation whenever He spoke to crowds. Jesus essentially walked around teaching people out of the curriculum He had written beforehand and sent ahead of His own physical arrival on earth. Matthew 13:34–35 says, "All these things Jesus said to the crowds in parables; indeed, he said nothing to them without a parable. This was to fulfill what was spoken by the prophet: 'I will open my mouth in parables; I will utter what has been hidden since the foundation of the world'" (ESV).

Many parables in Scripture compare the kingdom of heaven to things in nature, like plants, animals, mountains, and even precious stones, to better enable us to make human connections to our spiritual experiences and come to understand the character of God and His Spirit's activities in our lives. In the gospel of Matthew alone, the kingdom of heaven is compared to a treasure hidden in a field, a man sowing seeds, a net gathering fish, a man taking a journey, a king settling his accounts, and a landowner hiring laborers for his vineyard.

John's gospel explains how Jesus, who was with His heavenly Father from the beginning, spoke all things into existence and then came to earth and walked among the creation He had made.

> In the beginning was the Word, and the Word was with God, and the Word was God. He was with God in the beginning. Through him, all things were made; without him, nothing was made that has been made. . . . The Word became flesh and made His dwelling among us. We have seen His glory, the glory of the one and only Son, who came from the Father, full of grace and truth. (John 1:1–3, 14)

The Scriptures also inform us how Jesus' way with His disciples was to give them more extensive explanations of these parabolic lessons when He was alone with them so they could comprehend their deeper meanings and apply them to their lives. Even today, the Lord shares with His friends the deeper meanings of the Divine Correspondences hidden within His creation. This way, the spiritual world becomes more visible and tangible so that His children can understand and apply their lessons to their own lives and, in time, become more like Christ in character. I IMAGINE Jesus saying, "Come with Me and let Me show you what I have hidden here long ago to use to help and teach you now." The Holy Spirit speaks through the works of creation, continually teaching the truth that can be affirmed by God's written Word and applied to our lives in the present.

> Prayer is meant to be a Divine Dialogue, which requires both speaking and listening, both giving and receiving.

Repeatedly, Scripture says, "Whoever has ears, let them hear" what the Spirit is saying. These words speak of spiritual hearing, but in truth, believers have access to five spiritual senses, each corresponding to the five physical senses: divine hearing, seeing, taste, touch, and smell. "Taste and see that the LORD is good" (Psalm 34:8).

Perceiving the Lord's messages requires using our spiritual senses; this is why the faith practice of IMAGINE is just as important as the practice of ASK. Prayer is meant to be a Divine Dialogue, which requires both speaking and listening, both giving and receiving. Without our sanctified imaginations, we greatly struggle to perceive and receive the Spirit's answers and the good things the Lord wants to provide us with in response to our ASKS. So often, we miss what God is giving to us because we are looking for immediate and abundant provision. Yet, the Lord's way is often to give seeds that we must plant and tend before they can become abundant in our lives. If we do not have eyes to perceive these seeds, we will miss planting and tending them and then wonder why God seems not to provide for us. "Do not despise these small beginnings, for the LORD rejoices to see the work begin" (Zechariah 4:10 NLT).

Using our sanctified imaginations takes practice. Just as giving in to fear is more natural than choosing faith, using our physical senses is more natural than using our spiritual ones. By practicing the use of our sacred imaginations, we hone our spiritual senses, which then become more accessible to us over time. If we want to receive answers from God, we must first ASK. But once we have asked, we should expect the Lord to respond somehow. God's providence is continually operating in the world around us. The faith practice of IMAGINE requires taking time to consider the things the Spirit is illuminating in our path, connecting our perceptions to the reality of our experiences, and cross-referencing any conclusions we may draw with the truth of Scripture. God does not contradict His Word. Instead, He will use the many canvases in His creation to reach us with His love. Just as a story can be received in various forms—books, movies, plays, songs, and the spoken word—God offers hope in many forms so we will perceive the threads of His divine storyline being woven through our human one.

In the days following my encounter with the Divine Communicator, who revealed His presence as the Word hidden in the things of creation, using Leafy Sea Dragons, I began to understand that everything we see with our physical eyes in this world is merely a seed speaking to what will become fully abundant in the next. The Lord is continually sowing seeds of promise and offering wisdom for us to plant and tend in the soil of our souls for our life's coming abundance. By intentionally using our sanctified imaginations, we hone our spiritual senses and become less likely to miss the good gifts given to us in our times of need. Imagining requires time to consider, hear, and see in the unseen realms. This Divine Dialogue begins with asking and seeking God's answers in prayer. It means not only speaking to God but also watching and listening for His responses given in the things of earth.

GOD GIVES SEEDS

Sometime between awake and asleep, the Lord spoke a word to my Spirit, saying simply, "Seeds." I sensed this was in response to my recent ASK to understand how people find their purpose.

"Seeds?" I really had no idea what He wanted me to know about seeds. Still, I drove to our local hardware store and purchased every type of seed they had. I opened the seed packages one at a time. Then, I extracted a few seeds from each packet, taped them onto a piece of paper, and wrote the type of plant they would become. I was still confused, even with all the seeds I had bought. So, I got back in my car, drove to the next town to a large garden center, and bought every kind of seed on their enormous turn-style rack. I repeated the process but still gained nothing. *Lord, I know You are trying to show me something; please make whatever it is clear to me.* As I finished praying, I looked down and found that God had illuminated three seeds out of all the others. They all looked identical, but each would look entirely different when fully grown. They were all tiny and black and looked like poppy seeds. But only one of them was a poppy. The other two were turnip and basil seeds.

Turnipness, Poppiness, and Basilness

God was speaking to me about the foolishness of comparing our gifts in seed form when what they are BECOMING is still unknown. Poppy, turnip, and basil seeds become vastly different in maturity despite being identical in their infancy. Indistinguishable to the eye in seed form, they would become completely different plants in maturity in color, look, size, taste, and usefulness. As I considered these plants and how easily they are mistaken in their seed forms, I felt grief over how we harm ourselves and our relationships when we compare ourselves to others. How often do we feel insecure, jealous, or even proud when standing next to others, and how frequently do we compare ourselves based on falsehoods or things not yet revealed? It is foolish to compare or judge a gift or talent without considering the critical roles that faith, grace, and waiting will play in its growth into maturity. Few things hinder our success in assembling well with others more than comparing our gifts and anointings while in development. As I contemplated further, these three plants seemed to take on human characteristics. I considered the underground BECOMING of the turnip, the high and vibrant BECOMING of the poppy, and the seemingly mundane BECOMING of basil.

I phoned my mother to tell her about my thoughts through a character narrative, with Poppy, Basil, and Turnip as the story's lead actors. Turnip grew up in obscurity, unseen by anyone for most of her life. Turnip struggled greatly with self-pity and jealousy because she compared herself to

Poppy's summer bloom instead of focusing on the hope of her fall harvest. With her long, lean stem and vibrant red hues, Poppy grew prideful as she compared herself to the lowliness of Turnip and the commonness of Basil. However, the pressure to remain on top proved difficult and detrimental to Poppy. As her blooms would fade, she would find herself stuck in an exhausting trap, seeking to prop up the diminishing glory that had become tied to her identity. As for Basil, she seemed caught somewhere between Poppy and Turnip, tossed between a sense of pride and inadequacy depending on which one had been set as the object of her comparison.

> We are each intended to be an entire garden in the Lord.

My mother began to cry as I spoke. As an identical twin, she had compared every part of her being to her sister, Georgie, her entire life, expecting everything to become complete simultaneously. But by joining me in my IMAGINE exercise in this way, she realized that *she* had been all these characters at different times. She cried because she had focused for so long on her areas of inadequacy, always comparing her weaknesses to her sister's strengths. This little story gave my mother a profound new sense of freedom. She discovered new power to overcome her cruel inner dialogue and the false notions she had been fighting all her life.

In truth, *no one* is only a turnip. We all have a measure of *turnipness*, *poppiness*, and *basilness*. We are each intended to be an entire garden in the Lord. By comparing the gifts God gives and their way of maturing in us with that of others, we hinder ourselves and harm our relationships. Considering our journeys in this way helps us combat self-pity, jealousy, shame, judgment, and pride. Comparison is perhaps the most prevalent of all weeds that choke out our internal peace and hinder our flourishing.

We do not dare to classify or compare ourselves with some who commend themselves. When they measure themselves by themselves and compare themselves with themselves, they are not wise. We, however, will not boast beyond proper limits, but will confine our boasting to the sphere of service God himself has assigned to us, a sphere that also includes you. (2 Corinthians 10:12–13)

But until we receive the beautiful seeds of His truth and allow them to be planted and broken open within us, we will hinder ourselves from BECOMING all we were created and redeemed to be.

To Become What Is Intended

For a seed to become what it is intended to be, it must die, be broken open, and come undone. Until it loses its outer shell and ceases to be a seed, it can never be transformed and fulfill its own glorious destiny. "Very truly, I tell you, unless a kernel of wheat falls to the ground and dies, it remains only a single seed. But if it dies, it produces many seeds" (John 12:24). A wise monastic once told me that "some just want to be bigger, better seeds" rather than allow themselves to become something altogether new, fearing the breaking, humility, and sense of loss that transformation requires. It is not natural to give up what is known for what is unknown, yet this is the essence of faith and what the journey to glory requires.

Our experiences with God through His creation are gifts. But each of these gifts is not meant only for our receiving, but also for our BECOMING. The immeasurable beauty and untold mysteries of God's kingdom have been given to us for our stewardship. Yet, we rarely recognize this because the treasures God entrusted to us are often presented in seed form. If we're handed an acorn and told, "This is an oak tree for the shade you will need one day," we might be disappointed with the apparent work ahead, but it wouldn't take much imagination to believe in the acorn's potential.

Nevertheless, we miss this all the time as it relates to the seeds of potential God has given *us*. Most seedlings require tending until their leaves and flowers come forth and their purposes become known to us. Scripture warns us not to compare anything in its seed form. Assuming we know the destiny or potential before God reveals it can hinder our own BECOMING journeys and our belonging in relationships. "As servants of Christ and as those entrusted with the mysteries of God judge nothing before the appointed time; wait until the Lord comes. He will bring to light what is hidden in darkness and will expose the motives of the heart" (1 Corinthians 4:1, 5).

BECOMING IMAGES

Few places on earth draw me into the peaceful and wondrous presence of the Lord more than the seashore. Looking out at the horizon and considering the power and mysterious contents of the ocean inspires me to dream with God and envision more for life. Even as a child, I remember marveling at the extraordinary beauty and perfection of seashells when I would find them on my beach walks with my mother. But it wasn't until adulthood that I began to consider the truths of God's kingdom reflected in these mini wonders of the deep after "treasure hunting" for them with my own children. Little did I know that in the varietal and colorful homes of these marine creatures I would discover one of the most meaningful series of letters from the Creator that would shape me and my entire family—personal invitations to become more like the Lord in specific aspects of His character.

In the years of raising my children, God answered me often through their words and the activities we would engage in together, such as watching birds come to our feeders, tending our gardens, collecting walnuts fallen from trees, or finding seashells walking along the ocean shores. Thanks to a season of ministry partnership with the Haas family, who had a home by the sea, our family was granted the blessing of spending extended time on Sanibel Island. While Scott worked, I spent time homeschooling our four children, and our "after school" free time revolved around the sea and sand. Those days walking the beach felt holy as I began envisioning what could become of me and those I love. Each morning, when the sun rose over the waters, my mind naturally expanded as I considered the ocean's vastness. At each setting of the sun, my heart received the invitation from the lapping waves to rest: "Stand still and consider the wondrous works of God" (Job 37:14 KJV). Each vision of the future seemed to start in wonder, move to inquiry, and progress to genuine listening, seeing, and considering the wisdom God had sown into these mini-wonders of the sea.

GOD OUR ROCK

On an early visit to the island, I could not shake this odd but specific obsession with finding murex shells, especially the lacey variety. One day, I decided to ask God what makes them so unique and why it felt as though God Himself was inviting me to learn more about them. I thought it must be more than just how beautiful and strong they are. I asked the Lord, "What's so special about the murex, and why am I so drawn to them?"

After asking, I searched "murex" on the internet and found that it's not an ordinary shell. The creature of the murex shell produces the purple dye, which was used to color the garments of ancient priests and kings and the curtains of God's holy tabernacle.[3] Because each murex snail yielded little more than one drop of dye, the dye was extraordinarily expensive, "worth more than three times its weight in gold. This is why a Roman edict was issued in 301 A.D. reserving the dye for priests, nobility, and royalty."[4] According to the book of Philippians, Lydia, a woman who lived by the sea in Thyatira and was likely the first convert to Christianity in Asia, was called a "seller of the purple." This is undoubtedly a reference to the dye made by the murex. Lydia is believed to have used the money she earned from collecting murex and selling its dye to support Paul's missionary journeys. In some roundabout way, these humble creatures of old had held the resources that clothed God's anointed, empowered the spreading of the gospel, and supported the ministry of the one who penned one-third of the New Testament. What a unique shelled creature this was, indeed! I did not know it then, but God was beginning to answer my soul's longing for vision and for light to shine upon the word of my destiny in Christ. Seashells would prove they have much to teach us about the beauty of spiritual formation.

"Open Our Eyes"

In Aristotle's naming of the murex shell, meaning rock, I sensed an invitation to consider the connection between this sluglike creature's rocklike home and the safety found in God as My Protector and Stronghold. Psalm 18:12 affirms this: "The LORD is my rock, my fortress and my deliverer; my

God is my rock, in whom I take refuge, my shield and the horn of my salvation, my stronghold." God invites us to know Him as our abiding place where we are kept safe and where we become formed and transformed into His image. Knowing and applying these truths informed my spiritual understanding of the deeper meaning of this image in creation.

After pondering these things, I decided to implement a seashell study using an observational and philosophical practice known as phenomenology as a part of our homeschool marine biology class. Phenomenology comes from the word phenomenon, meaning wonder, and *logos*, meaning words or the study of something. Essentially, phenomenology is the study of God's Words revealed through the wonders of His creation. When the kids and I engaged in our homeschool study, we asked God questions like, "What are You trying to say to us about Yourself, Your kingdom, or our life situation through this little wonder You have presented to us from the sea?" Wonders in creation are meant to invite our souls to ASK for wisdom, seek His guidance, and knock on the door of God's dwelling place, knowing that He wants to impart more to our understanding.

One day, I laid out examples of every kind of seashell we had found and asked my children a few questions like, "Which of these shells are you most drawn to?" and "Which of these has characteristics that you see most in yourself?" We had been discussing how, since we were created in the image of God, and because the book of Romans teaches us that God reveals His divine attributes through the things in His creation, it must mean that we can see parts of ourselves in these things, too. Perhaps we are intended to see aspects of our future BECOMING.

My eight-year-old daughter Maya answered the question first. "I see myself strong like the big horse conch."

Surprised by her response, her older brother Cole immediately retorted, "Wow, Maya, I was just thinking you were something more fragile, like a paper fig."

Then came the young voice of comic relief, Maya's five-year-old little sister Leah, who said, "Maya's like a spikey sea urchin because she hurts my feelings."

The following day, Maya shared with me how she wished she knew of a shell that was all these things: strong, fragile, and even a little spiky because she knew these traits were all true of her. I encouraged her to ASK God, and maybe He would help her find such a shell, or better yet, one that revealed how *He* saw her.

Later that day, after we finished homeschooling, the kids and I went for a walk on the beach. While our eyes scanned the sand, I told the four of them how I could not believe I hadn't yet been able to find a single sand dollar, even though it was the shell I had been explicitly trying to find for two weeks. Everyone in the family had been seeing them "accidentally." But despite my best efforts, I had not found even one. While I was still speaking and staring down determinedly at the edge of the gentle waves rolling onto the sand, Cole spoke up as if directly on cue. "Mom, there's one right by your foot; can't you see it?"

I could hardly believe my eyes. I was staring right at a sand dollar, but somehow I had not "seen" it. I picked it up and commented about how sad it is that we often cannot "see" what's right in front of us. The kids and I giggled, but Maya took our not "seeing" what was right in front of us more seriously. She looked out at the expanse of the sea and said with the utmost sincerity, "God, open our eyes."

As soon as Maya spoke those words, her eyes glanced down to where the edge of the water meets the sand, and there she noticed, lying alone in the shallows by her foot, the most beautiful and perfect lacey murex shell any of us had ever seen. It was flawless—but more importantly, it was strong, fragile, and a little bit spiky, just as lacey murexes are meant to be.

We all knew that the Lord had answered Maya's ASK. She had found a shell much as she perceived herself, albeit with spikes that were more beautiful and less sharp. In a moment, the Lord also answered our deeper prayer in asking how He saw Maya; and He did so in a way that would invite her to become more like Him in these beautiful ways. However, perhaps the most important lesson for Maya in that experience with the lacey murex was that now she knew the Lord personally as the God who hears (*Yahweh*

Shammah) and answers her prayers. He answered the fun and contemplative questions like, "How do You see me, Lord?" and the more serious, repentant one, "God, open our eyes." Since that day, when any of us finds a lacey murex shell, which is always a wonderful thing since they are so rare, we think of Maya and how God answered her prayer that day on the beach in front of us all.

Diligent Seeking

Even as I write, I am struck by how we struggle to see God's movements and BELIEVE He is involved in our everyday experiences, especially when we are in sorrow or suffering. Why do we become blind to the reality that the God who made us, sustains us, and lives within us also communicates with us day by day?

> These love letters in creation invite our souls to explore more of God in our stories as they unfold.

His revelation will always align with His character. When you witness a lightning strike across the sky during a time that you are suffering, you may think God is seeking to strike you while you're down, but this is not God's way nor in accordance with His character. Jesus called the Holy Spirit the Comforter, and His Word promises that "A bruised reed he will not break, and a smoldering wick he will not snuff out" (Isaiah 42:3).

God's Spirit always speaks in the perfect balance of truth and love. If you diligently seek to know what the Lord is saying, He will be faithful in revealing it to you, but it will likely require an ongoing conversation with Him. It has been that way for me. Because the Spirit of God does not contradict Himself, it is essential to cross-reference your thoughts, considerations, and interpretations of God's living words and the messages in His creation with the truths found in Scripture. This work of searching the Scriptures will only bring greater confidence in His truth, love, character, and active presence in your life.

It's been over a decade since I began intentionally contemplating the attributes of God in the things I notice in nature to inform my BECOMING journey and invite the people in my life to do the same. What has become most curious for the kids and me is how we long for others to understand that the things they notice in creation are likely meant as Divine Correspondences sent by God, a kind of love letter for their soul. A setting sun, a shooting star, or a shell rolling up from the waves can bless, inspire, and even answer a prayer. These love letters in creation invite our souls to explore more of God in our stories as they unfold. Aspects of these mini wonders speak to the truth of God's Word and the messages He wants to impart to us. May we be awake enough in our own lives to recognize the Spirit's promptings so we do not miss the messages of God's truth spoken creatively in love.

THE GOD WHO SEES

They say that low tide two days after a storm is the best time to go shelling. On one such occasion, I was out with our three little girls, seeking to find some post-storm treasures. A few lovely lightning whelks, a handful of buttercup lucina shells, a couple of banded tulips, and even two small shark's eyes were among our acquired riches. The shark's eyes, also called moon shells, were found exclusively by four-year-old Annika that day. As the youngest and smallest in our family, we have joked that her fantastic ability to see the "eyes" in the sand is perhaps related to her short stature or her proximity to the ground. But now and again, I wonder if her unspoiled eyes of faith helped her see more readily what we so easily pass over. We often jest how Annika, my little shelling buddy, might have been able to identify more seashells than letters of the alphabet at that point.

It's How He Works

On our walk, we happened upon a woman holding a gorgeous moon shell. It was the largest one we had ever seen of the shark's eye variety. It was flawless and larger than the size of my fist. I commented on how beautiful it was. She responded, "It just came up to my feet right in the waves."

Even though finding this impressive shell may have seemed like luck to her, I view such things as providence. Because of my view of things, my heart wished I knew this woman's story, thinking there must be a reason God wanted her to know that she was being seen by Him this day in a particular way. Not wanting to sound strange, I restrained myself from asking her anything more and chose to walk on. As the girls and I continued to collect pretty shells, I found myself wishing that God would give me a moon shell as big and as beautiful as the one He gave to her. Sensing a slight twinge of envy, I confessed it to the Lord. Then, I told God that I was happy to wait as long as I needed to because I knew He would give me the messages meant for me at just the right time.

Almost twenty minutes later, there in the shallows of the surf, we passed that same woman again, the one who was holding that very special and very large shark's eye in her hand. This time, my compulsion to ask her the question was even stronger. If this was the Holy Spirit speaking to me, I did not want to ignore Him. If not, the worst thing would be looking like a fool to a stranger. And I have certainly been that before.

So, I mustered the courage and approached her once again. I told her that whenever the kids and I find a moon shell, we think of it as God's invitation to us to REMEMBER that He sees us and that we are never far from His care. I told her about the verse in Genesis 16:13 that reads, "Now I have seen the One who sees me," and then I told her, "I wanted you to know this just in case God was trying to tell you He sees you."

"I know why He would be saying this to me today," said the woman, with eyes now wide. "Yesterday was the first anniversary of my husband's death."

I could hardly believe it! *But of course, God was longing to give her real comfort*! I thought. *That's who He is and how He works*! But my astonished reaction was showing me that when God does something miraculous and allows me to know about it, I am surprised afresh every time. *The Lord is always so right in all His ways. This widow was definitely the one who needed such a special gift today.*

Before the woman and I parted company, my girls came running up and interrupted our conversation, exclaiming, "Mommy, Mommy, look! Look at this huge shark's eye Annika found." Annika's little hand reached up and gave me a big, beautiful shark's eye. I could hardly believe this now. It was the largest variety of moon shells our little shelling group had ever found. It wasn't quite as large as the widow's shell, but the coloring around the pupil of the spiral's eye was unique. It was a lovely shade of blue.

"Where did you find such a beautiful shark eye, Annika?" I asked. In her sweet little voice, she replied, "I just looked down, and there it was." When the woman saw our newly found treasure, she told us that the kind of moon shell we had in hand was called a "Frank Sinatra" because of its Ole Blue Eye. Before the kids and I parted ways with the woman, who had become precious in our sight just as she was in God's, we talked a little more about some Bible verses that we often connect to other shells in her hand. They were shells that reminded us of the Lord's guidance and protection given to those who acknowledge God and look to Him for help.

> The shells reminded us of the Lord's guidance and protection given to those who acknowledge God and look to Him for help.

Not many days after this beautiful encounter by the shore, I was reading the Bible and came upon what I believe to be other layers of His biblical truth for that widow. "May the LORD keep watch between you and me when we are away from each other" (Genesis 31:49). "I will instruct you and teach you in the way you should go; I will counsel you with my loving eye on you" (Psalm 32:8). I dove deep into the idea of God as the One who sees and provides. I found that the name of God as El Roi, which means the God who sees, is directly connected to the name of God as Shepherd, indicting His watchful oversight of His people, as a good shepherd watches over and provides for his sheep.

I never saw that woman again, but our encounter with her compelled me to look deeper. As I considered the moon shell's spiral, I came to believe in God as the author of all math and artistic perfection more profoundly than ever before. The moon shell's designer is the same One who created science, math, language, and music. Because these mollusks, like the other slugs and snails of the sea, lack a brain, the involvement of an intelligent designer in their intricate formation is evident to those with spiritual eyes to perceive it. The moon shell grows based on a logarithmic spiral, similar to the more well-known nautilus shell, based on a geometrical form known as the golden spiral—a logarithmic ratio that is replicated in many items throughout creation.

The golden spiral is indicative of the mathematical perfection with which the Lord created all of nature. This sacred geometry is found in places like spiral galaxies, the eye of hurricanes, the cochlea of the ear, the cornea of the eye, a seahorse's tail, and even the DNA molecule itself. The way the golden spiral corresponds to the acts of seeing, hearing, and providing, as well as to the coding of every living thing, speaks to me of how God sees us, hears our cries, and supplies our needs. These divine aspects correspond to the name given to God by Abraham. He named His Lord *Yahweh Yireh*, the One who sees, sees to it, and has become my sight. "But the eyes of the LORD are on those who fear him, and on those whose hope is in his unfailing love" (Psalm 33:18). "The eyes of the LORD are on the righteous, and his ears are attentive to their cry" (Psalm 34:15).

Taste the Goodness of God

Once we have become aware that God sees us, hears our cries, and will provide for our needs, we begin to enter a life cadence of looking to Him more quickly for help and asking Him for provision. Whenever Annika found a moon shell after that day, she would say, "God's face-timing me." This was Annika's modern version of the same sentiments spoken by Hagar in Genesis 16:13: "You are the God who sees me . . . I have now seen the One who sees me."

> The Lord invites us to come and dine with Him at His banquet table every day.

The faith practice of REMEMBER takes us from feeling hopeless to being hopeful again. ASK takes us from *hoping* God can to *believing* He can. IMAGINE takes us from thinking He *can* to believing He *will*. We can begin the Divine Dialogue by praying and asking, as Maya did, "Lord, open our eyes." We can also participate in the IMAGINE practice by entering into it from a different angle, that is, by first tasting the goodness of God's truths through the reading of Scripture and then searching for these same truths that are "speaking" out of the things in His creation. No matter how we use our sanctified imagination, it is all part of the scriptural invitation to "Taste and see that the LORD is good" (Psalm 34:8). Job 12:11 poses the question, "Does not the ear test words as the tongue tastes food?" When our wonder becomes a declaration of praise in response to the whispers we've perceived and the seeds we've received, we step closer to seeing our desolate spaces BECOME the abundant places God intends.

The Lord has invited us to come and dine with Him at His banquet table every day, to learn from Him, listen to Him, and glean from all His wisdom written on the countless scrolls of His creation. Whether through our neighbors, our children, our spouses, our circumstances, or the things of the sky, land, or sea, God always seeks to communicate His loving messages to us. The Bible invites us to IMAGINE, saying, "But ask the animals, and they will teach you, or the birds in the sky, and they will tell you; or speak to the earth, and it will teach you, or let the fish in the sea inform you" (Job 12:7–8). The Spirit of Christ spoke all things into existence, and if we attune our spiritual ears to hear, then all things in creation will begin to speak to us about Him. These are the echoes of eternity.

YOUR BECOMING STORY: IMAGINE

What have you heard or seen in the creation that resounds in your Spirit? Have you taken time to stop and consider how the object of your wonderment might correspond to God's written Scriptures, aspects of His divine character, or the needy places where you are seeking Him in your life? ASK the Lord directly to show you what He is trying to communicate. Does the Bible mention this thing by name? God is an on-time God and promises to answer the needs you've expressed to Him. Consider why He might be drawing your attention to a particular thing now, and begin to plunge into the depths of His infinite wisdom and love letters He has written into His creation.

"Echoes of Eternity"

I see the dance of Gilgal in the wings of hummingbirds.
I hear the robin's song of praise sung as faith assured.
I feel the Spirit's holy breath in gales and gusts of wind.
I meditate on ancient stones that tell where grace has been.

I witness love outpouring in cascades of waterfalls.
I consider the divinity in creatures great and small.
I glimpse the call to unity in the work of honeybees.
I wonder at the vast unknown in the dark and depth of seas.

I contemplate the Spirit's peace in doves so meek and mild.
I sense God's tender mercy when I hold an infant child.
I view in every spiral eye the perfect hand of grace.
I found the Star of David in a pomegranate's face.

I know from owls and frogs and cats God sees in dark of night.
I touch *Shekinah*-glory in the moon's reflected light.
I muse the tree of good and evil links to figs and wasps.
I wish these holy mysteries were easier to grasp.

I stoke the holy flame within that entered at rebirth;
For I can see the Word of God hidden in things of earth.[5]

PART 2

DIVINE EXCHANGE

5

TRUST

Broken and Incomplete Parts

While living in Russia as a college student on a study abroad just after the Berlin Wall came down, I witnessed the devastating aftermath of the collapse of a nation. It was 1992, and while much of the world, including the United States, was celebrating the fall of communism, Russia had begun deteriorating into a state of utter chaos. The seventy-year-old welfare system on which the entire Soviet society had long relied was falling to pieces. Its currency value dove into an unprecedented freefall, and the ruble was no longer worth the paper it was printed on.

"OBMYEN VALUTI" was printed on signs atop the kiosks that were popping up on nearly every street corner. One man would call out "change money" to passers-by from these ticket-booths-turned-mini-banks. Another counted bills and wrote in paper ledgers. These dime-a-dozen currency exchange booths were appearing at a rate that matched the number of people awakening to the devastating reality that their hard-earned money was growing increasingly worthless by the day. Every citizen would need to bring their Russian rubles to one of these money booths and exchange them for a more stable currency. Otherwise, they would end up broke and destitute in a matter of months. Each day that a Russian citizen held on to their devaluing currency, rather than trading it in for a more stable dollar, hoping this was a recoverable downturn, the more their liability grew. The ruble would never again become more valuable than it was then. The whole economy was collapsing and would prove unrecoverable.

To some, this old-world picture may seem unrelated to their present and personal circumstances. But for those who have experienced seeing their treasured things suddenly lost, destroyed, broken, or turned worthless, this will hit closer to home. Everyone eventually faces loss and brokenness in life. In fact, generational pain and loss cascade down all of our family lines. Its repercussions spread across every nation, making up much of the hard we experience in this life. Even though many of these things are beyond our control, we are still affected by them and have to deal with them. Our natural human tendency is to ruminate in worry or become transfixed by all the broken pieces.

But worrying does not heal our souls or repair our broken things. In fact, it further fragments us, and the accumulation eventually overwhelms us. The Lord invites all of us to entrust to Him what's broken or diminishing in our lives at any time. He promises to make our burdens lighter, restore what we've lost, redeem our sufferings, heal our wounds, and make all things new (Revelation 21:5, Matthew 11:28). Like the Russian people of that day, we must exchange what is devaluing for a more stable currency according to the Divine Exchange of God's higher economy.

A SHATTERED NATION

During those early days living in Russia, I noticed a kind of collective suffering that can only be known by those who live through it. Collective suffering changes how those in its grip measure the value of people and things. It also has a way of creating a common cry among its people. Whether it's a cry for safety after a natural disaster, recompense after war, recovery after economic depression, or mourning after a family tragedy, there is a common cry among the people in the aftermath of any large-scale suffering. Living in Russia, where everyone seemed blanketed in despair, wearing expressionless stares and rarely cracking a smile, I started asking folks about the disengaged manner of their people. I was always given the same answer: "*Tyazholaya zhizn*," which means it's a "heavy life." "Heavy life" was the name of the mantle worn by an entire society that shared a pervasive sense of loss stemming from back-to-back wars, extreme political oppression, and the collapse of their entire economy.

An invisible banner seemed to loom large over the nation, declaring, "Every man, woman, and child for themselves." The metros were filled with long-faced elderly widows selling their precious things, from family heirlooms to beloved pets. Parents pawned their children's used toys and clothing just to put food on the table. Orphans became street children in droves, and countless vulnerable people fell victim to unspeakable horrors. I tried to make the best of living there, but ignoring the darkness of my surroundings became increasingly difficult. My level of anxiety continued to rise, and self-pity began to take root in my heart. I was overwhelmed by the desolation. And even though I was not a permanent member of this Russian society, I unknowingly became one of its burden-bearers while living within its culture.

> I tried to make the best of living there, but ignoring the darkness of my surroundings became increasingly difficult.

Transfixed by Fragments

One day after class, I accepted a ride home from a Russian schoolmate. At a red light, our driver accidentally stopped his car on the trolley tracks. When the next tram came by, it violently swiped the side of our car right where I was sitting. The door next to me was crushed, the window by my face shattered, and I was covered in broken glass fragments. We all got out of the car and stood there stunned in the center of Nevsky Prospect, the busiest street in St. Petersburg. Immediately, an angry Russian police officer demanded that the driver get his car off the road and clean up the mess. Although many people had witnessed the accident, not one person offered us any help. While the policeman was still yelling at the driver of our car, I slipped between two buildings, took a seat on an alleyway stoop, and began picking the shards of glass out of my skin.

Within a few days of the collision with the tram car, I witnessed a fatal accident in front of the Hermitage Museum. It was a shocking scene where a female Italian tourist was killed by a hit-and-run driver while crossing the street on foot. The utter lack of reaction by the many bystanders was horrifying. *What could have bewitched so many people to leave them transfixed in such unmitigated apathy?* I wondered. Perhaps the shocking indifference to human suffering had something to do with its pervasiveness. Maybe it was compassion fatigue, and the people were too overwhelmed with their own hardships to have any mercy to spare. Whatever the reason, human life had become as devalued as the Russian currency itself. It was the first time I had experienced such profound disregard for human suffering and the devaluing of human worth, and tragically, it would not be the last.

CAN'T GIVE WHAT WE DON'T HAVE

I was twenty years old when I first came to Russia, and helping its people had been my focus since first arriving. But, after these accidents, I entered a state of self-protection, which led me to abandon my aim of assisting others. I saw this tendency in the people around me and wondered if perhaps the Russian people were so focused on their own needs and losses that they had no room to engage with other people's pain. It seemed too few were whole enough to help the shattered ones. Extreme hardship was everywhere. It did cross my mind that perhaps the Russian people lacked the compassion, care, and provision to share with others simply because they had not been receiving these things themselves.

We can't give what we don't have, just like we can't teach what we don't know. We learn through receiving. "We love because he first loved us" (1 John 4:19). Even empathy, mercy, understanding, patience, and comfort all require a receiving first. The Bible affirms this, saying: "Praise be to the Father of our Lord Jesus Christ, the Father of compassion and the God of all comfort, who comforts us in all our troubles so that we can comfort those in any trouble with the comfort we ourselves receive from God" (2 Corinthians 1:3–4).

After the 1917 Bolshevik Revolution, faith and trust were replaced by fear and skepticism among the Russian people, and these became the new batons passed down to future generations. This was due in large part to the communist government's rampage against any form of religion. It destroyed houses of worship and harassed, incarcerated, and executed religious leaders of all faiths. In this campaign to extinguish religion, "over 12,000 clergy were murdered outright– shot, beaten to death, hanged, or drowned—a secret 1930 police report put the number of Orthodox clergy who had died in prison camps at 42,800."[1] This doctrine of state-enforced atheism made the people terrified to engage in any overt religious practices. In consequence, this created a dearth of spiritual tools being taught in close communities. Even after decades of living in America, my Russian teacher Olga struggled to allow me to read biblical text during our language lessons out of a deep-seated fear grown from a lifetime of living under the terror of communism. The deprivation of spiritual teaching, faith understanding, and access to God's written Word had undoubtedly created the Russian people's spiritual poverty, which fed the lack of hope and smiles in this heavy-laden society.

Deprivation to Appreciation

Gripped by the reality of the Russian people's hardships and overcome by my own feelings of homesickness, I clung to every word written in every letter I received from home. Such letters had become a lifeline for me. At my lowest low, I got a letter from my grandmother, Mema, which had taken several weeks to arrive. Its words were so fitting that I marveled at its timeliness. "One must experience deprivation to experience true appreciation," wrote Mema, seeking to encourage me. These words resonated deeply. *There it is,* I thought. Finally, I had found some meaning behind why I was led into the muck and mire of this post-communist bedlam. *God must want me to become a more grateful person.*

To survive in this place, I decided I would need to take my eyes off of myself and my temporary circumstances, become more grateful, and focus on the difficulties others were facing. I reminded myself, repeatedly, that because I carried a blue passport, this would not be my reality forever, but for those carrying red ones, the heavy life of *tyazholaya zhizn* would not soon be over. I hoped this shift in focus would improve my outlook and lift my emotions.

Sadly, it did not. Not only would my heart not find the rest it sought, but my eyes were now open to such a great sea of suffering that I nearly buckled under its weight. Now that I had intentionally borne witness to their pain, I felt even more responsible and overwhelmed by it. I feared I was becoming reconciled to the heavy life of *tyazholaya zhizn*.

My despair soon led me to a new low. *Well, if this isn't rock bottom*, I thought, *I've definitely hit a ledge on the way down*. I could no longer ignore my need to lament all the pain and suffering. It was not something I could bypass. So, I did the only thing left to do. I cried. I cried gut-wrenching cries until my heart remembered God as my hope. Only then did I think to pray. "Lord, please help me! Show me where You are in this place! Open my eyes to see Your face and my ears to hear Your voice. If there is something You want me to do here, then show me what it is. And keep me safe while I am so far from home! In Jesus' name, Amen!"

> I had, at last, become committed to relying on His grace and keeping my focus on His loving face.

As I journaled that prayer, it felt as if my heavenly Father took my face in His hands, like a loving parent would, assuring me He was with me, that He would show me the way, and that He could handle all this *for me*. I had, at last, become committed to relying on His grace and keeping my focus on His loving face. The Spirit reminded me of the truth found in Isaiah 41:13, "For I am the Lord your God, who takes hold of your right hand, and says to you, 'Do not fear, I will help you.'"

All the worrying and ruminating I had been doing had become like mental static, making it impossible for me to hear the Spirit's voice speaking or perceive others rightly. Yet all along, God had been inviting me to entrust my fears to Him so I could hear His voice again and walk with a renewed sense of hope. By faith, I began participating in the Divine Exchange once again. But this time, it was not my own sin I was bringing for exchange but the brokenness caused by the sins of others and the burdens I had taken upon myself on behalf of others.

Jesus died on the cross for both our sins and our brokenness. Isaiah's prophecy foretold how the Messiah's self-sacrifice had been both the atonement for our sins and the healing of our wounds. "But he was pierced for our transgressions, he was crushed for our iniquities; the punishment that brought us peace was on him, and by his wounds, we are healed" (Isaiah 53:5). As overwhelming and incomprehensible the pain, sin, and brokenness in this world are to us, John 3:16 and 17 speaks about how all of it is not too much for the Lord to handle: "For God so loved the world that he gave his one and only Son, that whoever believes in him shall not perish but have eternal life. For God did not send his Son into the world to condemn the world, but to save the world through him."

I took the time right then and there to entrust my earthly currencies of fear, worry, brokenness, loss, and pain to God. In return, the Lord's Spirit refilled me with hope, comfort, and a deep sense of His love. I went to bed praising Him.

THE ILLUMINATED WAY

Walking home from my class at the Economics Institute, I stopped by a bakery located on St. Petersburg's main drag, Nevsky Prospect, near the location of the car accident that took place only a few days earlier. Despite my best attempts at placing my order at the *Bulochnaya* kiosk, I somehow managed to pay for an enormous backpack-sized bag of crackers instead of the small handful I wanted for snacking while studying.

"*Eto slishkom manoga*—that's too much," I repeatedly said to the stern-faced Russian woman standing behind the counter. But to my dismay, she kept filling the plastic bag with freshly baked salted crackers. She handed the bag firmly to me, saying in Russian, "You ordered this much, so you get this much. *Dosvidanya*—goodbye." With my enormous plastic bag of crackers in hand and feeling conspicuously like Old Saint Nick, I crossed Nevsky Street to find "greener pastures," relax, and get some homework done.

I found a lovely place to sit on the lawn in front of the stately Kazan Cathedral. Sitting there with my schoolbooks on one side and my giant bag of crackers on the other, I felt happy. I was very grateful that the strange incident at the bread store had not upended me today as it would have before entrusting my burdens to God. As I sat cross-legged and barefoot on the grass, I heard songs of worship being sung in English rising from the other side of the lawn. Hearing praise sung in my heart language for the first time since coming to Russia filled me with even greater joy.

I began to sing along. Then, I got up and walked across the lawn toward the crowd that was gathering. It felt like I was returning home from some long and arduous journey. As I drew closer to the crowd of Russians gathered around the worshipers, a kind-faced, English-speaking man met me. He introduced himself as Pastor Jack Hibbs. When he learned I was an American, he shared that he had come with his church group and began introducing me to his team members from Calvary Chapel, who welcomed me warmly. I offered to help translate so more of his team could converse directly with the Russian people who were gathering.

Communion and Philanthropy

As we stood there together, I heard a voice that seemed to echo from out of the crowd and draw my attention. At first, these words were easy to ignore as they were spoken in an almost imperceptible whisper. They were the very same words I had heard every day since coming to Russia. And just like everyone else, I had learned to ignore them. But today, the negligible voice seemed to grow louder to me.

"*Ya galodnaya, pomogite, Ya galodnaya,*" were the words being quietly repeated, which meant, "I'm hungry. Help me. I'm hungry."

No one else seemed to notice, but I could no longer ignore it. It was the voice of a small elderly woman standing nearby me.

She spoke again. "*Ya galodnaya, pomogite, pozhaluysta*—I'm hungry. Help me, please."

I knew full well her words were meant precisely for me. This *babushka* had a certain cloaked dignity and a venerable grace as she humbly expressed her need. If I had not known Russian or had not just experienced spiritual cleansing through prayer only days before, I would have missed her pleas as everybody else did. Her words spoke of her need, yet my Spirit heard something higher. She was like a Divine Correspondence sent by God to me, which read something like this in my inner spirit: "Standing before you is My response to your prayers and requests to see Me and be used by Me in this world. This woman is an image meant to show you the way to walk. Can't you see My divine hand and provision in the broken bread that you carry?"

"*Vozmite, pozhaluysta,*" I said. "Please, you take them." I insisted on giving the bag of crackers I had been carrying to the old woman; they were undoubtedly meant for her receiving.

After bowing her head and making the sign of the cross, she took the bag of bread crackers into her small, weathered hands and repeated several times, "*Spasibo, Bolshoye spasibo.* Thank you, thank you very much."

"*Pozhaluysta,*" I said again to this woman to convey its double meaning—both "You're welcome" and "Please." I wanted to express both senses of the word because while she had received something to satisfy her hunger, she had also

> From broken glass to broken bread, I had just experienced another cycle of grace in my life.

lifted my burden. The interaction with this widow taught me the higher law of philanthropy. I was giving what I was never intended to carry alone or for long, and my burden became lighter in sharing.

Having this new communion experience on the same street where I had been covered in broken glass from the car accident just a few days prior felt both ironic and providential. The two locations may have only been a few steps apart, but the faith journey they represented was significant. It began with me in need, covered in literal glass fragments, but it ended with me serving as a vessel of provision for another's needy condition. From broken glass to broken bread, I had just experienced another cycle of grace in my life.

But from a higher heavenly perspective, this communion experience was taking place on a land that was undergoing its own profound redemption. Kazan Cathedral was initially built as a center for Orthodox worship, but tragically, it was turned into the Hall of Atheism under communism.[2] Now, this land was being sanctified once again by our songs of praise and the partaking of *holy* communion. "Although the Lord gives you the bread of adversity and the water of affliction, your teachers will be hidden no more; with your own eyes, you will see them. Whether you turn to the right or to the left, your ears will hear a voice behind you, saying, 'This is the way; walk in it'" (Isaiah 30:20–22).

Living in Russia's crumbling society without my usual support system forced me to seek the Lord to find any sense of peace, joy, or safety. The more I was personally affected by the societal degradation, the more critical it was for me to use the faith tools I had received while growing up. Relenting, turning away from the chaos, and looking to God as a calming and centering presence gave more light to my path so I could proceed safely. Though I had been a temporary member of this "heavy-life" society where even human beings had lost their value in the eyes of the culture, the restoration of my inner peace and joy caused me to see the people once again as image-bearers of the Most-High God.

MOSAIC PITCHER

Only God can assign true value to people or things. When we allow broken people to determine the value of someone or something, we often miss their true worth and discard what should be embraced, treasured, and protected. People who are covered in brokenness and weighed down by worry often reject the things God treasures most highly. Once we do the faith work of exchanging our hurts for healing and lies for truth, our eyes are opened to the actual value of things and people, even what the world rejects as unworthy. God taught me the importance of not allowing other people's rejection to determine something's worth through the gift of a simple glass pitcher. As the old adage goes, "One man's trash is another man's treasure."

When I was twenty-seven, I interviewed for my first job on Capitol Hill. When the time had come for the final interviews given by the bipartisan chairs of the congressional caucus, the pool of applicants had been whittled down from eighty-eight to two. As one of these last two candidates, I spent considerable time sitting with the other finalist in each congressional waiting room before the interviews, and I had grown quite fond of her. Though I was ultimately chosen for the position, I viewed her not as a competitor but as a friend. I hoped we would stay in touch. I even invited her to my wedding, which was just around the corner.

> Only God can assign true value to people or things.

Though she did not come, she sent a lovely gift. It was a beautiful glass mosaic water pitcher with gold, blue, and purple blown-glass sections affixed by melted golden resin lines. I thought it was magnificent and looked forward to using it to entertain as a newlywed. I ran into her in the Hart Senate Office Building sometime after my wedding and told her how much I treasured the gift she had sent.

"It's one of my favorites," I told her.

In utter surprise, she spontaneously blurted out, "Really? I got it at a yard sale for fifty cents!"

It seems I had overestimated her fondness for me and the relationship we had forged in those waiting rooms. Her words caused me to question how I could ever have treasured the item she had given me. My perception of the pitcher's value changed in a single moment. So, when I got home, I shoved it to the back of my cupboard and forgot all about it.

Several years later, I had the chance to lead a congressional fact-finding trip to Romania. After completing our official business there, the embassy staff took us around to show us some of the finest artisan galleries in the country. We were taken to a unique shop that was filled with pieces made using some of the most exquisite artistic techniques. When I walked in, I almost fell over because across the entire first wall of the shop were items made precisely like the fifty-cent pitcher now buried in the back of my cupboard. My purple, blue, and gold glass mosaic pitcher wasn't worthless after all. Seen here in its proper environment, I could appreciate the pitcher for the masterpiece that it always had been.

Even though I had now learned the actual value of my pitcher, it remained unused in my cupboard for many years. It would not be until seven years later, when I came into a season of profound suffering, that thoughts of this pitcher would resurface. I pulled it out and filled it up to see if it could even hold water. Seeing its usefulness and beauty and remembering its story filled me with the hope that perhaps the things I perceive as having little value in my own life might somehow be valuable to God, even beautiful, and become useful again.

Around this same time, I learned that the woman who gave me the pitcher had recently committed her life to Jesus and that her faith had been influenced by a woman I attended Bible study with for several years. *Wow, talk about a closed-circle testimony playing out!* In response to this positive news and the revelation of the pitcher's value, I decided to purchase a set of wine glasses made using this same Romanian technique. I did this as an act of faith, hoping God would use me to hold the new wine of His kingdom and to share its joy with others.

GATHER THE FRAGMENTS

Nearly two decades after living in Russia, the Lord spoke the words, "Gather the fragments" to my soul. This inner whisper had come not long after I had envisioned my backyard covered in broken glass pieces.

I could not remember ever hearing the phrase "gather the fragments" before, and I had no idea what it meant. I wasn't even sure I knew what a fragment was, so I looked it up. A fragment is defined as a small part broken off or separated from something. I realized that the broken pieces on the ground of my life met this description of fragments, but I sensed there was more. When I typed the three words together in an internet search, I was astonished to find that they had been spoken by Jesus to His disciples just after the feeding of the five thousand. John 6:12 states that "when all had eaten their fill, [Jesus] told his disciples, 'Gather up the leftover fragments, that nothing may be lost'" (ESV).

Aside from the resurrection of Christ, the feeding of the five thousand is the only miracle found in all four Gospels. Its teachings are familiar to most believers and vital for learning how God honors our offerings of faith. But it is also a story that reveals how God values our broken parts and how He operates in the world on behalf of those under His care.

As the story goes, a large crowd had gathered on the hillside and remained there listening to Jesus teach that entire day. When it got late, the people turned hungry, and Jesus took pity on them and performed a miracle for their provision. First, He asked the people to share what they had. He was given two small fish and five barley loaves from a young boy. Next, Jesus took these few items and held them up to heaven in prayer, asking His Father to sanctify and multiply them.

Every person in the crowd not only received plenty to eat but there was such an abundance of provisions that there were even leftovers. The excess was discarded by many and was left strewn upon the hillside once the crowds departed. Jesus instructed His disciples to gather up all these leftover pieces before they met up with Him again.

Because I was reading these verses in a time of personal grief and exhaustion, I was struck by the condition of the disciples and what seemed to be Jesus' insensitivity. Jesus and His disciples had just been reunited after a long period of traveling from town to town in ministry, often facing stark rejection by people. Not only this, but they had just heard the horrific news that their mentor, friend, and cousin of Jesus, John the Baptist, had been beheaded for his faith.

Each Piece Has Value

Considering all this, it seemed insensitive, unnecessary, perhaps even cruel, to require the disciples to clean up the hillside when Jesus instructed, "Gather up the leftover fragments, that nothing may be lost." I knew this could not have been based on frugality on Jesus' part because He would soon multiply bread and fish again at the feeding of the four thousand. But through prayer and divine listening, I came to understand that this call to salvage the discarded and scattered pieces was not because Jesus lacked concern for His friends but because of His love for them and because of how highly He values every part of their stories.

Jesus knew His disciples' need for comfort and rest. These were things He also needed in His depleted human condition and grief. Jesus was seeking to reveal heaven's high regard for everything made holy by the Father, no matter its acceptance or rejection by people. Each fragment was once a part of something the Lord had made holy; therefore, every piece would retain its value forever, no matter how poorly people treated it in the present. His disciples, who had been sent out like loaves of bread to be shared, were now being taught that the pieces rejected by others were still valuable to God and useful in His work.

Once the disciples did what the Lord had asked and gathered every broken and rejected piece of leftover bread, these pieces filled up exactly twelve baskets. I am keen to believe that each basket represented one of the twelve disciples, and the bread fragments signified the parts of their stories that others had minimized by taking what they wanted and carelessly rejecting the rest.

In my broken, weary, and sorrow-filled state, having experienced much rejection along the way of ministry life, the spiritual implications of the words "gather the fragments" made me begin to hope for the redemption of my brokenness. This story came alive and became personal to me in a new way. Having the Spirit whisper to me the words, "Gather the fragments," in this season revealed His great love for me.

God knows when we are weary and grieving. His Word shows us how highly He values the broken, lost, and rejected things in our stories. Just as Jesus called His disciples to collect every leftover piece, believing each had value, the Lord calls all His children to engage in this work of gathering, by faith, that which has been discarded.

Since the beginning of time, people have taken what they wanted from holy things and rejected the leftovers as worthless once they have had their fill. Nevertheless, whatever has been consecrated to God, no matter its current condition, remains precious and highly valuable to Him. Each fragment identified in our stories is meant to be gathered and presented at the Divine Exchange, at the foot of the cross of Christ, for its redemption and remaking for further usefulness. Wisdom calls us to be skeptical of the value placed on the pieces of our lives by others who may not have spiritual eyes to see. We are to trust God's measurement of worth over that of people's. Each fragment picked up and handed to God will begin to cycle in grace and, in time, experience a redeemed usefulness.

ENTRUSTING FRAGMENTS

Despite what God had taught me through Scripture and the image of the mosaic pitcher, I had not yet truly considered what I had been rejecting and misvaluing in my own life. Even though God had directed me to "gather the fragments" and had helped me make the connection between the leftover bread on the hillside and the broken pieces in my life, I was still slow to do what God was asking of me—to identify and release my own brokenness into His redemptive economy.

It would take the accidental shattering of a six-foot mirror leaning against my living room wall to compel me to do this work of entrusting the broken parts of my own identity. This incident became a personal invitation to consider what these broken pieces might represent in my life. As I collected the shards of broken glass, I began "naming" each one—assigning the wounds, hurts, and lies I believed about myself to each piece of the shattered mirror. I traced a few of the fragments onto the pages of my journal and asked God to redeem each one I had named. My inner world, displayed before me in this external way, made trusting God more tangible and practical and proved quite liberating.

The Potshard Gate

The Lord takes the heart condition of His people very seriously and is notorious for providing a visible, tangible illustration of our condition so that we can see the truth of what He is seeing. In the book of Jeremiah, the Lord rebukes the religious leaders for their focus on acquiring more for themselves while minimizing the pain and brokenness of the people.

> From the least to the greatest, their lives are ruled by greed. From prophets to priests, they are all frauds. They offer superficial treatments for my people's mortal wound. They give assurances of peace when there is no peace. (Jeremiah 6:13–14 NLT)

The Lord later called the prophet Jeremiah to take a vase and shatter it in front of all of the Israelites at the gate called "Potshard" to give the people a picture of what their brokenness looked like and to warn them what would happen to them should they remain in their wicked ways (Jeremiah 19:11).

God wanted all the people to be able to see their broken state in a way they could no longer ignore. He was tired of religious leaders treating mortal wounds as flesh wounds and declaring peace where there was only suffering, sin, and heartache. This is precisely what God wanted me to understand about the state of my own soul and about others around me. The mirror shattered so I could see with my own eyes what He already knew to be true.

> We are invited to re-entrust these pieces to God so they can become useful in His time.

In Russia, I learned the importance of becoming healed in order to become a vessel of healing for others. The more people experience healing themselves, the more able they are to help others heal. Conversely, as the saying goes, "Hurt people hurt people." Too often, wounded people wound other people with their own broken parts. Like an injury to our physical bodies, the brokenness in our souls that we leave "unentrusted" to God will eventually cause more harm to us, our relationships, and our decision-making. Although we do our best to keep up the appearance of perfection and wholeness by revealing only those more complete and beautiful parts of ourselves, our fragments "still speak," and usually not when spoken to.

Even though much of the pain we experience in this life does not come from our own making, we still bear the responsibility, as the disciples did, to gather the pieces by picking them up off the land of our souls. We are all invited to re-entrust these pieces to God at the Divine Exchange so they can begin to cycle in His grace, be redeemed, and become useful in His time. Brokenness isn't something that can be avoided in this life. Of course, there are sorrows we can avoid by staying away from willful sin. Still, sometimes, we just get knocked off the counter, so to speak, by external forces and find ourselves shattered on the floor.

Some of these tribulations come from devastating life events that leave our souls walking on paths of broken glass. The cascade of our pain may have been triggered by a single event, like the betrayal of a friend, the suffering of abuse, the loss of a loved one, the failure of health, the undermining of an endeavor, the ending of a relationship, or even the collapse of a social system, as in the case of Russia. Perhaps the brokenness we carry has come from accumulating the fragmentation of others, a kind of secondhand trauma, where we have served as a burden-bearer for their pain. Nevertheless, our lives are not meant to become defined by fragmentation. At any point, we can seek the Lord's presence and entrust every piece to His love and care.

The Broken and Unfinished

Years later, when I looked back and read my journals showing the things I had entrusted to God, I realized just how much had been redeemed and made beautiful in God's keeping. New and confident beliefs had come alive in me, affirming the promise in 2 Timothy 1:12, "I am convinced that he is able to guard what I have entrusted to him until that day."

Not every broken thing I named in my journals had experienced full redemption. But all had been actively cycling in grace and increasing in wholeness. In a spiritual sense, some of the sharper edges had become smoother, like sea glass, because these once sharp shards had spent time tumbling in the waters of God's Word. But my most significant victory was getting unstuck from places I was formerly stuck. The TRUST work had also made room for new seeds to be planted in the soil of my soul.

It is marvelous how God invites all of us to entrust our cares and hurts to Him. Doing this work eventually leads to the once burdensome and depreciating things in our lives returning to us more whole and highly valued. "For we know in part and we prophesy in part, but when completeness comes, what is in part disappears" (1 Corinthians 13:9–10). "He who began a good work in you will carry it on to completion" (Philippians 1:6). The Lord alone can bring abundance to everything that He first planted in our hearts and complete every partial thing we entrust to Him.

We all need to consider our soul's condition. What's been broken? What's left unfinished? Where are the wounds? What areas are not flourishing because of the debris crowding out the light and hindering growth? We should also consider what methods we have used to deal with our brokenness in place of trusting God. Perhaps our wounds have made us more self-protective and unwilling to risk loving fully. Maybe the broken pieces have been turned into weapons. Or perhaps we have used them to erect walls of self-protection that are keeping us alone in our pain.

Our stuck areas are often the ones covered in the fragments of former hurts. Too often, instead of seeking God's healing, we foolishly try to patch our wounds and our broken relationships through insufficient means, which only extends our suffering and delays our healing. We hide away our broken things and cover them over with a put-on smile, all the while deteriorating on the inside.

In these states of need and brokenness, the fragments of our lives seem to cry out to be healed, redeemed, and reconciled to our more significant and eternal stories in Christ. So, even when we reach the loneliest of lonely places, whether through a slow erosion or a sudden shattering, there is still a great reason to hope.

The Lord invites us to come to Him with every fear, shame, insufficiency, hurt, sin, lie, loss, and pain. Our Maker is also our soul's Physician, the One who came to heal us and reconcile all things. Everything we entrust to God becomes a piece of raw material in His capable hands for His reassembling into a beautiful mosaic. The Lord truly does work *all things* together for good (Romans 8:28). Every piece and part we release to Him will become glorified in this life or the next. This activation by entrusting also changes our souls in the *now of life*. "May the God of hope fill you with all joy and peace, as you trust in Him, so that you may overflow with hope by the power of the Holy Spirit" (Romans 15:13).

As I considered God's way as the Great Re-Maker of broken things, I marveled at how His persistent hand works, even throughout the generations and in every nation. The intricate mosaics that covered the surfaces of so many Russian cathedrals I had visited returned to mind. To think they had remained standing through two World Wars, under decades of communist oppression, and the banning of Bibles, and how, through these miracles, God's Word could not be silenced. The fragment-covered walls continued to speak praises to the King of kings and to tell all the people of His love.

YOUR BECOMING STORY: TRUST

What is broken in your life? What areas are still incomplete that you long to see whole, reconciled, or redeemed? Name these parts, one by one, as a way of entrusting them to God for restoration, reconciliation, and remaking. What brokenness has come down from your ancestors that you want to be free from? What family secrets, bad patterns, or effects of family tragedies have carried over to your generation that have not yet been redeemed? What part of your life feels incomplete, neglected, or stuck? What lies have you believed that have undermined your sense of worth or harmed your relationships?

As you consider these questions, you may find it helpful, as I do, to trace and name broken pieces of pottery, glass shards, or sea glass as a tangible way of entrusting your fragments to God for healing, completion, and redemption.

"Trust Prayer"

I choose to trust God with every . . .
sorrow, hurt, and loss, broken relationship,
experience in need of redemption and season of life.

I choose to trust God with my . . .
dreams, gifts, talents, abilities, work, and endeavors,
loved ones, family struggles, health, and heart,
weaknesses and strengths
finances and giving, ministry calls,
unmet desires and passions, wants and needs,
fears and anxieties, and my past and future.

I choose to trust God to be . . .
merciful in my weakness
forgiving in my repentance,
And faithful to help me discern the truth.

I choose to trust God that He will . . .
remember, lead, answer, provide, protect, heal, and lift up,
redeem, complete, and restore me in all areas of brokenness,
and that of my loved ones at the right time.

I choose to trust God . . .
when trials come,
when others come against me,
when I can't see the way,
when I lack the strength to go on,
when those I love stray,
when the difficult seasons seem not to end, and
when the way forward seems unclear.

I choose to entrust the pieces (parts and people) . . .
that I want to cling to as too precious to release,
that I want to ignore as unimportant,
that I want to throw out as unbecoming,
that I want to hide or deny out of shame,
that were stolen from me, and
that were lost when the storms came,
believing all will be restored and made beautiful one day.

TRUST

I choose to trust that God will . . .
reward me for the things I do unto Him in secret,
bring life in my spirit with every death to the flesh,
give me beauty for the ashes that I give to Him,
comfort every part of my aching heart that I entrust to His care,
and give me the grace to accomplish all that He requires of me.[3]

6

REDEEM

Fears and Sins

My Mema wore the same gold necklace every day when I was growing up. It had a raw gold nugget hanging from it as a pendant. It seemed odd to me that a woman as refined as my grandmother would wear such an unrefined thing. So, I asked her about it. "Mema, why do you wear that gold nugget around your neck?"

Her response was stranger than her jewelry. "This represents my sin," she said.

Sin would be the last thing I'd want hanging around my neck, I thought. But Mema explained that finding sin in our hearts is as good as finding gold. It is only through discovering and confessing our sins to God that we can remove the impediments to BECOMING truly rich in faith. Even though I did not fully grasp what she was saying back then, the memory of that conversation stuck with me. It would come to mind often, especially when I had sin to address. It encouraged me to confess my sins instead of hiding them away out of shame or blaming others for my predicament.

WEARING THE WORD

In adulthood, I came across two Scriptures that spoke to the brilliance behind Mema's gold nugget necklace. Proverbs 3:3 says, "Never let loyalty and kindness leave you! Tie them around your neck as a reminder. Write them deep within your heart" (NLT). Mema did just that. She wore a word of truth around her neck that brought life to her soul, reminding her how to access the flow of God's grace continually. But it was Revelation 3:17–18 that provided the explicit theological backing for Mema's gold nugget necklace, affirming how confessing sin leads to the receiving of greater treasures. It addresses the rewards of redeeming our sins through God's way of Divine Exchange by recognition, confession, and repentance.

> "You say, 'I am rich; I have acquired wealth and do not need a thing' But you do not realize that you are wretched, pitiful, poor, blind, and naked. I counsel you to buy from me gold refined in the fire, so that you can become rich; and white clothes to wear, so you can cover your shameful nakedness; and salve to put on your eyes, so you can see. Those whom I love, I rebuke and discipline. So be earnest and repent. Here I am! I stand at the door and knock. If anyone hears my voice and opens the door, I will come in and eat with that person, and they with me." (Revelation 3:17–20)

This interaction with Mema taught me a great deal about the freedom we can experience by engaging in the Divine Exchange of God's economy. These Scripture verses also revealed that those who are wealthy are often the poorest in God's eyes. They address not only the sins we commit but also what are called sins of omission. Sins of omission refer to the good we fail to do when it is in our power to do it. James 4:17 says, "If anyone, then, knows the good they ought to do and doesn't do it, it is sin for them."

DIMINISHING RETURNS

Mema often spoke of her struggle with accumulating too many things in her house and the burden they were to her, weighing down her heart and occupying her mind. She lamented this sin, warning us, her grandchildren, not to fall into this same trap. She would say, "Let go and let God," for our sake and hers. Still, it was a family trip to an arcade that would provide me with the clearest picture of how important it is to use God's Divine Exchange in a timely way.

I fondly remember the summer when all my cousins and I decided to pool our Jungle Land Arcade tickets and trade them in for a silver pendant for Mema that said #1 GRANDMA. From her reaction and how proud we acted, you would have thought we had given her a piece of jewelry from Tiffany's. Mema placed it around her neck right below her gold nugget necklace from Pepa. To her, this new treasure represented something beyond what money could buy: her grandchildren's love and admiration. To us, it represented trading in everything we earned to show our love for someone who loved us all.

The Exchange at the Cross

As every parent knows, the exchange of money for tickets at an arcade is a bit of a racket. There are more losses than wins, little return on money spent, and plenty of frustration when tickets don't come forth from the machines, especially when players next to us hit the jackpot. But the brilliance of an arcade is how it can teach the importance of timely stewardship. You see, game tickets earned are worth something only after they are exchanged at the ticket counter, and they become worthless the minute the player departs the arcade.

Life on earth is a lot like an arcade. Failing to redeem our tickets gives us a vivid picture of the losses we face when we fail to steward our time, talent, and earthly treasures before we depart from this life. Arcade tickets embody the saying, "You can't take it with you." When we entrust our burdens and perishing things to God, He replaces them with heavenly treasures like peace, joy, and the power of His grace.

> "Do not store up for yourselves treasures on earth, where moth and rust destroy, and where thieves break in and steal. But store up for yourselves treasures in heaven, where neither moth nor rust destroys, and where thieves do not break in or steal; for where your treasure is, there your heart will be also." (Matthew 6:19–21 NASB)

In God's economy, the exchange place is not found at a ticket counter but at the cross of Christ. Thankfully, the exchange rate of the cross is exponentially more in our favor because we get credit for both our wins and our losses. Better still, the person we are pooling our tickets with is Jesus, and He's already won every game. Plus, His Father owns the place. Both worldly economies and God's economy have limited time offers for making our exchanges. It becomes too late to exchange earthly treasures for heavenly rewards the moment we pass from this life.

Timely stewardship is an essential part of our journeys toward freedom. The more sins of commission and omission we accumulate without making use of the cross, the more burdens we carry and the more impoverished we become. At the Divine Exchange, we release the perishing and broken things of earth, and God provides life-giving gifts and priceless heavenly treasures in exchange. In Malachi 3:10, the Lord even encourages His people to test His Divine Economy's rate of return, saying,

> "Bring the whole tithe into the storehouse, that there may be food in my house. Test me in this," says the LORD Almighty, "and see if I will not throw open the floodgates of heaven and pour out so much blessing that there will not be room enough to store it."

Even though we cannot fully grasp His merciful and gracious ways, the Divine Exchange is something we would be wise to invest in regularly for our soul's freedom and the blessing of all.

WEEDS

When I was about eight, I asked my mom why I needed to keep confessing my sins if God had already forgiven all of them. But because Mom was a new believer, it was a difficult question for her to understand, let alone answer. She did her best and gave me one of those typical Christian-parent answers about how it is just part of obedience. But my question compelled her to ASK that same question directly to God.

Soon after, our family left on a two-week vacation, and Mom essentially left that question hanging on her "spiritual clothesline." When we returned home, my mother realized, as she looked out the kitchen window, that God had responded to her ASK. Below our second-story window, we found that my mother's gardens had become entirely overrun by weeds. The weeds had gotten so bad that all the potential beauty and abundance in her previously well-tended gardens were in jeopardy of being lost.

I distinctly remember Mom calling me over to the back window and explaining the correlation between her weedy garden and our souls and how both can become overrun when not tended regularly. From that point forward, weed pulling carried the double meaning of physical weeds in our garden and unconfessed sins in our hearts. If we don't give the necessary time and effort to pull the weeds, what's in our gardens gets crowded out, leaving little room for new plantings God might intend for our lives. This way of thinking about my soul as a garden has always stayed with me.

RECKONED DEAD

It is a genuine marvel how God uses our life circumstances to teach us about our needy conditions and His ways of grace. But it's even more remarkable when the Lord seems to go out of His way to provide circumstances for teaching our children complex spiritual things in a way they can understand and apply. Explaining the importance of bringing sin into the light, "reckoning the flesh dead," and receiving the riches of God's kingdom proved harder to explain to my kids than I remembered it being for my mom or Mema. At least, that is, until God sent the "gift" of the flies.

I dreaded the coming of the warmer weather, knowing with summer came the flies. Because the house we moved into when our children were young was located near farmland and adjacent to a pond in rural Pennsylvania, flies became a regular part of our first few summers there. It was a real headache when doors or windows were left open. These pesky creatures are unwelcome at any picnic, let alone inside our home when trying to make dinner. I REMEMBER being exasperated and crying out to the Lord, desperate for relief from the flies. Not many days later, He gave me an idea of a way to get my kids to help me with this pesky problem.

I called the kids to the living room and told them, "For every fly you kill, I'll give you a quarter, but this only applies if I don't have to ask you to do it. You can use a fly swatter, the new bug-a-salt gun [that shoots salt to kill them], or even your hand, preferably with a tissue. Twenty-five cents to the one who makes the kill and cleans up the fly guts." On days when the flies were terrible, or we were hosting company, I would increase the reward to fifty cents a fly.

This fly experience gave me a beautiful way to teach my children about the upside-down nature of God's economy. I explained how His blessings could replace our sins, just like cash-in-hand took the place of dead flies. Realizing that something as foul as flies is more valuable when reckoned dead taught us all an important spiritual lesson. Honest and straightforward confession before God reckons our sin dead even quicker than swatting a fly, and the rewards of the Divine Exchange are far superior. Our youngest, Annika, still remembers the days of the flies as the days she made seven dollars.

This experience gave life to the verse found in Romans 5:20, which tells us that as sin abounds, grace abounds even more. The flies helped my kids understand that even though grace increases wherever sin increases, just like they got more money for more flies killed, this does not make us want more sin in our hearts any more so than we wish for more flies in our home. They understood that sin, like flies, is just a part of life on earth. And even though we cannot stop them all from entering our house, no matter how diligently we try, we can keep them from taking over, defiling our spaces, and stealing the peace inside our homes. We must acknowledge their entry and choose to combat them until they are reckoned dead—both sin and flies. This experience brought a new understanding of why the enemy of God's people is called Beelzebub, which translates to "Lord of the Flies."

MISSING THE MARK

Thanks to my Mema and my mom, I learned that unrecognized and unconfessed sin keeps us stuck and blocks us from experiencing many of the Lord's blessings in this life. Our biggest problem isn't the existence of sin; it's allowing sin to remain in our hearts. When we first come to know Jesus, we lose our identity as a sinner, but this does not mean we become practically sinless or free from the struggles of sin. Even Paul, the apostle, dealt with the ongoing wrestling with his own sin, an inner battle he memorialized by writing a biblical tongue twister for the rest of us, "For what I want to do I do not do, but what I hate I do. . . . For I do not do the good I want to do, but the evil I do not want to do—this I keep on doing" (Romans 7:15,19).

Sin is an archery term that means missing the mark, and it happens as often as an arrow misses the center of the bullseye. Missing the mark of perfection is an ongoing part of every human life, even after coming to faith. Sin often seems more prevalent once we come to faith because now that we're living in God's light, the spots from the world are more easily seen. Everyone looks clean in the dark. It's the light that reveals our imperfections most.

> When we're living in God's light, the spots from the world are more easily seen.

First John 1:8–9 addresses the importance of believers admitting they still sin and the call to continued confession for ongoing cleansing, "If we claim to be without sin, we deceive ourselves, and the truth is not in us. If we confess our sins, he is faithful and just and will forgive us our sins and purify us from all unrighteousness." It is pretty freeing to realize that confession is something meant to happen regularly. Sanctification refers to the ongoing process of being made holy through a day-by-day faith walk with Jesus. It involves the practice of confessing our sins as much as entrusting our brokenness, setting up stones of remembrance, asking our questions, and trusting God to answer us in His time.

THE WAY OF BECOMING

COMMON IMPEDIMENTS

I remember coming home when I was around the age of nine, just after an incident with a schoolmate. I marched into the room where my mom was and announced: "This time, I did nothing wrong—I did absolutely nothing wrong, and I didn't deserve what she did to me."

My mom, in her classic style, responded, "Then your job is to forgive."

Oh, brother, you've got to be kidding me, I thought. "I don't want to forgive. I did nothing wrong," I told her.

Somehow, I had associated forgiveness with something we only give if we need it from that person in return—like in a fair trade. But Mom asked me to do all the giving up!

"But honey," Mom continued, "if you don't choose to forgive, you will be doing something wrong, and it will harm you."

> The way to forgive when forgiveness is hard begins with remembering God's unmerited forgiveness of us.

Mom didn't want me to cut myself off from the blessings of the Lord's presence. At least I know that now. All I knew then was that I did not want to forgive. I tried to hold on to my unforgiveness as if keeping it was benefiting me somehow. Mom assured me it was not.

She continued, "Then, ask God to help you want to forgive and start with saying, 'Help me, Lord, to want, to want, to want, to want . . . to forgive;' and eventually, I think, you will want to forgive."

I certainly did not enjoy being convicted like this when I was a kid. But now, I am exceptionally grateful for this kind of training. Nothing has brought as much peace and joy to my soul as applying these truths when I stray from the Way. Forgiveness is key to keeping the doors to the Divine Dialogue open. "If I had cherished sin in my heart, the Lord would not have listened; but God has surely listened and has heard my prayer" (Psalm 66:18–19a). It is reasonable to choose mercy and forgiveness based on our need to receive these things ourselves. "And when you stand praying, if you hold anything against anyone, forgive them, so that your Father in heaven may forgive you your sins" (Mark 11:25). When I do not feel like extending mercy to someone who has hurt me, the Spirit will often remind me of Matthew 5:7, "Blessed are the merciful, for they will be shown mercy." It reminds me that choosing to be merciful to others is a way to store up mercy for ourselves, and I always seem to need it.

It is not someone else's sin that defiles our hearts or separates our souls from the power of God's Spirit. The hurt and sin we hold on to, the unforgiveness we harbor, and the bitterroot we allow to grow up in us impede the flow of God's grace to us, in us, and through us. "Above all else, guard your heart, for everything you do flows from it" (Proverbs 4:23). When sin is allowed to remain and grow in us, it will eventually crowd out the light and lessen the amount of freedom, power, and hope we desperately need to overcome our troubles, weaknesses, and worries. Therefore, let us pray as King David did, saying, "Search me, God, and know my heart; test me and know my anxious thoughts. See if there is any offensive way in me, and lead me in the way everlasting" (Psalm 139:23–24).

Forgiving someone doesn't necessarily mean we suddenly enter back into the same relationship with that person, particularly if there has not been remorse or repentance on their part. Reconciliation with others often requires the rebuilding of trust over time. Nevertheless, the Word of God encourages us to do our part: "If possible, so far as it depends on you, live peaceably with all" (Romans 12:18 ESV).

THE BEST BATH

When my daughter Maya was six years old, she came upstairs from playing with her younger sister, Leah, in the basement and said, "I can't do it. I can't forgive her anymore. I don't have enough love."

I thought, *Here it is*. Maya needed the power of Christ to live in her so she could continue to experience the flow of His grace when she came up against her limited human resources.

I shared the gospel message with her in the context of her current need. We spent time talking about how Jesus made a way for us to gain access to more of His love and patience so it could come out from the inside of our hearts. She was so ready. I invited her dad to join us so we could all pray together. It was a beautiful time, and Maya experienced a miraculous infilling of love for her little sister. The next few days were glorious until they were glorious no more.

Maya came in from playing with her sister and loudly proclaimed, "It didn't work; there's no more left." Maya had plumb run out of patience and grace for her little sister again. Now would be the time to explain a different theological truth to Maya in a way she could understand.

"Okay, Lord, give me wisdom," I prayed.

Just then, our ten-year-old son, Cole, came walking down the stairs. He had overheard the conversation with Maya and said, "Hey, Mom, can I take a crack at this one?"

Out of curiosity and with a bit of relief, I responded, "Absolutely!"

Turning to Maya, Cole said, "When you give your life to Jesus, it's like taking the best bath of your whole life. But you still have to wash your face every day."

> Confession of daily sins is a critical part of soul care.

It sure seemed like solid theology to me. Like with Maya, the loss of grace did not begin with her sin but instead with the trespassing of her little sister. The answer to her internal problem wasn't going to be found in making her sister change but in accessing more of God's grace through forgiveness and cleansing and choosing to walk forward in love and patience.

RECOVERING INNER PEACE

We do not lose our inner sense of peace because the Lord has gone away from us but because we have stopped depending on Him and started looking to something else for fulfillment or rescue. The way to regain our lost sense of inner peace and joy is to go back and deal with the things that led us astray in the first place. When we lose our inner peace, it can be helpful to try to recall the last time we sensed God's peace and empowering presence before fear and anxiety took their place. We can always ask the Holy Spirit to show us when we last felt covered in God's peace and how it was lost.

It was always a group recovery mission whenever my mother would lose a contact lens before the days of disposable lenses. She has terrible eyesight, so it was always a serious matter. When she'd drop a lens, she'd say in her no-nonsense mom voice, "Don't anybody move; I just lost my contact." Then, we would gingerly get on our knees and help her search. All future activities were dependent on its recovery. Who cannot identify with the confusion when we or someone close to us cannot see clearly?

Spiritual Lenses

When we lose our spiritual lenses, we stop seeing those around us accurately, and because of the disquieting of heart and confusion in our minds brought on by the cloudiness, we often look for someone to blame. This further propagates a bad pattern, where outside factors affect our inner life, and then our inner life causes harm to others. We need to learn the warning signs when we are heading in the wrong direction, when our spiritual eyes are growing dim, and our spiritual lenses are becoming increasingly cloudy. My tell is that I feel frazzled, anxious, and confused. When I am no longer seeing clearly, it will be accompanied by a loss of my internal sense of peace. When I feel my inner peace waning, I realize I may have set up impediments to experiencing God's presence. I have, essentially, lost my spiritual lenses. In this state, I've been known to do strange things, like putting the milk in the cupboard and putting the cereal in the fridge. But if not quickly addressed, something funny can turn serious—and the people around me can become negatively affected by my disorientation.

This is the point at which I need to ask for a second touch from Jesus' hand, just as the blind man at Bethsaida needed a second touch to see people clearly. After the first touch of Jesus' hand, the man said, "I see people, but they look like trees walking around." Then, Jesus touched the man a second time, and his sight was completely restored. It is not that Jesus couldn't perform a complete healing with a single touch, but that He was making a more different critical point through this second touch.

Just because we may have come to believe in Jesus and chosen to make Him the Lord of our lives, this doesn't mean that from time to time, we don't need another touch from His healing hand so we can come to see other people clearly. Perhaps it is meant to show us that we all need to return to Jesus for more healing when we aren't seeing properly. Part of the work of deep inner healing of the soul is finding the root of the problem that caused us to lose our inner peace in the first place. This kind of soul therapy and spiritual healing can take some digging. But the digging is worth it. My mom was big on making sure we did not just pull the weeds from their tops or stems but rather by their roots. She was quick to take us out to the garden and show us how quickly weeds return when we don't get the root.

"Kerry, what's the root?" she would ask, so I would look deeper at the attitudes behind my actions and the beliefs that led to my behaviors. One of Mom's regular prompts to help us in our sin-mining was to remind us that "judgment comes out of jealousy."

Fruit and Root

If judgment is the fruit, jealousy is the root. Comparing our area of lack with another's area of plenty is an invitation for jealousy to take root. Few things are more invasive to our lives and ruinous to our relationships than giving envy a foothold. "For where you have jealousy and selfish ambition, there you will find disorder and every evil practice" (James 3:16). The way of repentance is looking to God and asking Him to meet our needs and quell our fears. Asking God can serve as an antidote to jealousy and judgment.

> "You can't keep the birds from flying overhead, but you can keep them from nesting in your hair."

The diabolic twins of jealousy and judgment are like seeds from the same enemy of our souls sent to sow discord in our hearts. But as my Nana Richards used to say as a reminder of the part human choice has to play, "You can't keep the birds from flying overhead, but you can keep them from nesting in your hair."

If we are quick to confess the "little" internal sins rather than justifying or nurturing them, the Lord will be faithful in extracting them, making room for love and relationships to flourish more in our lives. Confession of daily sins is a critical part of soul care, particularly confessing the hurts and offenses instead of keeping a "record of wrongs," as this is sure to invite bitterness to take root. Bitterness and unforgiveness become landing pads for agents of darkness that are ever seeking to invade our minds and terrorize our souls. The way to forgive when forgiveness is hard begins with remembering God's unmerited forgiveness of us. "Be kind to one another, tenderhearted, forgiving one another, as God in Christ forgave you" (Ephesians 4:32 ESV).

The story Jesus told about the wicked servant and his master found in Matthew 18:32–34 warns us just how serious the business of forgiveness is to God and the terror unforgiveness will bring about in our lives.

> Then the master called the servant in. "You wicked servant," he said, "I canceled all that debt of yours because you begged me to. Shouldn't you have had mercy on your fellow servant just as I had on you?" In anger his master handed him over to the jailers to be tortured, until he should pay back all he owed.

SPIRALS OF FEAR

Need, fear, and desire are the origins of nearly every choice we make. These things are not bad in themselves. They are natural human tendencies and emotions. What makes them bad or good is determined by what we seek for their relief or fulfillment. Either we can choose to look to God for help and ascend by faith, or we can look to self or other things of this world and begin a negative downward spiral that ends in brokenness and despair.

These are two of the clearest patterns in which humans engage. The one empowered by faith leads to our soul's BECOMING by grace in positive ways, and we refer to this pattern as a Cycle of Grace. The other leads to negative, harmful, and unbecoming things in our lives and relationships, and we refer to this pattern as Spirals of Fear. In fear, we naturally turn to self-sufficiency to solve our problems.

But when our efforts or identities are revealed as insufficient, we become more anxious and ashamed of our failures and weaknesses. If, at this point, we would remember that the fleshly self was never meant to be our sufficiency and rightly turn our gaze back to the Lord, we could avoid unnecessary pain and heartache. Nevertheless, we often press harder into control and get exhausted, or we turn to other people, hoping they can save us from our problems. But every external thing or person will eventually prove insufficient to save us. If we cannot see that pride or idolatry has gotten us here, we will turn and blame the things or people we have set up to rescue us. Shame and blame play critical roles in keeping us in these downward fear spirals. So, whether we have played god or made gods out of other people or things, we will continue to become even more fearful, resentful, and fragmented if we don't confess where we've gone wrong and strayed from the Way.

> The good news is that we can return to the Lord for help and redemption at any point.

Failing Patterns

An idol is anything other than God, to which we turn our heads and fix our gaze for too long. Sadly, our human tendency is to flip back and forth from idol to idol, from god-playing to god-making, from prideful self-sufficiency to idolizing other people or things. As long as we remain in these failing patterns, we will spiral more and more, faster and faster, until we create hurricanes that tear us apart inside and harm those close to us. When our spiraling in fear creates these hurricanes, the debris from our lives begins to fly and decimate those nearby. Shame turns into despair, and blame turns into bitterness. Our brokenness grows alongside sadness, worry, and vulnerability in these harmful patterns. In these states of vulnerability, it is natural to begin wielding our broken parts like weapons out of self-protection. Our untreated wounds start to fester and spread to other parts of our spiritual bodies.

The good news is that we can return to the Lord for help and redemption at any point. When our mind is distracted because of an unconfessed sin that is impeding the dialogue between our soul and God's Spirit, we can ask God to show us where we may have gotten off track so we can correct it for the sake of our soul and relationships. In essence, this is a recovery mission to help regain our spiritual lenses. According to 1 Chronicles 16:11 (ESV), this is meant to be something we do regularly. "Seek the Lord and His strength; seek his presence continually."

These patterns are avoidable. But stopping them requires a willingness to call sin by its proper name of sin and stop being afraid to find it, admit it, confess it, and turn from it. We should be more scared of staying in these fear-spirals than humbling ourselves enough to discover where we went wrong. We can turn back, ask God to meet our needs, heal our relationships, and empower our work so we can begin to cycle in grace again. Lamenting our brokenness and repenting of our sins are like the two shoulders of the same body, both equal and necessary for running our races well.

THIS IS YOUR LIFE

When I turned forty-seven, a wise and creative friend, Hyatt Moore, encouraged me to reflect on my year gone by, just as he does each year on his birthday. It would prove the perfect year for it because I had just gone through a significant time of weed pulling in my soul. This gardening work had been going on for some time, culminating at the twentieth anniversary of the Congressional Angels in Adoption Awards, a program I had helped create.

I expected to see many familiar faces from my years working in DC, but I had not expected to run into people associated with nearly every era of my life journey, some going back as far as the seventh grade. It was a "This is your life, Kerry," organized exclusively by the Lord Himself. The irony was that the people God brought before me represented times when I felt I had been unable to sufficiently "please" them, no matter how hard I had worked or how much I had sacrificed. These encounters were unsettling for a highly relational person like me because they brought a deep sense of relational failure and personal shame.

One Finish Line

Despite their jarring effect, it was clear that these "happenstances" were providential, so I began asking the Lord about them. "What are You trying to show me? I know it's something. But what, I certainly don't know. I can see Your 'ironic' fingerprints all over this, Lord, so please enlighten me; I don't want to miss what this is about!"

After the Angels in Adoption gala, I took time for the deep reflection my friend Hyatt had encouraged me to do. It all proved beneficial and illuminating. I saw that the greatest hindrance to my personal development had been the weighty and entangling sin of idolatry. I had to call this specific soul impediment by its truest name of sin and then cast it off through confession and repentance. I suppose it was not the "worship of a golden calf" variety of idolatry. No, it was a more subtle form that cleverly disguises itself as "people-pleasing." People-pleasing rarely gets pegged as one of the more severe soul problems. It is often even made the object of praise by self and others. But wow, does this sneaky sin of people-pleasing take a grave toll on the soul! And let me be clear, people-pleasing pleases nobody in the end. "Am I now trying to win the approval of human beings or of God? Or am I trying to please people? If I were still trying to please people, I would not be a servant of Christ" (Galatians 1:10).

As I took this look back over the years, I realized how extraordinarily gracious God had been to me. He still brought about His purposes in and through my life. But if I had understood the extent of internal confusion this people-pleasing habit had been causing, I could have come through many life experiences with less inner turmoil and fragmentation, both personally and relationally. Pleasing God is often in contradiction with pleasing people, even when the people are believers, and sadly, even those we love and who love us. Therefore, we risk dividing our minds and efforts when we try to please both God and people. Running toward two different finish lines in the same race is a soul-separating endeavor that tears us apart.

Around this same time, our son Cole was running in the district cross-country meet on behalf of our local high school. For many weeks leading up to the race, he intentionally prepared himself in body, mind, and soul. Outside of the rigorous practices and the countless miles that his coach had him and the other runners log, Cole made his own mindful choices to only take healthy things into his body and to do all he could to "get out of his head," as his coach calls it. Cole seemed to have a laser-like focus on running his best race.

The evening before his race, Cole, serendipitously, had a chance to speak on the phone to a dear family friend, Sally McRae. Sally has known Cole since he was a toddler when she worked with Scott in the adoption and orphan-care ministry of Show Hope. Sally, known affectionately in the running world as "Yellow Runner," happens to be one of the world's top 100+ and 200+ mile ultrarunners and runs for Team Nike. When Sally learned that Cole would be racing the next day, she advised him that when he goes to the starting line, to "keep in mind what a privilege it is to get to do something like this, to be healthy and strong enough to run like this, and to be sure to run out of a sense of joy and gratitude, not out of obligation to someone or something." Her words resonated with him.

Leading up to race day, I asked Cole what we, as spectators, could do or say to help him in his race. Cole explained how he tends to block out peripheral voices because he's focused on the singular task of running. He said he gets a general sense if the spectators call out words of encouragement or critique. He explained how critical comments and fear tactics can have the negative effect of making him run slower because of the extra effort it takes to get out of his head.

"Honestly, Mom," Cole said, "when I'm running, I don't think there is some magic word to yell. Maybe matching my running energy with the same energy in cheering would help. Oh, and please don't think I'm ignoring you when I run past you without looking. I might glance at you for a second, but I won't turn my head because it slows me down. I need to keep looking straight ahead and focus on finishing my race."

Wow! Now, that's some deep spiritual wisdom being unwittingly spoken through my son, I thought. His words provided living revelation to the

Hebrews 12:1 verse that his father had pronounced over his race early that day, which says, "Let us throw off everything that hinders and the sin that so easily entangles. And let us *run* with perseverance the race marked out for us, fixing our eyes on Jesus, the pioneer and perfecter of faith." Cole's words also brought down specific questions from my spiritual clothesline that I had asked of the Lord. Namely, "What hinders me from running my race to the fullest?"

I found myself thinking of endeavors God had entrusted to me in seed form, things He had long been calling me to tend and see to completion, but which I had neglected or even abandoned altogether because I was listening to the critical voices of people instead of the voice of God. I started confessing my sin of looking and listening to the wrong things instead of looking to God. It was incredibly freeing to realize that the sin problem was mine because this meant I could rid myself of the problem that had brought me so much pain and hindered my BECOMING journey.

> I was listening to the critical voices of people instead of the voice of God.

The words "Let us" in Hebrews 12:1, which read, "Let us throw off everything that hinders and the sin that so easily entangles," call us to participate in this work for ourselves. It does not say, "Let God lay aside for you" or "let your parent, pastor, or spouse remove that weight." It says, "Let us." Becoming unencumbered is not something that others can do for us. It also isn't something God will do for us without our participation in the process.

My job was to lay aside the worry of what other people thought of my work and focus on what God thought of it. When I did this, I became free from the bondage of seeking to please people and not offending them, thinking that this was what pleased God. I wrongly thought these things were the same, but they are not. Redeeming our sins is how we cast off the burdens and heavy weights we are not meant to carry. We are invited to take up a lighter one by remaining focused on the Lord. No one else can do this work of clearing our sins. "Let us throw off" means we must do our part in this work of faith.

None of us can stop people from having expectations of us, nor can we prevent them from thinking or saying critical things. But we can choose to listen to the Voice of Truth and walk as the Spirit leads us. It is in this way we are freed to become what God intends. Allowing the expectations or critique of people to become fixed before our eyes slows us down, makes our journey more laborious, and divides our hearts and minds. Through my son's cross-country race, God reminded me of the dangers of idolatry and how it can keep us from succeeding in our spiritual journeys because our eyes are not singularly focused. We are meant to remain fixed on Jesus alone, who is already at the finish line, and listen exclusively to the Holy Spirit, our soul's Head Coach, who can lead our races most efficiently. "Train yourself for godliness; for while bodily training is of some value, godliness is of value in every way, as it holds promise for the present life and also for the life to come" (1 Timothy 4:8 ESV).

Gaze on Him

I had been listening to many voices, and not only that, but I had made a habit of paying particular attention to the critical and hard-to-please ones. The problem isn't in hearing these voices but in giving them more credence than the Lord's voice, thinking that trying to please the naysayers is a form of humility. It is not. Instead of seeing the value in fighting to get these critical voices out of my head, I would press into them and even turn my head toward them, remaining fixated until they showed their "pleasure" with me and gave me their approval. Man-pleasing slowed me down and zapped the power I needed to run my race unhindered. God has given us the ability to keep our hearts fixed upon His face and not turn our attention to the right or the left. The power to remain steadfast lies within us and is made manifest by focusing our gaze on the Author and Finisher of each thing in our lives. "Do not turn aside from any of the commands I give you today, to the left or the right, following other gods and serving them" (Deuteronomy 28:14).

God is waiting to receive His children and reward them for their faith at the finish line. Still, we can allow ourselves to be harmed by our sins along the way and end up far wearier in the final legs of our race than was ever intended. By focusing on created things, we divide our power and lessen our momentum as our attentiveness becomes split between the finish line and peripheral end goals. Turning our expectations toward the creation, whether to things or people, ministries, or even our own efforts as an ongoing source of any kind, is a form of idolatry and will always lead to disappointment and resentment.

My mother would often say, "Idolatry leads to hate." I so see this! Whatever we set up as an idol will fail us and eventually fall. If we do not repent for placing our ongoing expectations on people or things that should only be placed upon God, we will blame them when they fail us. At first, we may be disappointed. But disappointments can quickly turn to resentment and ultimately to hate if we refuse to repent of our part in setting them up in the first place. The way to remain safe in our relationships with things and people is to recognize their goodness and be grateful to God for them. Look to God and praise Him for everyone and everything. People and things were intended to help us know God more, just like studying art helps us know the artist better. Though it is much easier to use our physical eyes to see than our spiritual eyes, God calls us to return our spiritual gaze to Him so that we don't stop running our purposeful race and miss out on the glorious ending He is writing in each of our stories.

YOUR BECOMING STORY: REDEEM

Here are a few questions to consider to help identify things you may need to confess to the Lord for His forgiveness for your soul's freedom and healing.

What do you keep repeating in your mind that someone has done to you?

Where did your hurt turn into unforgiveness or bitterness?

In what ways has your fear or discontent turned to jealousy or criticism of others?

What are you afraid of?

How might your fears be controlling you or leading you to control others?

Have you dealt with insufficiency or the shame we associate with it?

Have you sought the Lord and entrusted your needs to Him, or have you hidden out of self-protection, doubled down in control, or blamed others?

Where have unmet expectations of someone or something made you critical and resentful?

Where has your mourning crossed into self-pity, thinking you suffer more than others?

How have you cared more about pleasing people than pleasing God?

I encourage you to write an honest prayer of confession to the Lord. Begin by confessing what the Spirit has revealed to you, whether they are sins against the Lord, your own flesh, or others. Then, ask God to forgive and cleanse you in the name of Jesus. First John 1:9 says, "If we confess our sins, he is faithful and just and will forgive our sins and purify us from all unrighteousness."

"Divine Exchange"

For my eyes to see Your glory
For my ears to hear Your voice
Fill my life, invade my story,
I repent, make my choice,
I turn to You.

I will buy from You
Gold refined by fire.
I will buy from You
Oil for my eyes.
Clothe me in the robes of Your mercy.
For Your glory, heal my soul,
Make me holy.

For my hands to heal the hurting
For my feet to bring Your peace
That's the grace in my returning.
You're my joy. You're my strength.
I turn to You.

I trade these ashes for Your beauty.
I trade this sadness for Your joy.
I trade this sin for Your forgiveness.
My loss is gain in Your Divine Exchange.[1]

7

STAND

Storms and Trials

In Paul's letter to the Ephesians, he calls on believers to clothe themselves in the armor of God so that "when the day of evil comes, you may be able to stand your ground" (Ephesians 6:13). The words "day of evil" always seemed a little excessive to me . . . until one day, the gates of hell themselves came against my family, and every one of my beliefs was tested.

My brother's wife, Jenn, and I were both pregnant at the same time. It was the first week of January 2008, one week before Jenn's due date and three weeks before mine, when my husband Scott's brother-in-law, Jim, had a heart attack. Scott packed his suitcase and flew out to South Carolina the next day to be with his sister and help care for their baby so she could be with her husband in the hospital. Meanwhile, my parents came to help me care for our two young children while Scott was away since I was so far along in my pregnancy. Soon after Scott left and my parents arrived, my sister-in-law Jenn went into labor.

My parents, my two kids, and I immediately left our house in the Poconos, which was about an hour from the hospital. We wanted to make it back to our hometown when my brother Bobby and Jenn's baby would be born. On the way home, our son Cole became violently ill and started vomiting in the car. Just then, Bobby called my father. Dad picked up and said, "Bob, I can't talk; Cole just threw up everywhere. Call you back." In the chaos of the moment, Dad didn't hear his son's reply. Bobby had yelled out on the other end of the phone, "Wait, Dad!"

When Dad called him back, Bobby was sitting alone in a hospital room, not knowing if he would ever see his wife or infant son alive again. Jenn's epidural had gone to her heart, and both mom and baby had flatlined. They'd been rushed out of the delivery room, and Bobby still had no word on their condition. When we finally arrived at the hospital, we found Bobby holding his newborn son alive while still waiting to hear whether his wife would survive. Ultimately, through a series of long-shot medical interventions intermingled with a series of divine interventions, both son and mother were miraculously saved.

WHEN DARKNESS FALLS

As I lay down in bed later that night, it occurred to me that I had not felt my baby move all day. I figured I was just distracted by the day's trying events. Scott flew back home late that night. Exhausted, I fell asleep praying for God's help and protection. The following day was January six, Scott's birthday, Orthodox Christmas, and the holy day of Epiphany, which was both strange and fitting considering the integration of human storylines that would continue to play out.

My mom offered to watch our kids so Scott and I could catch up and have a private birthday brunch for him. When we sat down, I shared my worries with him about not noticing any baby movement. Scott took me straight to the hospital, where we were taken to the labor and delivery floor. Through an ultrasound, we were informed that what we had feared most had actually come to pass: our baby no longer had a heartbeat.

It's difficult to describe the pain that overswept me in an instant. I began to cry out in utterly despairing grief—at a level that was beyond my understanding. It was as if I were witnessing myself wailing from outside of my body. My brother, Bobby, could hear my cries from their hospital room just across the hall. He did not know it was his sister crying, but he began to pray, knowing that this sound must be a mother who had just lost her child; the cry he heard was unlike any other.

I had only ever heard this "otherworldly" sound of distress when I witnessed a Ugandan woman fall apart at the news that her baby had been stolen. While in Africa, I learned that this weeping and screaming combination was known as keening. The people there had grown quite familiar with its sound, as terrorists had abducted tens of thousands of children in that region in recent years.[1] I, too, felt my child had been stolen.

Two Doors Apart

I was placed in a wheelchair and taken down the hall to where a second ultrasound would confirm our baby's death. Scott walked beside me, and we both began quietly worshiping just to keep breathing. Three years earlier, the miscarriage of our daughter Malaya had taught us the importance of singing praise just to regain our breath when the pain is all-consuming. This type of worship was not some kind of celebration in the high notes of life but a choice to cling to God as our Breath-Giver in the low notes of life for our survival.

When the second ultrasound confirmed our child's passing, we also found out for the first time that our baby was a girl. The nurses took us to a room only two doors down from my older brother, where his wife and baby were recovering. The contrast could not have been more stark: I could not have imagined that our family would experience "the House of Rejoicing" and "the House of Mourning" two doors apart in the same hospital.

> Only God could be what we each needed now.

Doctors informed me that labor must be promptly induced. After the life-threatening complication that had almost taken my sister-in-law's life, I decided to forgo having an epidural. As I climbed into the hospital bed to begin the laboring process, Scott said, "I'm sorry, Honey . . . I can't help you now."

"I know you can't," I replied straightaway. This was another understanding I had gained earlier, albeit in lesser trials. If this had happened in our first years of marriage, I would have had greater expectations of Scott to be some kind of savior rather than my companion in the suffering. It is natural to look to our spouse to fix what ails us. But I knew only God could be what each of us needed now. Our baby girl was in a place only He was familiar with.

I slid my body to one side of the bed and invited Scott to lie beside me while I labored to release the shell that no longer housed our baby's spirit. The pain that accompanied my labor, without the epidural, was a strange comfort to me, as it provided a physical embodiment of the profound grief I was feeling over the loss of my child.

During one of the relief points in the laboring process, we talked about what we should name our daughter. Though we would not be raising her, we had already learned the importance of naming the children carried in my womb. We wanted to find a name that would minister to our broken hearts when we spoke of her. The Spirit led us to the sixty-first chapter of Isaiah, which discusses Christ's ministry to those who suffer. We chose the name *Isabella Grace,* or *Bella* for short, based on God's promise to give "beauty for ashes" (KJV). Her full name affirmed this promise of beauty for ashes: Bella means *beautiful,* Isabella, *consecrated,* and Grace, the *empowering presence of God.* By faith, we trusted that our daughter was now consecrated in the empowering presence of God and that her legacy would be one of beauty in exchange for the ashes we would entrust to our Lord at her burial.

> Integrity is about holding firmly to the things we have already come to believe so we can remain standing despite the hurricanes, and even while we wrestle to overcome our unbelief.

Later in this long laboring process, I asked Scott, now sitting in the chair beside the bed and reading his Bible, "What are you reading?"

"Ecclesiastes 7:3," he answered. "'Sorrow is better than laughter because sorrow has a refining influence on us'" (NLT).

I can't quite understand that right now, I thought. But I held on to the words, hoping they might make sense later.

Silently, my mind turned inward, and I entered into the practice that had become familiar over many years . . . to bring my wrestling to God and to ask Him my questions directly.

First, I wondered if this was happening because God loved me less than others. So, I asked Him. And His Holy Spirit answered by reminding me of children I had known and come to love through my orphan care ministry, who had also suffered deeply. The Spirit asked me to consider His love for a girl I knew named Jeanne.

BETWEEN THE ASKED AND ANSWERED

Jeanne had suffered unimaginable horrors most of us could not even imagine. As a nine-year-old, she had witnessed her parents' brutal death during the Rwandan genocide against the Tutsis in 1994. She was later brought to the United States by a Rwandan foster family. In truth, she had been separated from her many siblings—including her own twin sister—to experience labor exploitation and to be abused by the family's father. When I met Jeanne, the Lord filled me with inexplicable love for her, and over many years, she and her siblings, who still lived in Africa, became like family to me. I had witnessed firsthand how profoundly God loved them and how He could—and *did*—redeem their suffering for the salvation of many.[2] Their stories taught me that God had been with them through their hardships and that His love was more immense than even the most profound human suffering.

So, when I asked if God loved me less and He answered me by reminding me of Jeanne, it revealed that He had not stopped loving me any more than He had stopped loving her.

Soon, another question surfaced: *Lord, did You take my baby because of my sin? Is this how it works even after repentance and salvation?* I wondered, so I asked Him. God reminded me of His servant Job and how he, who was called the most righteous man on the earth during his lifetime, had lost all ten of his children in a single moment when the day of evil came upon him. Even then, Job did not sin against God. Instead, he recognized the Lord's sovereignty in his ultimate sorrow, saying, "Naked I came from my mother's womb, and naked I will depart. The LORD gave and the LORD has taken away; may the name of the LORD be praised" (Job 1:21). The Scriptures reveal that Job's soul remained intact through his tribulation period because he was determined not to speak against God and maintain his integrity (Job 27:5). Integrity is about holding firmly to the things we have already come to believe so that we can remain standing despite the hurricanes in our midst, and even while we wrestle to overcome our unbelief. Remembering Job's innocence juxtaposed with his profound suffering comforted me and helped me continue to STAND in faith.

Still, I wondered: *When all this has passed, will I be so damaged on the other side that I won't even recognize myself?*

In reply, a vision came to my mind's eye. Glancing over to the labor and delivery room corner, I saw a blazing fire with people standing inside it. I knew the story of Shadrach, Meshach, and Abednego and how they had been thrown into Nebuchadnezzar's fiery furnace, so I assumed it was them I was seeing. But as I looked closer, I realized it wasn't them. Instead, I saw Scott, Jesus, and me standing together in those flames. The vision brought me deep comfort and caused a small new flame of hope to stir deep in my soul. But the pain of our loss, as my body labored in delivery, still hung over me like thick darkness.

"Later, You Will Understand"

In this cloudy haze, I asked Scott, "Honey, what are you thinking about?"

He replied, "I can't seem to get the lyrics of one of Steve's songs out of my head. I keep hearing, 'You are being loved right now. There's a song being sung over you by the One who breathed life into you. You are being loved right now at this very moment.'"[3] Scott paused. Then, he spoke again. "It sounds strange, I know, but it keeps replaying in my mind."

How could this be love? How could God be singing over us right now in our devasting loss? I couldn't imagine.

Still, I chose to hold on to this idea because of what Jesus had told His disciples. "You do not realize now what I am doing, but later you will understand" (John 13:7). I understood some things at that point in my journey, and other things I still did not. The fact that God loved me all the time was something I believed theoretically, but at that moment, I didn't feel very loved. Still, God reminded me of how I had felt His love flow through me for others who were suffering and didn't feel loved. Numb and overwhelmed as I was, I knew my God had answered me before, so I chose to wait for Him to bring understanding again.

The day we left the hospital, we received an email from Steven Curtis Chapman, with whom Scott was working in ministry. Steve was on a writers' retreat in Ireland with several other worship leaders when he heard about the loss of our baby. He asked the other retreat participants to pray with him. That night, God impressed the verses Hebrews 6:19–20 on the heart of another worship leader, Matt Redman, concerning our loss. "We have this hope as an anchor for the soul, firm and secure. It enters the inner sanctuary behind the curtain, where our forerunner, Jesus, has entered on our behalf."

> We have this hope as an anchor for the soul.

Matt and Steve began to pen a song based on that verse the following day. Then Steven and his son Caleb stayed up late into the night recording the song so we would have it as a source of comfort as soon as we returned home from the hospital without our baby girl.

And so, it turned out that Scott had spoken prophetically when he felt the reality that the Maker of heaven and earth was singing over us. The truth of Scott's words emanated through the song written and recorded called "Close to Your Heart," based on Hebrews 6:19, where hope in Jesus Christ is referred to as "an anchor for the soul."[4] I was grateful for the comfort this song brought me in the early days after our loss. I would repeat lines from the lyrics frequently as a way of soothing my soul and when trying to fall asleep in the hard weeks that followed.

ANCHORED AND CROSS-TIED

The more I listened, the more another question began niggling within me: *What good is an anchor in a hurricane?*

Indeed, what we were experiencing was no ordinary storm; it was a hurricane. This was the day that evil had come against my entire family, threatening three of its members and taking the life of our baby girl, Isabella Grace. At delivery, we learned that there was a knot in her cord, which had suddenly tightened and cut off her supply of oxygen.

The grief felt like it would consume me; it felt as though I was drawing closer and closer to the eyewall of the storm. I wondered if the brokenness was permanent and whether I would return to wholeness.

So, I continued to take my grievances to God in the form of questions. Dialoguing with Him was already part of our way together. My thoughts and questions went something like this: *You created language, every Word, every created thing, water itself, even the molecules that comprise water, and the atoms that make up all things. You created boats and even the idea of boats, anchors, and people making boats and being in boats. So, if You called our hope an anchor, allowed this hurricane to hit us, and inspired these men to write this song, then please help me understand what this means for me now. What good is an anchor when trying to survive a hurricane?*

Boats and Docks

I searched for God's truth regarding anchors and storms in science and language. The document I discovered was a transcript from a lecture given to boat owners at the National Marine Hurricane Preparation Symposium on how a boat can survive a hurricane. Even though it was not a spiritual message, it read like a parable to me.

The lecturer, David Pascoe, began by saying,

> The dock anchoring brochure was picked up twice as often as the information on direct anchorage. But this will change over the course of the year when the marinas discover that a boat on an anchor mooring is ten times more likely to survive than a boat tied to a dock. As a matter of fact, the dock has a much better chance of surviving if boats are not tied to it during a hurricane. Almost all docks will survive a hurricane when no boats are tied to them.[5]

The message was expressed in maritime jargon. But as I read the document, the Holy Spirit seemed to play the role of simultaneous translator, causing me to comprehend the deeper spiritual meanings of the illustrations mentioned. "Boats" were human souls. "Docks" represent things we can see with our eyes in this world. Tying our hopes to something we can see is like hitching a boat to a dock in a storm. Placing our hopes in the truth of Christ and God's Word is the same as dropping anchor into the depths of the sea by "direct anchorage."

Whenever we see a storm coming, we must consider the strength of what we have tied our hopes to for survival. Suppose it is something we can see with our eyes, as docks can be seen, like our homes, jobs, ministries, wealth, health, stuff, looks, past successes, or reputations. In these cases, we must know that these things will not keep us safe through life's great tribulations, such as the death of a child, divorce, betrayal, disease, abuse, war, disaster, or facing our own mortality.

God calls us to evaluate what we have become wrongly tied to as a source of hope or security. Whatever it may be—anything we tether to other than the Lord—only gives us a false sense of safety that will fall apart when the storm comes, putting *both* us and what we are tied to in jeopardy. The untethering process requires self-examination and the cutting loose of harmful soul-ties that would tear us apart in a hurricane. In times of crisis involving life and death, when it is beyond the ability of things and people to save, the only thing that will keep our boats in one piece is to anchor directly into the unseen presence of God.

> Anything we tether to apart from the Lord only gives us a false sense of safety.

I began to see that this way of anchoring is precisely what it means to STAND *when the day of evil comes.*

As I read further, I learned ways to minimize loss and damage in a storm, which I found particularly relevant to our relationships with other "boats," that is, people.

It read, "The domino effect occurs when one boat on a canal breaks loose and crashes into others, resulting in a chain reaction that ends up with boats piled up at the end of the canal."[6] Pascoe used the example of the aftermath of Hurricane Andrew, where hundreds upon hundreds of boats were piled up at the end of the canals due to this domino effect.

The lecturer warned, "Therefore, consider whether your boat will be vulnerable to the domino effect when contemplating whether to cross-tie to another boat. If possible, try to check on the anchorage of the boats upwind from you. If someone's done a lousy job or has been tied to weak or rotten docks, then, chances are, his boat is going to wreck yours."[7]

Where Hope Is Anchored

When Scott told me, "I can't help you," I already knew I could not anchor my hopes in Scott. He could not answer my soul's most pressing questions nor care for our daughter, who was now gone from this earth, and he could not heal my broken heart. We both needed to anchor directly into Jesus ourselves. And so we did. We could lie side by side and cross-tie to one another for support and comfort, sharing things God was ministering to us individually. But we would need our own sustenance and rescue by being anchored in the Lord for our souls' wholeness and integrity.

This maritime expert also wrote, "You'll probably stand a better chance if you can use anchors to stand off from the dock, or find a better location, rather than being a sitting duck at the end of the canal." Pascoe emphasized this: "If you don't know how well they have anchored, it's better to stand off alone, but be aware that you will face an inevitable disaster if the storm comes and you are tied to a boat with no anchor."[8]

Because boats represent people, these maritime realities about anchoring in a storm confirm that it is better to be alone, away from the crowd, than around many other people who have not chosen to place their hopes in Christ when a storm is coming.

Though being anchored alone is better than being with others who have failed to anchor themselves in the deep, the best thing is what marine experts call the *neighborhood team effect*:

> If you can generate a neighborhood team effect, so much the better. But you have to get all the boat owners involved and ensure that all the boats are well secured by their own anchors. Many boats survived the eye of Hurricane Andrew despite fronting directly on Biscayne

Bay, with a 10-foot storm surge, by a combination of cross-tying and anchors.[9]

According to maritime experts and God's Word, the best way to survive a hurricane and remain standing is through a combination of anchoring in Christ and cross-tying to those who are also anchored in Him. If we want our boat, that is, our soul, to survive with its integrity still intact on the other side of a great storm, we must choose to anchor into Jesus and cross-tie with others who have also anchored in the depths of the Lord themselves.

FELLOWSHIP OF THE SUFFERING

God not only provided these profound truths that would minister to my soul in this season of tribulation but also the vessels of His grace in the form of others who had suffered with whom I could cross-tie. From early on in my pregnancy, when I asked the Lord for a name for our child that reflected our season of life, He only gave me the name Jacob. So, for a time, I thought we were having a boy. But a few months before my due date, my sister-in-law Jenn announced they were having a boy and naming him Jacob. *Hmm,* I thought. *Maybe God is just speaking to me about my nephew.* But as it turns out, God had more to share with me about the name Jacob in light of my story.

Even though my Rwandan friend, Jeanne, had not yet heard we had lost our baby, she emailed me telling me how the Lord had put me on her heart and called her to pray for me. She quoted directly from the book of Isaiah, referencing me as a type of Jacob and saying God had given her this verse for me:

> But now, this is what the LORD says—he who created you, Jacob, he who formed you, Israel: "Do not fear, for I have redeemed you; I have summoned you by name; you are mine. When you pass through the waters, I will be with you; and when you pass through the rivers, they will not sweep over you. When you walk through the fire, you will not be burned; the flames will not set you ablaze. For I am the LORD your God, the Holy One of Israel, your Savior." (Isaiah 43:1–3)

When God spoke the name Jacob to me, He was speaking prophetically so that, in time, I would understand more about my soul's wrestling. Jacob's wrestling with God was about his journey of relenting before God's power and *becoming* changed in the process.

God's beloved possession, as Israel. Just as God was with Jacob, He was faithful to see me through the raging fires and the violent waters. I was not burned up, drowned, or destroyed. Instead, God sang over Scott and me in the storm. He answered all my desperate cries and questions. He reminded me again and again of His presence and His love. Yes, death comes to us all and all our loved ones. But only those who press in to ask, seek, and knock will receive the answers, healing, and provisions they seek. Sorrows and sufferings are like seeds planted in our souls. If these seeds are watered with God's Word and given the light of His wisdom, they will, in time, grow up and produce fruit that can be shared for the comfort and nourishment of others.

A Life Raft

The weeks following our daughter's death were extremely tough, with waves of grief befalling without notice. I usually felt the Lord's comforting presence draw close to me during these times. But when I would cross out of mourning and into self-pity, thinking no one else could understand my pain, the comfort I needed would often seem far off. I cried to the Lord, who showed me how to find His comfort again. He took me to 1 Peter 5:9, which says, "Resist him [the enemy], standing firm in the faith, because you know that the family of believers throughout the world is undergoing the same kinds of sufferings." I sensed the Lord was encouraging me to remember that I am not alone in my suffering and that there was wisdom and support to be gleaned from those in His body who had gone before me.

I remember sitting at my dining room table when my breast milk came in and thinking, *I should be nursing my baby, not planning her funeral.* In this time of grief, my father's brother Vic called to offer the other half of their baby brother's grave for Isabella to be buried. My Grandmother—Mema— who had been a spiritual mentor to me, had lost her youngest child, Billy, at the age of two in a drowning accident. My uncle Vic had witnessed it but could not save his brother because he was only three years old himself at the time and could not swim yet either. Other people cannot save us from experiencing pain and suffering, but they can make the road we walk a little easier and the loads we carry a little lighter if we let them.

My Isabella and Mema's Billy would share a grave plot because both were small, having died so young. In time, I realized that God meant the sharing of this burial plot as far more than a way of lightening my hardship. It was an image of the spiritual understanding that Mema had entrusted to me over the years, which had come out of her wrestling with God, combined with the spiritual insights that came out of mine. The Lord showed me that I was experiencing a unique kind of fellowship of mothers who have suffered the loss of their children. Mema and I joined this fellowship outside of time. Through its initiation, I began applying the many lessons she had taught me out of her seeking and finding God in the darkness. In a way, Mema had handed me a life raft before I knew I would need it. Only the Lord knew that she would be with Him when her life lessons would need to be applied to mine. I sensed that somehow and someday, the mixed ashes of our children will become part of the beauty that will adorn the head of Christ's resurrected bride.

STRESS WOOD

Knowing that storms come on us suddenly, it is critical to gather provisions and develop healthy relationships in advance so that when the storms come, we can remain standing. The analogy of anchoring in Christ and cross-tying to other believers can also be found in creation, inviting us all to apply the concepts to our lives. A tree's anchor is its taproot, which is first sent straight down deep into the soil to secure the tree before it can rise. Next, it sends out its branching roots that eventually intertwine, or cross-tie, with the branches of other trees underground. Branching roots can be pervasive. Take, for instance, the branching roots of a single well-developed oak tree, which can even go out for over a hundred miles if laid from end to end. But no matter how impressive a tree's branching roots may be, just like some people's extensive social networks may seem impressive, neither a tree's branching roots nor a person's social networks will be sufficient to save them if the storm blows too strong. It may actually be their downfall; as one goes, so go the others, falling like dominoes if they lack proper taproots. Remember, the taproot is the tree's main anchor. The more trees in an area with deep taproots and healthy branching roots that are intertwined with other deeply rooted trees, the less likely it is that the forest will become decimated in a hurricane.

Rooted and Grounded

God desires His children to live in healthy spiritual communities so they can experience His character and love through the people with whom their lives are intertwined. When the apostle Paul speaks of a healthy community, using the terms "rooted" and "grounded" in Christ, it should evoke the image of the underground root systems in a thriving forest. Paul prayed,

> . . . that He would grant you, according to the riches of His glory, to be strengthened with power through His Spirit in the inner self, so that Christ may dwell in your hearts through faith; and that you, being rooted and grounded in love, may be able to comprehend with all the saints what is the width and length and height and depth, and to know the love of Christ which surpasses knowledge, that you may be filled to all the fullness of God. (Ephesians 3:16–19 NASB)

For trees to become deeply rooted and grounded, wind is essential. Without the wind, trees grow weak, thin, and underdeveloped in their root systems. When exposed to strong winds, trees form something called stress wood, which is necessary for their survival. Stress wood, also called tension wood or reaction wood, enables trees to grow toward the light for optimal sun exposure and to remain standing strong in a storm. Stress wood vastly improves a tree's ability to withstand hurricane-force winds. Even though trees can grow much more quickly when shielded from the wind, they will not develop stress wood and, therefore, will not be able to sustain the weight accompanying their height. This was proven in a scientific experiment called Biosphere 2, where the trees were shielded entirely from wind and, as a result, did not develop the core strength they needed to reach maturity and sustain themselves.[10]

So it is with us. The small trials we face daily test the composition of our faith and reveal whether or not the hope we are holding on to is secure and able to withstand when the winds of life pick up. Standing is meant to be something we do every day in small ways. Daily anchoring into the presence of God amidst the "ordinary" trials of daily life, like annoyances in relationships, aging, or minor illnesses, gives us a chance to grow stronger and become more deeply rooted. Seeking to remove every force that comes against us is like asking God to stop the wind from blowing through the trees.

Even before this experience of such painful, personal loss, I struggled with the Bible verses in Romans 5:3–5 that call us to rejoice in our sufferings. Paul says, "We also glory in our sufferings, because we know that suffering produces perseverance; perseverance, character; and character, hope. And hope does not put us to shame." I could see how suffering can lead to perseverance and even to character development, but hope? It just did not compute. At least, not until my desperation for a new kind of eternal hope forced my own taproot to drop deeper into the things of God and, in time, caused my mind to rise higher toward the things of heaven. Once again, I returned to the parable of the trees. They must send their taproots deep before their trunks can be raised to the heights and remain standing.

Standing is something we practice both in the storms and extended times of waiting. *Stand* means occupying a place, being on one's feet, or "being ready." Standing is not about using our energy or will to move forward, but rather, getting up, staying up, and getting back up so we don't lose ground in life's buffeting or times of waiting. Romans 12:12 describes the proper posture for spiritual standing: "Be joyful in hope, patient in affliction, faithful in prayer." Two closely related words can help us better engage in this faith practice of standing—withstand and understand.

To *withstand* means to have the power and ability to remain standing when things come against us and test our resolve. The ability to withstand is based on what something or someone has already become, what they consist of, and what provisions they have been able to gather before facing the storms, battles, or times of waiting. Essentially, what are we standing *with*? The more reconciled and integrated our souls become, the better we can withstand what tests us.

Understanding means standing in the midst of, beneath, or within, and it is something we gain by receiving, putting together, or grasping. Therefore, the biblical call to gain understanding requires investigating truth and putting our thoughts and experiences together with the truth of God's Word. This faith work we do before coming into a trial curates the provision, protection, and confidence in Christ we need to get through it.

On Guard and Alert

We are called to remain alert and on guard, trusting even when God seems silent, absent, or when our hopes have been deferred. To encourage my faith in the times of waiting, I hung a giant wooden sign in my home with a quote found etched on the wall of a German concentration camp during WWII. It reads, "I believe in the sun even when it is not shining. I believe in love even when I cannot feel it. I believe in God even when He is silent."

Knowing what we have already become in Him according to our understanding of His love and truth can give us the confidence and courage to STAND in trials or times of waiting. Our understanding of the Word and our confident beliefs in Christ are like spiritual armor that covers and protects us.

> Put on the full armor of God, so that when the day of evil comes, you may be able to stand your ground, and after you have done everything, continue to stand. Stand firm then, with the belt of truth buckled around your waist, with the breastplate of righteousness in place, and with your feet fitted with the readiness that comes from the gospel of peace. In addition to all this, take up the shield of faith, with which you can extinguish all the flaming arrows of the evil one. Take the helmet of salvation and the sword of the Spirit, which is the Word of God. And pray in the Spirit on all occasions with all kinds of prayers and requests. With this in mind, be alert, and always keep praying for all the Lord's people. (Ephesians 6:13–18)

These verses teach us that by being clothed in God's righteousness, peace, truth, and the memories of His savings, as well as being equipped with tools of faith and the Word of God, we will be able to STAND our ground when the strong winds buffet and turmoil encompasses us like a hurricane. God's grace in these forms will be sufficient for us to remain standing; it calls on the "spiritual stress wood" that has been developed in our souls. Four pieces of spiritual clothing need to be intentionally "put on": the belt of truth, the breastplate of righteousness, the helmet of salvation, and the shoes of peace. Not only are we called to "put on" certain things, but we are also called to "take up" spiritual tools, which involve deliberate actions of faith. They are the shield of faith, the sword of the Spirit, and words of prayer.

The sword of the Spirit, which is the Word of God, is the only offensive weapon mentioned, and it is the power by which you can push back the darkness. By taking up our armor, anchoring in the living presence of God, and cross-tying with other believers who are likewise anchored and "standing," we can defend ourselves against evil.

> The call to every believer is to be faithful in every possible way we can and to STAND on the Lord's promises.

Indeed, once we are clothed and armed, God tells us three times that we are simply called to STAND, "So that when the day of evil comes, you may be able to stand your ground, and after you have done everything, to stand. Stand firm then" (Ephesians 6:13–14a). He is the One who will do the fighting for us. Our job is to keep watch, remain steadfast, and continue in prayer. "You will not have to fight this battle. Take up your positions; stand firm and see the deliverance the LORD will give you, Judah and Jerusalem. Do not be afraid; do not be discouraged. Go out to face them tomorrow, and the LORD will be with you" (2 Chronicles 20:17). The call to every believer is to be faithful in every possible way we can and to STAND on the promise that it is the Lord who fights our battles and will bring about our rescue.

Going into battle with God makes me think of how a father often dances with his young daughter. Though both may be twirling around the floor, he is doing all the work while she stands on his feet, merely along for the ride. The same principle was at work when the Israelites overcame hardship and won their battles and when God told David to pick up five smooth stones. And with one stone and slingshot, David felled the giant (1 Samuel 17:49–50). God allowed Joshua to bring down the walls of Jericho by simply walking, praising, and blowing a ram's horn (Joshua 6:20). Moses only had to touch the waters of the Red Sea for God to part them (Exodus 14:21). And he needed only to strike the rock as God said so that water would flow from it (Exodus 17:6). The power to overcome was not in the stone, sling, horn, or staff. His power is in the grace He provides to those willing to take tiny, obedient steps of faith: anchoring in the deep, picking up our battle gear, remaining clothed in His righteousness, surrendering to His providence amidst the hurricane, and then doing all we can to STAND while the Lord delivers the victory.

> God is our refuge and strength, an ever-present help in trouble. Therefore we will not fear, though the earth give way and the mountains fall into the heart of the sea, though its waters roar and foam and the mountains quake with their surging. There is a river whose streams make glad the city of God, the holy place where the Most High dwells. God is within her, she will not fall; God will help her at break of day. Nations are in uproar, kingdoms fall; he lifts his voice, the earth melts. The LORD Almighty is with us; the God of Jacob is our fortress. (Psalm 46:1–7)

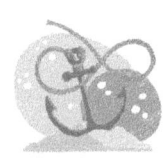

YOUR BECOMING STORY: STAND

Each of us must be equipped for the storms that life brings us. Whether the "slow erode" or the "sudden shattering" of a hurricane—suffering is ubiquitous. Everyone experiences some measure of "the day of evil," and thus Paul's command rings out to each of us: *"And after you have done everything. . . stand"* (Ephesians 6:13).

It behooves us to examine ourselves and ask: *Am I ready for a hurricane? Do I know how to* STAND?

Four keys are necessary for a believer to prepare to STAND in the day of evil.

First, consider your "boat," or soul. It must be cleaned and ready for action. Walking in forgiveness for those who have wronged you, entrusting your hurts to the Lord for healing, and confessing your sins regularly are critical to accessing intimacy with God and experiencing the blessings of His empowering presence. Be relentless in "dialogue with God" in both the high and low notes of everyday life.

Second, assess your anchorage. *What are you anchored to?* This requires unfettered honesty and openness, allowing the Holy Spirit to search your heart. What do you cling to for comfort and security? Success? Relationships? Finances? Reputation? Stuff? Your soul's anchor must be dropped into the depth of God's love and faithful presence. Take the time to cut the soul-ties that will harm you in a storm. Cast off the idols and distractions so that nothing takes the place of God as the Savior of your life.

Third, assess your "cross-ties." Are you living in a healthy, faith-filled community, able to experience the "neighborhood team effect"? God has provided His body as a means for loving and strengthening you, including during the worst storms one can endure. Consider the fellowship that can be found with those who have gone before you in their own journeys of suffering and come out the other side with wisdom to share. If you are not in honest, consistent, and healthy relationships with other believers anchored to God's presence, consider asking the Lord to connect you in new ways to His living body and help you invest in relationships that will bear eternal fruit.

Fourth, embrace the winds of daily life. Build your "stress wood" and prepare for the larger storms. How have you seen God amid your suffering? How has your suffering produced godly character in you or given you more of an eternal perspective? Ask yourself what your faith consists of. What are you made of? Consider the integrated beliefs you have on board your soul that have served as provision and protection during times of trial. What Scriptures can you attach to these experiences; what of God's Word has been proven true in your life?

"I Will Stand"

In the dark
Do You hear me?
In the loss
Do You see me?
In the night
Time moves slowly.
In the wait, will You hold me?

In hopes and fears
In unmet dreams
In troubled days
That You'll redeem

I will stand on Your truth,
My heart stands.
In Your Word, I place my hope.
My soul waits for You, Lord,
My soul waits.
In between the asked and answered,
Even when I'm bruised and battered,
I will stand and wait and trust in
   You, Lord.

In the light
I can see You.
In the warmth,
I can feel You.
In the day,
Hope comes quickly.
In the wait,
You have held me.

I guard my soul.
I keep the walls.
I will not doubt,
When darkness falls

I've done all that I can do.
Now, I'll watch and wait for You.
Like the sunrise in the East,
Rays of love will bring me peace.
In the wait, I've grown stronger.
I will fear the dark no longer.
I will watch for Your coming,
More than those who wait for
   morning.[11]

8

PRAISE

High Notes and Low Notes

My Uncle Tommy Richards was like a living embodiment of PRAISE to me. He grew up playing nearly every musical instrument, often performing alongside his father with two of history's most famous jazz musicians, Jimmy and Tommy Dorsey. Uncle Tommy was a spectacular drummer and played for deployed soldiers during World War II and the Korean War through the USO. But it was not his musical ability that made his life such an example to me; it was his constant way of thankfulness and how he treated others. Uncle Tommy joyfully showed respect to every person simply because they were made in the image of God.

At ninety-three, Tommy was a little unstable on his feet. Still, he insisted on standing when anyone entered or exited the room and shaking the hand of anyone who approached him. When he came to watch our children's swim meets, I encouraged him not to stand up in the viewing area of the indoor pool, fearing he would fall. Yet, Uncle Tommy could not help but maintain his lifelong habit of rising whenever the door next to him opened and someone entered. Respect and thankfulness were deeply ingrained in his soul; they had become inextricable parts of his essence. So, even though his eyesight, strength, and hearing were failing in his later years, to the end of his days, Tommy still saw far more clearly than most.

For most of my life, Uncle Tommy lived far away from us. My parents would often speak about how hard it must have been for him to care for his wife, Sally, who had gone blind and had suffered from dementia for over twenty years. Yet, whenever we saw him, Tommy was filled with gratitude, not self-pity. Sally did not recognize him for most of the last ten years of her life; still, he never neglected to treat her as the bride of his youth. He smiled kindly, thanked profusely, spoke graciously, and interacted gently with her and all others, regardless of age or condition. Thankfulness was the drumbeat that marked his life, and this rhythm proved itself by helping him keep his promise to his wife: "For better or for worse, in sickness and health, until death do us part." A thankful heart before God is a powerful thing. "I am under vows to you, my God; I will present my thank offerings to you" (Psalm 56:12).

As people age, they become more of what they are, and what they have chosen to mark their lives becomes more evident. Many people are like Johnny-one-notes in their old age, playing the same "note" over and over again. Tommy's character was not marked by the sour notes of pride, bitterness, or self-pity but by the sacred rhythms of PRAISE and thanksgiving. His life made me question what my life speaks and what it will be marked by in my old age.

NATURE'S BELLS OF PRAISE

While out for a walk in the spring, many years after surviving our own long season of hardships, I pondered the highs and lows of my life. This led me to ask, "Lord, how do You see me at this point in my journey?"

But before I got any sense of a reply, I saw, out of the corner of my eye, lilies of the valley peering up from behind their broad leaves in a patch along my garden walkway. I stepped closer and saw that many of them were in full bloom. I was amazed by how they had multiplied since their planting here years earlier. Somehow, I had missed seeing them in bloom every springtime before. I wondered why. Was it because they were so small and easily hidden? Maybe it was because I was always too busy to take the time to look. Whatever the reason, I was delighted to greet them now.

But appreciating lilies was not a new experience for me. Lilies of the valley were my favorite flowers growing up. I first noticed them while walking home from middle school along my neighbor's sidewalk. I remember loving their sweet, crisp scent. But I also remember being a little sad, thinking about how easily these beautiful flowers are overlooked. Gathering my first bouquet and delivering it to my mother made me feel like some successful forager or treasure hunter.

Hidden Treasures

Today, as I picked some of the lilies of the valley from my garden, I imagined their tiny, white, bell-shaped blooms as musical notes playing upon a scale, each stem like a little PRAISE song to its Maker. I brought them inside and placed them on my writing desk in a vase. At the time, I was working on a devotional article on PRAISE. Perhaps this is why I perceived them as little songs. Then again, we are clearly told in Scripture that God made all of His creations to PRAISE Him; even the mountains and trees were made to rise in PRAISE to their Maker. "The mountains and hills will burst into song before you, and all the trees of the field will clap their hands" (Isaiah 55:12).

Finding these lilies was not random; it was God's response to my ASK: "Lord, how do You see me at this point in my journey?" What had seemed like a distraction on a prayer walk was the Spirit prompting me to look and see. Doing so required lowering myself, narrowing my focus, and discovering hidden treasures, which, in the end, would give me a higher, broader, and longer perspective of the musical stems threaded through my story.

Isaiah 45:3–4 affirmed this perspective: "I will give you hidden treasures, riches stored in secret places, so that you may know that I am the LORD, the God of Israel, who summons you by name." The hidden nature of these flowers speaks to how PRAISE often involves searching for beauty hidden in the shadows of our own lives. The Lord Himself says He searches the whole world to find authentic worshipers hidden among all humanity. "A time is coming and has now come when the true worshipers will worship the Father in Spirit and in truth, for they are the kind of worshipers the Father seeks" (John 4:23).

Still, I struggled to believe that God could view my life as something as joy-inspiring and sweet-smelling as these flowers. My joyful childhood seemed overshadowed by the years that tears had become my regular companion.

As I considered these new connections between the joy of PRAISE and the sorrow of tears, I started to view the blooms as both white bells rising and tears falling. The beatitudes of Jesus affirmed this connection between tears of sadness and the joy that can be found in His comfort, saying, "Blessed are those who mourn, for they will be comforted" (Matthew 5:4). Knowing that the word "blessed" also meant happy made me wonder if perhaps true happiness and sadness are seen by heaven as intertwined in this earthly life. The Bible verse about the positive influence of suffering, which Scott had read to me during our own loss, surfaced in my mind. "Sorrow is better than laughter, for sadness has a refining influence on us" (Ecclesiastes 7:3 NLT). Back then, I could only hold these words lightly in my hand, but now they were BECOMING soaked into the fibers of my soul. I praised the Lord for the lilies.

In this moment of PRAISE, formerly disassembled things began to assemble. I recalled the words of Reverend Andrews, my parents' pastor, who had come to our hospital bedside just after Isabella's stillbirth and prayed, "This baby girl has been committed to Your keeping, Lord, and baptized in the waters of her parents' tears."

> "Can't you see *My* tears in the falling rain? I am weeping with you."

Then came the memory of the night I went out for a drive alone in a torrential downpour, not long after our daughter's passing, and ended up in an empty field on top of a mountain crying out to God. "Why me? Why did You allow this pain? Do You even see my tears? Do You even care?" Even now, I can recall the echoes of His heavenly voice that spoke back to my heart that night as I watched the rain falling on my windshield: "Can't you see *My* tears in the falling rain? I am weeping with you."

Just as Jesus' compassion was seen in how He wept over the death of His friend Lazarus, I could see the Lord's deep compassion for me in the rain (John 11:35). His presence with me that night pulled my heart out of a pit of despair and my mind back from the cliff-edge of hopelessness. God doesn't ask our PRAISE to be pain-free. For this, I also praised Him.

PRAISE AS BREATH

The deeper I dove into PRAISE, the more enthralled I became by its layered nature. And I was astonished to see how often PRAISE had preceded God's answers to my prayers and how it seemed to open the doors of heaven and cause new strength to pour into me, empowering me to persevere. I saw this most clearly after my first miscarriage of our daughter, Malaya.

Upon our return from the hospital, Scott didn't say anything for a long while. He had no idea how to comfort me, nor could I find words to express what I needed. But in time, Scott came and found me upstairs lying in bed. He chose to lie beside me, reach out, and gently hold my hand. At some point, he began to sing quietly. As he sang, the room seemed to fill with cool air, making it easier to breathe somehow. At first, I missed the connection between Scott's singing and the air that filled my lungs. It was only when he stopped singing that I realized how the overwhelming heartache had swelled again and how all the oxygen seemed to evaporate from the room. My chest felt heavy, and I could hardly breathe.

"Keep singing," I said, out of desperation for breath. Scott began singing "God of Wonders." With his singing came the cool air again, filling the room and my lungs and lifting the heaviness from my chest. The connection and the effect were undeniable. I was experiencing the presence of God's Spirit as the breath of life through the praises of my spouse.

Ironically, the joke in our home was that Scott "couldn't carry a tune in a bucket." Clearly, the Spirit's breath-giving presence has nothing to do with the caliber of our singing voices but, instead, the faith that stirs our hearts. Though I had heard it said that PRAISE to God is our very life-breath, it was not until that day, experiencing it in such a personal, tangible way, that my belief in this truth became sure.

Breathing Praise

PRAISE is as essential to our spiritual life as breath is to our bodies. It enlivens us, revives us, and sustains us daily. Like breathing, PRAISE is something meant to be done continually. "I will bless the LORD at all times; his praise shall continually be in my mouth" (Psalm 34:1–3 ESV).

I used to wonder how it could be possible to PRAISE the Lord continually, at least on a practical level. But as I dove into Scripture, I found connections between the words that mean life, breath, wind, and Spirit in Hebrew. Some Jewish scholars even believe that the sounds that the mouth makes when breathing, with the inhale of *Yah* and the exhale of *Weh*,[1] are ever declaring the Name of God as *Yahweh*, which means the BECOMING One, the One who causes to become.[2] This connection between breath and praise began to satisfy my understanding of how it is possible to PRAISE continually, tears included. Still, I found even more layers as I continued searching.

> Like fresh air, the Spirit's life indwells us, causing us to be and to become more like Christ in character.

Inspire means the breath of the Spirit coming upon us, *respire* means the Spirit's breath moving within us, and *aspire* means the Spirit's breath working through us.[3] Like fresh air, the Spirit's life moves toward us, rests upon us, indwells us, and works through us, causing us to be, and to become more like Christ in character. The root of the English word "spirit," which is *spir* or *spirar*, can also mean the stem of a flower, the spire of a church, or the trunk of a tree.[4] Undoubtedly, the Lord was teaching me about the role of PRAISE in spiritual formation and the call to become like beautiful lilies singing songs from the valleys, trees anchored in the storms, and sacred spires pointing heavenward.

PRAISE IN THE HIGH AND LOW NOTES

When God's promises have been fulfilled, we more naturally PRAISE Him. But it is praising Him by faith while still in difficulty that provides the strength we need to endure and find peace in the waiting. PRAISE ushers us into the very presence of God when we feel far off. "Enter his gates with thanksgiving and his courts with praise; give thanks to him and praise his name" (Psalm 100:4). PRAISE and thanksgiving serve as master keys that provide access into the doors of the Divine.

Human life comprises many kinds of songs, happy and sad, some played in major keys and others in minor. But every song must have high and low notes, for it is in the variation where its uniqueness is found. Though PRAISE comes more naturally in the highs of life, it is between the asks and the answers that PRAISE is most vital; it is indispensable for life on earth.

It is, however, helpful to understand the nuances of PRAISE through the different Hebrew words used in the Bible so we can PRAISE authentically, even in trials.

- *Yadah* is a Hebrew word indicating a confessional form of PRAISE spoken in recognition of our need for God's higher perspective when we cannot see clearly.[5] This is precisely what I had done in asking God to share His view of me and my journey.

- *Baruk* declares the truth of God's worthiness, even in the darkest of nights.[6] This is how Job could authentically PRAISE the Lord in the loss of all of his children and possessions at one time (Job 1:21).

- *Shabach* is the choice to PRAISE God by declaring His goodness to the next generation, like sharing our stones of remembrance. *Shabach* is the form of praise that calms tumultuous waves and holds us back from foolishness.

- *Todah* is the simple "thank you" of PRAISE; it can mean giving a thank-offering, giving PRAISE sacrificially, or even shaking hands in agreement.[7] We can express *todah* to the Lord for any act of His kindness.

- *Taqa* means to PRAISE by clapping, blowing a ram's horn, hammering a tent peg, pledging oneself, or beating a drum. *Taqa* brought the walls of Jericho tumbling down (Joshua 6) and marked the life of my uncle Tommy.

- *Zamar* is a form of PRAISE connected to playing instruments, mainly strings, or using our vocal cords for humming. We find *zamar* in the unconscious humming people do to keep a hopeful cadence, a whistling while we work, or the buzzing of a bee.[8]

- *Gil* or *Karar* can indicate PRAISE through joyful movement, be it dance, spinning, or twirling in gladness. It is the rejoicing that accompanies the closing of a circle in our lives; it is the kind of PRAISE King David engaged in when he danced before the arc of the Lord.[9]

- *Halal* or *Hallelujah* means to shine, celebrate, commend, give light, make clear, or jubilantly PRAISE.[10] This is how we PRAISE in the high notes of life when God's help and rescue have become evident and when our ASKS have been answered.

PRAISE does not require ignoring the truth of our realities, nor does it imply pretending things are good when they are not. Instead, PRAISE beckons a good and almighty God to intervene in the bad, empower us in our lowly condition, and allow us to bring Him glory no matter our earthly circumstances. An essential spiritual competency is learning to PRAISE in both the darkness and in the light, in the depths and on the heights. PRAISE can provide strength and protection for any leg of your spiritual journey.

The Robin's Song

The Lord drove this point home through an image He gave to my friend Bethany Haley while we were together on a BECOMING retreat. After asking the Lord how her soul could survive both the storms of life she was in and the next ones she saw coming, Bethany went out for a walk to engage her sanctified imagination and to practice listening prayer. Straightaway, she saw an unusually large robin standing in the middle of the walking path ahead of her, staring intently at her as she approached it. Bethany realized the Lord was inviting her to consider this creature and its ways.

Returning from her walk, Bethany dove into scientific articles about robins and discovered them to be a living parable teaching the power of continual PRAISE. The robin is a bird that represents many different aspects of PRAISE: it is the first bird to sing in the morning and the last to sing at night. While other songbirds sing after a storm, when the danger has passed and the provision of worms and grubs is most easily attained, the robin is the only bird that sings by faith when it sees a storm coming. It is singing in anticipation of the Lord's promised provision that the rain will bring. Robins even sing while they go out in the rain to harvest the abundance that would come to them in no other way than through the storm. It is no surprise that robins have a reputation as the faithful harbingers of spring.

LILY OF THE VALLEY ANOINTING

On my way to teach all twelve faith practices of BECOMING together for the first time, I had asked the Lord to give me whatever anointing I would need to succeed in this endeavor. In my spirit came the words, "Lily of the valley." But, at the time, this meant little to me. *How can a flower be a spiritual anointing?* I wondered. *I must have misheard.*

When the time came for me to teach, I noticed sitting on the table beside me was a vase filled with at least a hundred stems of lilies of the valley. I couldn't believe it. *Seriously?* I thought in amazement. Our insightful hosts must have put them there. Still, they were a loving confirmation of God's presence and a revelation of how He had gone before and prepared this place for me.

Our retreat concluded with an anointing prayer, during which every woman received a different oil variety. I overheard one woman say she'd gotten a bottle of the lily of the valley oil. Naturally, I joined her group. It seemed right to receive a tangible anointing from this particular flower. When the prayer concluded, one of the ladies in our group, Kristyn Brodersen Smith, came over to speak to me.

"While walking the grounds and praying earlier today," she said, "I sensed the Lord was talking to me about you, but I only got one word—'Married.' This didn't make sense to me since you're already married; that's why I didn't say something earlier." It seems the prayer time had reminded her to share with me, hoping maybe it meant something to me.

But I did not know what it meant either. Still, I made a mental note and thanked her for sharing. Then, I took my utterly exhausted self to bed.

Our host told me that my bedroom was the same room where Corrie ten Boom had stayed in the past. Corrie was a Dutch Christian and Holocaust survivor who had been imprisoned for helping many Jews escape the Nazis during World War II. She was an author I admired for how she practiced her faith, especially in times of great suffering.

"It's All Yours"

Lying in bed, I thanked God for all He had done during our retreat. But I did wonder why I felt so empty. Teaching the tools using my life stories had taken a lot out of me, emotionally and mentally. Still, this empty feeling made me wonder if I had done something wrong despite receiving many encouraging words from retreat participants. My mind drifted to the words of Corrie ten Boom.

> When people come up and give me a compliment [saying]—"Corrie, that was a good talk," or "Corrie, you were so brave," I take each remark as if it were a flower. At the end of each day, I lift up the bouquet of flowers I have gathered throughout the day and say, "Here You are, Lord, it is all Yours."[11]

When we give our thank-offerings to the Lord as a sacrifice of PRAISE, we not only bless Him with a beautiful bouquet of spiritual flowers, but we also free our hands to be replenished with new seeds for future plantings. I had done what I had been called to do. In time, God would show me that my emptiness was natural and essential. Momentary emptiness accompanies release. It comes just after we hand over our "bouquet" of praises to the Lord and before we receive new things from His hand. This reciprocal hand-off teaches us that the Divine Exchange is essential to the faith practice of PRAISE. It also reminds us that "all things have been created through him and for him" (Col. 1:16b). All this helped me understand the connection between the Scripture card placed on my bed by our hosts and the idea of new things that regularly come from God's hand. "You make known to me the path of life; you will fill me with joy in your presence, with eternal pleasures at your right hand" (Ps. 16:11). Even though, at the time, I did not fully grasp all these spiritual implications, my heart calmed, and I fell asleep.

Garments of Praise

After returning home from the retreat, my mom surprised me by transplanting some lilies of the valley from her garden into mine. It was not lost on me that my newly beautified yard had once symbolized the unbecoming aspects of my life based on my vision of it covered in broken glass. In seeing the transformation of my actual yard now, ten years later, and realizing its connection to the redemption of my brokenness, I could confidently BELIEVE the promise found in Isaiah 62:3–4 (ESV) regarding my soul's BECOMING,

> You shall be a crown of beauty in the hand of the LORD, and a royal diadem in the hand of your God. You shall no more be called Forsaken, and your land shall no more be termed Desolate, but you shall be called My Delight Is in Her, and your land Married; for the LORD delights in you, and your land shall be married.

There it was again, the word "married." But in this context, marriage was being used in connection to the condition of the land and a person's soul, not just referring to the marriage between a husband and wife. It took some time for me to understand that God was also speaking about the marriage that happens inside of a person, the progressive integration of their soul and spirit, and the growing intimacy in their relationship with God through asking and receiving, wondering and discovering. This spiritual marriage requires an ongoing and necessary dance between faith and grace in order to produce the deeper intimacy and greater integration our souls long for.

I was also fascinated to discover that both PRAISE and lily flowers are described in Scripture as garments. "Consider how the wildflowers grow.

They do not labor or spin. Yet I tell you, not even Solomon in all his splendor was dressed like one of these" (Luke 12:27). The Message paraphrases this beautiful connection between the expression of PRAISE and the image of a garden's cascading flower blossoms in Isaiah 61:10. "For as the earth bursts with spring wildflowers, and as a garden cascades with blossoms, so the Master, GOD, brings righteousness into full bloom and puts praise on display before the nations."

In all this contemplating, I realized that the verse Scott and I had claimed as a promise at our daughter Isabella's passing, describing the Lord's ministry on earth, had been cycling in grace and coming to pass over time.

> To comfort all who mourn and provide for those who grieve in Zion—to bestow on them a crown of beauty instead of ashes, the oil of joy instead of mourning, and a garment of praise instead of a spirit of despair. They will be called oaks of righteousness, a planting of the LORD for the display of His splendor. (Isaiah 61:2b–3)

I praised the Lord because now I could see that the beauty of worshipers, comforted through PRAISE, become a display of God's splendor, even Divine Correspondences telling of His love to the world. Through this image of my garden's redemptive transformation, I confidently believed the Lord was fulfilling His promises to me.

EMPTY TO OVERFLOWING

I thanked my mom for planting the lilies in my yard.

"You should thank Aunt Bonnie," Mom said, "She's the one who planted them behind our house as a little girl when she lived here with Mema and Pepa."

I phoned Aunt Bonnie, my dad's younger sister, to ask her if she remembered planting them. She did.

"They were a gift from a poor farm girl I befriended on the school bus," she said, indicating she had received them not long after her little brother Billy drowned.

There it was! The deeper truth, the longer story, the higher view. My soul knew it when she said it. These lilies were not just about my story but about a more extensive one involving the storylines of God's redemptive grace throughout the generations of our family. It was about Mema and Pepa's pain and tears, the broken hearts of their children who lost their baby brother, and all the ashes of loss that had been taken to the place of the cross in hopes of healing and redemption. God was inviting me to see my life as part of a much longer song involving others who had come before me. It brought to mind the words of Reverend John Donne that address our interconnectedness as human beings,

> No man is an island, entire of itself; every man is a piece of the continent, a part of the main. . . . Each man's death diminishes me because I am involved in mankind. Therefore, send not to know for whom the bell tolls; it tolls for thee.[12]

Suffering is indeed a communal reality, but so is resurrection. We also see resurrection imaged through the lilies springtime rising up through the valley. "Our earthly bodies are planted in the ground when we die, but they will be raised to live forever" (1 Corinthians 15:42 NLT). Oh, how I wish I could turn up the volume on this message sung by the flowers every spring so that when I find myself lamenting the wintery seasons of mortality, I will never do so without this sense of hope. John 5:28–29 says we should "not be amazed at this, for a time is coming when all who are in their graves will hear his voice and come out—those who have done what is good will rise to live."

Into the Soil of Our Souls

The garden from which the lilies were taken had been in my family for five generations. My great-great-grandfather, R. L. Marks, a Jewish immigrant and clothing merchant from Lithuania, had purchased the plot in 1905. Now, transplanted from my ancestral land into my yard, these flowers served as a parabolic image of how the teachings of my ancestors had become integrated into the soil of my soul. When the stories of God's faithfulness told to us by our ancestors take root in us and begin to flourish, it is truly beautiful to God. "One generation commends your works to another; they tell of your mighty acts" (Psalm 145:4).

After Mema's death, her children chose to have the Grove Church steeple permanently lit so that it would shine through the darkness every night in honor of her life of faith. Just as flowers bloom in PRAISE to their Maker and the Word invites us to imitate them, this illuminated *spire* was meant to *inspire* our family and community to look heavenward in times of darkness. "We will not hide them from their descendants; we will tell the next generation the praiseworthy deeds of the LORD, his power, and the wonders he has done" (Psalm 78:4).

I started wondering if this was God's way with all believing families, where there is a redemption that comes down the family line over time. So, I searched the Scriptures to see what I could find in the biblical lineages. I was amazed to discover this was one of God's repeating patterns. The names of nearly every builder selected to reconstruct Jerusalem's walls and gates in the days of Nehemiah revealed a generational redemption. Because it was the tradition in the culture of that day to name their children after their season of life, we find generational redemption stories through biblical lineages continually unfolding in Scripture. But of all the generational praise songs of ascent, Samuel's is perhaps the most compelling. Hidden in the meaning of each name in Samuel's family line, we find step-by-step instructions that mirror *The Way of Becoming*.

Song of Ascent

Samuel was the last of the great Israelite judges in a line that began with Moses. He was also the prophet God had chosen to ANOINT Israel's first and second kings—Saul and David. But Samuel's story did not begin with him. His family's generational PRAISE song of ascent recorded in the Bible started with Samuel's great-great-grandfather, Zuph, whose name means "honeycomb."[13] Despite the meaning of his name and the idea of hard work that constructing a honeycomb invokes, Zuph's honeycomb was void and empty. He had no honey in his life. We know this based on the name he gave his son, Tohu, which means "void, empty, unformed, or desolate."[14] Just as many of our families' stories start in hard and impoverished places, Samuel's family story also began in a valley of desolation.

It seems that Zuph worked like a busy bee, trying to better his life, but found his efforts come to nothing. The sweetness he desired did not come forth from his toil. How many of us can relate to this? We see this common condition addressed by the prophet Haggai.

> "You have planted much, but harvested little. You eat, but never have enough. You drink, but never have your fill. You put on clothes, but are not warm. You earn wages, only to put them in a purse with holes in it." This is what the LORD Almighty says: "Give careful thought to your ways." (Haggai 1:6–7)

We do not want to find ourselves like Zuph, exhausted from work while lacking the sweet honey that only comes from grace-empowered efforts. Therefore, we must be sure to engage in the practices of PRAISE and worship to experience God's love and wisdom, as imaged by honey. It seems that Tohu, Zuph's son, made God his focus and began to worship Him and Him alone. We understand this based on the name he gave his son, Elihu, which means, "God will be my God."[15] In Elihu's name, I hear the proclamation of *shabach* PRAISE and the authentic worship of: "Lord, I believe; help my unbelief." From Elihu came a son named Jeroham, meaning "one who has experienced God's mercy and lovingkindness."[16] This name indicates the point at which God's faithfulness was recognized and praised, having been remembered, no doubt, in its B-Roll form.

Elkanah was next in the family line, and his name means "God has purchased, God has redeemed."[17] The practices of the Divine Exchange are apparent in his name and indicate a generational turning point where sin and brokenness were redeemed for God's blessings. It says Elkanah married Hannah, which means Grace,[18] and that he also married Peninah, which means Pearl.[19] His marriage to Pearl speaks of our call to remain faithful to what we have already become in Christ through the transforming of our fragment parts into precious pearls. His marriage to Hannah speaks of our call to remain committed to seeking the Lord's grace in every *neediness of the now.*

Elkanah and Hannah had a son named Samuel, which means "God has answered my ASK."[20] This was the point of closure in a multigenerational cycle that began in emptiness and progressed to fulfillment by grace through faith. Samuel's birth marked the high note of a long PRAISE song of ascent that started as a lament in the valley of despair but rose over five generations to the mountaintop of *Hallelujah.*

The Scriptures say that Samuel lived in the land of double abundance all of his life. This land, named *Ramathaim-Zophim*, means ripe pomegranates and honey-filled honeycomb, or *Ramah* for short, meaning exalted.[21] At last, the honeycomb constructed in the days of Samuel's great-great-grandfather, Zuph, had come to its longed-for ends, a home filled with the sweetness of love and wisdom. It is fascinating how God's ordained pathway out of desolation and into abundance was hidden before our very eyes in these scriptural names.

Generational Patterns

Samuel's life is a wonder-filled image representing the rewards of generational PRAISE and the patterns of faithful living. Not only do the names of Samuel's ancestors affirm *the how of faith* and the practices involved in ascending, but his annual circuit is broken into parts that directly parallel *The Way of Becoming.*

It says that Samuel continued to ABIDE in this land of double-abundance and to make a circuit each year from Ramah to Bethel (meaning *House of God*)[22] to Gilgal (*the Wheelwork*)[23] to Mizpah (*The High Place of Watchfulness*)[24] and then back to Ramah (*Exalted*) to complete each circuit.

Samuel's annual circuit is similar to how we are meant to cycle in grace, moving from our current need to remembering God's faithfulness, which emboldens us to ASK and IMAGINE and, in time, transforms our hope into a new and confident belief.

On Samuel's trek, his first stop at Bethel, meaning the *House of God*, is representative of the Divine Dialogue, which indicates our engagements with our heavenly Father through speaking and listening prayer. Gilgal, the *Wheelwork*, represents the Divine Exchange, where we trade in our sin, brokenness, weaknesses, and sorrow for the riches only Christ can provide. Mizpah, the *Watch Tower*, represents the places of hope to which we ascend as we walk by faith, transform by grace, and become Divine Correspondences of His love for the world. Samuel's place of abiding at Ramah, meaning *Exalted*, represents the place of our soul's retreating into God for rest, restoration, and rejoicing. It is where we can feast on the abundance of His goodness before we "go out" again to minister and begin a new Cycle of Grace to travel further along *The Way of Becoming*.

May the wisdom that these ancient circuits offer lead us to experience the victory God promises for those who will make PRAISE their strength.

In time, new treasures of double abundance would be born into our home, and with them, the praises of *Hallelujah*. We named our daughters Leah Joy, signifying how God had led us *by His Shepherd's staff to a place of joy*, and Annika Faith, declaring that life is lived *by grace through faith*.

PRAISE RISING

Of the first eight practices that comprise worship, including BELIEVE, REMEMBER, ASK, IMAGINE, TRUST, REDEEM, STAND, and PRAISE, PRAISE stands out among them because it requires intentional, external acknowledgment of the Spirit's work. Psalm 150:6 affirms this mandate to PRAISE, saying, "Let everything that has breath praise the LORD."

The faith practices of worship and PRAISE are meant to be practiced together, alternating between the two in an ongoing rhythm. We find this alternating relationship between PRAISE and worship imaged in the instructions God gave to Moses on how to design the garments of Israel's temple priests (Exodus 28:33–35). Golden bells and pomegranates were to be sewn around the hems of their robes in an alternating fashion. Pomegranates represent the abundant fruit that comes from abiding in practices of worship, and golden bells represent praises given for the glory of God.

In spiritual formation, worship is the faith work that catalyzes forward movement, but PRAISE is what brings the upward movement and helps our spirits rise. Every journey from the valley to the mountaintop requires both a "going around" and a "going up." Also, the closer to the top, the steeper the terrain; therefore, the more revolutions needed to complete the ascent. But without the bells of PRAISE, there can be no upward movement. It would all be merely circling without rising. The more praises and thanksgiving we express to God, the more we rise as we go.

We can also see this alternating way of PRAISE and worship imaged in the building of a house. Through hard work, the building stones are hewn and made ready for placement, just as our stones of belief require the work of faith to become prepared for fitting and display in our spiritual dwellings. PRAISE serves as the mortar placed between each stone that holds the house together and allows it to rise.

Sometimes, we are called to stay low and be hidden like the lilies behind their tall, broad leaves. But sometimes, the hand of God raises us up, like a freshly picked flower, and sets us in a place where our lives can declare the praises of His Name more publicly. When the Spirit calls us to rise or go out, we need not be afraid because the power of His promises goes with us. "Do not fear, for I am with you; do not be afraid, for I am your God. I will strengthen you; I will surely help you; I will uphold you with my righteous right hand" (Isa. 41:10). God's goal in raising us is not just to remove us from the valley or transform us for our own sake, but to empower us to represent God's love and light in the world so that others will praise His name. "Let your light shine before others, that they may see your good deeds and glorify your Father in heaven" (Matthew 5:16).

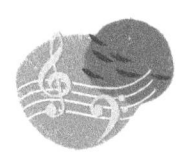

YOUR BECOMING STORY: PRAISE

Ask the Lord to show you how He sees you, knowing His answer will lead you to PRAISE.

When have you turned to the Lord in the low notes of your life rather than choosing to turn away from Him in your pain? If you find yourself in a valley of loss or pain now—ASK the Lord to breathe the breath of PRAISE into your lungs, even in the midst of it.

What is the drumbeat of your life? The Bible teaches that "The mouth speaks what the heart is full of" (Matthew 12:34). Is your life marked by the drumbeat of thanksgiving or the Johnny-one-note of complaint? One brings joy and strength to the soul, but the other steals these blessings away. What can you identify right now that you are thankful to God for providing?

Review the various biblical words listed in the chapter to help you differentiate the ways of PRAISE and engage authentically in it, no matter your life's condition. Which form of PRAISE could find a more significant place in your life?

"Praise in the Low Notes"

Lord, how can we begin to praise
When tears fill up so many days?
Must we rejoice, must we be brave,
So you will deem our words as praise?

With wholeness broke and beauty marred,
Thanksgiving feels so very hard
We want to praise but not pretend
So you will hear and rescue send.

We need not lie to You who knows,
That every song has highs and lows
Even the Psalms begin with angst
But rise like spires and end in thanks.[25]

PART 3

DIVINE CORRESPONDENCE

9

ANOINT

Gifts and Healing

While attending a community event in our town park, I ran into Laura Corbeil, a woman I had only recently met at a Bible study. Laura's love for God, life, and people seemed to flow from her like falling water. But today, she was not her usual effusive self. Laura was sad.

"What's wrong?" I asked.

Laura shared that she'd just heard from her obstetrician that she would likely lose the baby she was carrying. If not, he would be born with significant abnormalities.

It was springtime 2010, and at the time, Laura and I were both pregnant. This was my third pregnancy after having suffered the stillbirth of our daughter Isabella. Sadly, my subsequent two pregnancies had also ended in miscarriage. Hearing Laura's report gutted me. The three consecutive losses I had recently experienced had bent me toward fear and skepticism and made it difficult to muster hope for her situation. I tried to say the right things; I told her how sorry I was and promised to pray for her and her baby. We hugged, then parted ways.

THE WAY OF BECOMING

A PROMPTING

As I lay in bed that night, the fragility of new life weighed heavily on my mind. I worried about Laura and her baby and the baby in my womb. At last, desperate for sleep, I released all my concerns to the Lord in prayer. But I awoke in the middle of the night with Laura and her baby still on my heart. The Spirit seemed to be asking me why I had not prayed for her when we were together. I even pictured myself laying hands on Laura to anoint her with oil for her baby's healing. This idea was strange because I had never anointed anyone before. But in a way, the strangeness of the idea also reassured me that the inner voice suggesting that I anoint Laura came from the Lord and not my own mind. No matter how awkward it might be to do this, especially to someone I hardly knew, I felt prompted to go to her home and pray for her in person. Ignoring my own second-guessing, I decided to go through with it the following day.

In the morning, I searched for supplies around my house. I found a large bottle of plain olive oil in my pantry and a small Tupperware container. At first, I questioned whether regular olive oil in Tupperware would be sacred enough. But since it seemed to match my level of expertise with the practice, it fit somehow. I did not know any special prayers for making the oil holy, so I prayed a simple prayer and hoped God would honor it.

> Faith is the action of hope.

There were two immediate obstacles to overcome: I did not know Laura's phone number, nor did I have access to a car that day. But I was determined to obey the inner voice that had set me upon this strange mission. I realized that I *did* know where Laura's house was, and . . . I had a bicycle. So, off I went with my Tupperware container of oil, my own pregnant belly, and my daughter Maya strapped in the toddler seat on the back of my bike.

I rang the doorbell, and despite the unexpected intrusion, Laura greeted us enthusiastically with a gracious smile. I explained why we'd come and how I felt called to anoint her and pray for her baby. She immediately responded with gratitude and welcomed us into her home. Though I was out of my comfort zone, Laura made it seem like everything was just as it should be. *Thank the Lord for Laura,* I thought.

In my fumbly-bumbly way, I rubbed a bit of my pantry olive oil on Laura's forehead and said a simple prayer. Then, the thought occurred to me to anoint her belly. I debated the appropriateness briefly. But since I was knee-deep in such a foreign undertaking already, I asked her if it would be okay. Laura was delighted. So, I did. We ended our relatively brief time by praying together. Then Laura hugged me, and we said our goodbyes.

We did not see one another again during the remaining months of our pregnancies. I was relieved when we both gave birth to healthy babies. She had a baby boy named Charles Thomas, and I had a baby girl named Leah Joy.

Over the Bridge Called Hope

At a birthday luncheon for a mutual friend, Laura and I finally saw each other again and met each other's babies. When we sat down, I told her I could not imagine how anxious she must have been through the remaining months of her pregnancy, worrying about whether her child would survive.

In a state of genuine surprise, Laura responded emphatically, "No! I wasn't anxious at all! I knew God had healed my baby when you prayed for us!"

I was speechless.

Before I could say anything more, Laura asked, "Didn't you know my baby was healed when you prayed for us, Kerry?"

"No, I had no idea," I answered.

For the next few weeks, I repeatedly tossed the situation in my mind until finally, I asked the Lord about it. *How could Laura have known? How could she have believed so confidently? And how had that confidence overpowered her fear?* I was astonished by all of it.

This experience made the Scripture in Mark 9:23 come to life, "Everything is possible for one who believes." Laura believed anything was possible for her. Through my dialogue with the Spirit and reading Scripture, I was comforted that my own struggle with unbelief was not the hindrance to my prayer for Laura that I had feared it would be. Instead, God showed me His pleasure with my willingness to step out in faith despite my struggles. James 5:15 says, "The prayer offered in faith will make the sick person well."

I began to understand that *faith is the action of hope*. I had acted in hope. I *hoped* I was hearing the Lord. I *hoped* the olive oil in the Tupperware container was sufficient. My actions of biking, anointing, and asking the Lord to heal Laura's baby came out of my *hope* that God would be present and respond somehow. Laura and I had walked over that bridge called hope together by faith, going from the land of need to the land of belief. God had used my fumbly-bumbly efforts to show me that this is what faith, exercised in genuine Christian community, can look like, where imperfect and uncertain efforts bring one another before the throne of grace. God honored His promise in Matthew 18:19, which says, "If two will agree with what anyone asks in the name of Jesus, it will be done for them." I acted in hope. Laura believed. We agreed. And God healed her son.

THE ANOINTED ONE

After this miraculous experience, I dove deep into the study of this practice to understand what the Bible had to say, particularly the role of anointing in the life of Jesus and His disciples. To anoint literally means to massage with oil, and *Messiah* means *the Anointed One*. Jesus, the Messiah, was fully anointed with every spiritual gift. Still, He was anointed with oil in a physical sense by people during His life on earth. His spiritual anointings as eternal King, Priest, and Prophet were symbolized through the three gifts given by the Magi after His birth. The gold represented His eternal kingship, and the oil resins of frankincense and myrrh spoke of His eternal standing as priest and prophet. Surely, Jesus' parents, Mary and Joseph, would not have let these precious gifts be wasted, mistaking them as only symbolic. They would have wisely used these oils to anoint their child.

Jesus was also anointed in adulthood in preparation for new phases of His earthly ministry, such as before His crucifixion and again before His resurrection. Mary of Bethany rubbed Jesus' feet with her hair, using expensive oil before His death (Matthew 26). Even though others called her actions wrong and wasteful, Jesus said that Mary's extravagant act of devotion to Him would be remembered forever (Matthew 26:13).

Anointing was an essential part of Jesus' way of discipleship. When Jesus sent the disciples out in pairs, giving them authority to minister, He gave clear instructions on what to take with them and what to leave behind, and one of those must-have items was anointing oil.

> The anointing oil embodies the power Jesus' disciples take with them after spending time with Him.

> "Take nothing for the journey except a staff—no bread, no bag, no money in your belts. Wear sandals but not an extra shirt. Whenever you enter a house, stay there until you leave that town. And if any place will not welcome you or listen to you, leave that place and shake the dust off your feet as a testimony against them." They went out and preached that people should repent. They drove out many demons and anointed many sick people with oil and healed them. (Mark 6:8–13)

Reading this made me reexamine what I considered essential for a mission trip. Choosing to take oil over money, a travel bag, or extra shoes seemed impractical to me. But to Jesus, it was practical, medicinal, and spiritual. The anointing oil embodies the power Jesus' disciples take with them after spending time with Him.

Like Jesus and His followers in those days, we are also meant to receive spiritual anointings from the Lord and allow them to soak into us and fill us up like lamps being filled with oil. This way, when we go out to minister, we shine with His light and have oil to share for the illumination of others.

STRUGGLES OF UNBELIEF

As a Christian, I believed the many accounts of physical healing recounted in the Bible (e.g., Mark 6:13; John 11:1–44; Luke 8:43–48). Still, I struggled to embrace this practice wholeheartedly because some of my prayers for healing had not yet been answered, at least not the way I had hoped.

My older brother, Bobby, has been a Type 1 diabetic since childhood, and my younger brother, Tommy, has Stargardt's disease, a juvenile form of macular degeneration. Because the Lord has not healed either of them in the way I have asked, I have struggled with measures of unbelief. When Bobby's islet cell transplant failed, it hit us hard. When Tommy's eyes got worse instead of better, taking away his ability to golf and drive and causing him to be declared legally blind before his own wedding, I wondered if God had even heard our prayers.

I know it is natural to wonder if the suffering we experience is because of our sin. Even the disciples wondered this and asked, "Rabbi, who sinned, this man or his parents, that he was born blind?" I am comforted by Jesus' answer when He said, "Neither this man nor his parents sinned, but this happened so that the works of God might be displayed in him" (John 9:2–12).

I used to think that if God healed someone, it would happen instantly and completely because that is what typically happened in Scripture when Jesus prayed. But I learned that when Jesus' disciples prayed for healing, a different Greek word for healing was often used: *therapeuo*, which means healing over time, indicating a progressive recovery. This is where we get our English word therapy. Understanding these nuances in biblical healing has helped me remain engaged in anointing prayer even after disappointments.

Seeing God Working

Without a doubt, I have seen God working in and through both of my brothers' lives. I began noticing small miracles, bits of healing, and ways they had already defied many odds associated with their diseases. I was reminded of all the significant medical advancements that have taken place in their lifetime, which have, at times, even proven lifesaving. I sometimes think that the anointing Bobby needed most was the one God gave him at birth. His love of extreme sports, especially skiing and mountain biking, had helped sustain his health and was even credited with reversing his retinopathy. As for Tommy, the Lord restored the game of golf to him through the Blind Golf Association, where he became the US National Blind Golf Champion.

When I think of my brothers' ongoing struggles with their diseases and why God has not fully healed them, I can see a correlation with God's explanation to Paul, the apostle, as to why He had chosen to withhold full healing from his beloved apostle. "My grace is sufficient for you, for my power is made perfect in weakness." I appreciate Paul's response, too: "Therefore, I will boast all the more gladly about my weaknesses, so that Christ's power may rest on me" (2 Corinthians 12:9). I have witnessed Christ's power rest on both of my brothers' lives.

Sometimes, the Lord removes us from the trials, and sometimes He walks with us through them. Either way, we still need to ASK for sufficient grace and remember that whatever troubles we face, Scripture promises, "The LORD himself goes before you and will be with you; he will never leave you nor forsake you. Do not be afraid; do not be discouraged" (Deuteronomy 31:8). Even if the healing we seek does not happen immediately or entirely in this life, anointing prayer is a practice worthy of further exploration and implementation, able to affect things in the spirit realm that we might not fully know until we are with the Lord.

ANOINTED TO ANOINT

The verse, "Taste and see that the Lord is good," makes me think, "Try it; you might like it." Our willingness to try a particular faith practice has a lot to do with our exposure to it. Engaging in an unfamiliar worship tradition can take some humility because of our lack of proficiency in it. It might, however, be the very thing our souls need most in our journeys toward wholeness. God may bring a specific practice before us at a particular time for this very reason. Pressing past the awkwardness of anointing someone for the first time and learning more about it as a faith practice brought me to a transition point in my own spiritual journey.

My curiosity for anointing would be reignited by encountering a missionary man from Nicaragua whom I met on a ferry boat ride. Michael Buzbee and I had both come to attend the sixtieth birthday celebration of our mutual friend, Bill Haas. After exchanging pleasantries, Mr. Buzbee asked if he could pray for me before we disembarked from the ferry boat. It seemed off-topic from our initial conversation, but his prayer proved ideally suited and sequential to the spiritual narrative playing out in my life.

That evening at dinner, I saw Michael again, and he motioned for me to come over. When I did, he handed me a small bottle of anointing oil and said, "This oil was Ms. Ruby's. She was a spiritual mother to me, and she just went to be with Jesus. Now it's yours to use."

Seriously? How is this happening!? I wondered. Michael hardly knew me and couldn't possibly know the path I was on with anointing. No one but Laura really did. He shared about "Ms. Ruby" and how she had lived and ministered among the poor next to the largest city dump in Managua, Nicaragua. As he spoke about Ms. Ruby's legacy, I worried I would prove disappointing to this man if he knew how limited my experience was in the practice of anointing. Still, I received his encouraging words and Ms. Ruby's oil bottle with gratitude and brought them home with me. The oil would remain in a kitchen drawer until my child's neediness called for its use.

"Mommy, remember how today's lesson said that people will say the things in their hearts out loud?" asked seven-year-old Maya. "Well, I have potty words in mine." Her eyes now welling up with tears. "I heard kids saying them, but I don't want to say them in front of my little sisters."

"Oh, Honey, don't worry. We can pray and ask the Lord to clean your heart and mind," I explained. She seemed relieved to know there was a solution to her inner turmoil. But before we prayed, I remembered the little glass vial of anointing oil sitting in my kitchen drawer.

"Maya, would you like to invite your daddy down, and we can ANOINT your head with oil and pray over you?"

"Sure," she said, though I am not sure she fully understood.

Scott joined us, and it proved to be a special time for us all. Together, we anointed our daughter and prayed that the Lord would cleanse the thoughts of her heart and mind.

"I feel clean inside," Maya declared, smiling and hugging us both.

We praised the Lord for doing what we had asked. But soon, we would learn that He had done even more than we had asked or imagined.

Early the following day, Maya came to find me so she could share the dream she had during the night.

"It felt so real," she said. As she began to speak, the Spirit prompted me to pay attention and reminded me how Maya had been anointed for the cleansing of her mind and heart just the night before. I wrote down her words, and I'm glad I did. Her dream would prove prophetic in our family's story.

The connection between anointing and her dream was too clear to deny. Having the events of her dream unfold over the next few years proved to be a comfort and an affirmation, knowing that God already knew what would take place. I had witnessed a fulfillment of the Lord's promise found in Revelation 3:18 (ESV), which says, "I counsel you to buy from me . . . salve to anoint your eyes, so that you may see." I was also reminded of the vital role that cleansing through anointing can play in becoming a ready vessel for the Lord's noble use. "Those who cleanse themselves . . . will be instruments for special purposes, made holy, useful to the Master and prepared to do any good work" (2 Timothy 2:21).

I was getting to know God more intimately as the One who pours His power upon His people. "In the last days, God says, I will pour out my Spirit on all people. Your sons and daughters will prophesy, your young men will see visions, your old men will dream dreams" (Acts 2:17; Joel 2:28). I was in awe of the multifaceted nature of God's wisdom and power that comes through anointing. I saw how it heals, cleanses, empowers, fills, and imparts good gifts. After that, I kept the oil bottle handy and used it often on our children's booboos and troubled hearts.

REVELATION OF HIS LOVE

Even though I had been anointing my children more regularly with oil, it was not until I attended a sacred art retreat retreat with my parents at the Community of Jesus, a Benedictine monastic community, that I would be anointed with oil for the first time myself. My problem with ice pick headaches had begun to flare up again. They had started five or six years earlier, around the time of our daughter Isabella's stillbirth. At the retreat, my mother noticed how uncomfortable I seemed, so she asked if I was willing to have the clergy pray and anoint me for healing. That is when it dawned on me that I had *never* been anointed despite knowing the biblical call to do so. James 5:14–15 says,

> Is anyone among you sick? Let them call the elders of the church to pray over them and anoint them with oil in the name of the Lord. And the prayer offered in faith will make the sick person well; the Lord will raise them up. If they have sinned, they will be forgiven.

Even though these headaches were most inconvenient, they would prove a part of God's timing and the spiritual catalyst my soul needed for its most remarkable transformation.

The following day was All Saint's Day, and members of the church community gathered to commemorate those who had recently passed away and to remember them before the Lord by name. I heard my Mema's name, Beverley Marks, read aloud, as she had been a part of their community. Hearing her name made me feel close to her and part of a greater fellowship outside of time.

> Anointing with oil connects us to the generations of Christ followers who have gone before us.

Following the service, the clergy invited me into a small stone room at the front of the church. Here, they would pray and ANOINT me. I knelt on the kneeling bench in the center of the room as one of the clergy removed a glass bottle of oil from a cut-out in the stone wall. The cathedral had been modeled after a fourth-century basilica, which reinforced the way that anointing with oil connects us to the generations of Christ followers who have gone before us. Time seemed to slow down as I knelt to partake in the beauty and holiness of this ancient practice. My mom was invited to join those who gathered around me, and together, they laid hands on my shoulders, head, and back. One church leader anointed my head with oil while another spoke prayers over me.

I don't remember much of what was said, but I'll never forget the physical feeling that came over my body during that prayer time. It felt like liquid joy was pouring into me and filling me up from my toes to the top of my head. It was a foreign sensation but warm and welcomed.

What in the world is happening to me? I assumed I was the only one who could feel what was going on inside of me. So, when one of the priests said, "I can feel joy emanating from her," I nearly fell off the kneeling bench.

How could he feel what was happening inside of me? God must be really real and really here! I thought in amazement.

Spiritual touch is as real and powerful as spiritual sight and spiritual hearing. And God's powerful presence does not differentiate between the faith of women in a living room and the prayers of clergy in a cathedral. First Peter 2:9 speaks of how all who have placed their trust in Christ and walk in His ways are considered part of His holy priesthood.

> You are a chosen people, a royal priesthood, a holy nation, God's special possession, that you may declare the praises of him who called you out of darkness into his wonderful light.

As I left the stone room, I was encouraged by one of the clergy to stay alert because the Lord would reveal more.

Utterly Broken and Wholly Filled

Later that morning, I ran into my dad at the monastery bookstore. "Hey, Ker-bear," he said. "I bought two tickets for the three o'clock organ concert."

"That's great. I hope you and Mom enjoy it," I responded.

"No, honey, I want you to take my ticket because I'm too tired to go. I need a nap before the next teaching session. Go with your mother for me."

It was not so much an invitation for me but a rescue mission for him. And though I wasn't a big fan of organ music, I agreed to go to the concert for my dad.

Our seats were front and center in the beautiful Church of the Transfiguration. Here, we could see the fine details of the magnificent mosaics that ran the length of the floor's center aisle to the mosaic apse, which was composed of over two million pieces of tessellated glass depicting the risen Christ. After the organist played a few classical pieces, I noticed in the program that the next song's title was "Wasserflussen of Babylon," which means "Waters of Babylon." I mused, then decided *it's good that Gregorian Prayer Chant is sung in Latin and not German since German has words like Wasserflussen*. I mention what I was thinking to show how "earthbound" my thoughts were at the time because what happened next would be my soul's transcendent opposite.

I closed my eyes to blink, and at that very moment, I was given a most magnificent vision from the Holy Spirit. I kept my eyes shut tightly to take it in fully. In the foreground of the vision, I saw a river. On the other side of that river was a vast hillside covered by what appeared to be freshly cut golden grass. Standing upon that golden hillside was a beautiful little girl who looked about five or six years old. I knew instantly this was a vision of my daughter, Isabella, who had died at birth. Here, before my spiritual eyes, she wore a long white dress, and her hair fell to her shoulders in loosely wound curls. She was looking at me just as I was looking at her.

My heart was utterly broken and wholly filled at the same time. I kept my eyes closed so I would not lose sight of her. At first, my heart was begging Jesus, whose presence I could feel, to let my daughter stay and not take her away from me again.

Now drenched with tears, the wetness of my shirt made me aware I was still earthbound. I sensed my daughter was waiting patiently for my sake, but she was also complete and content. At first, I didn't want to release her. But only a few seconds later, I found myself so filled with love that I no longer needed her to remain with me. Love had made me complete.

I opened my eyes to release her. Then, I quickly closed them again to see if I could still see the vision. But now, behind my eyelids, there was only darkness. Only the tears that had soaked my shirt remained. The organ continued playing just as before, but *I was changed*. Something in me had become complete in that holy moment, as an all-encompassing love had filled me.

It would take some time for me to unpack this experience. At first, I told no one. It seemed speaking human words would somehow diminish its perfection. Over time, however, I came to see this vision as a partial fulfillment of the promise we claimed at our daughter's passing, taken from Isaiah 61:3, which says God will give "beauty instead of ashes." The depiction of the freshly cut golden field on which our daughter stood would also prove a proclamation of a coming harvest in ministry. And even now, the memory and details of this vision are still more real to me than anything I have ever experienced in the physical realm.

A TIME SUCH AS THIS

Anointing people made sense to me, but anointing *things* seemed decidedly strange, even though it was practiced throughout the Bible. In Exodus 40:9, God tells Moses to "take the anointing oil and anoint the tabernacle and everything in it; consecrate it and all its furnishings, and it will be holy." Also, Genesis 28:18 says, "Jacob took the stone that he had put under his head and set it up as a pillar and poured oil on top of it."

These were the kind of Scriptures I would normally pass over as inconsequential to my life, at least until the day I sensed God inviting me to ANOINT the spec home that had gone up next door. It felt strange to think of praying over an empty house. But I decided, *Why not? It couldn't hurt.* After crossing over my front lawn, I placed my hands on the western side of the building and asked God to bring a family of His choosing to live here. I prayed they would be a blessing to us and that we would be a blessing to them.

A few months later, while working in the garden bed in front of my home, I met Amir and Hila Kershenovich. They said they were considering buying the house next door. In our first conversation, I learned that Hila was from Israel and Amir was from Mexico. The two met in Israel while he was working there as a pediatric neurosurgeon. Hila mentioned her concerns about living in a small town because so much of the social life depended on gatherings with friends, and she didn't yet have any here.

"I can be your friend," I told her. Then, I shared how my family had been in this town for many generations and that it would be my pleasure to introduce her to my family members and friends. Hila and Amir purchased the home and later shared how our conversation had been instrumental in their decision. We became friends, and our friends became their friends, and their friends became ours. Over the next several years, our relationship proved the mutual blessing I had prayed it would be, but in ways far more significant than I could have imagined at the time.

Using Faith Tools

Even though my headaches had subsided after the anointing prayer at the monastery, I still had scans done at our hospital. The MRI showed that I had two tumors on the meninges of my brain. They were incidental findings seemingly unrelated to my headaches. Still, I would need the expertise of my neurosurgeon neighbor, Amir, who just happened to have extensive experience with meningiomas. I shared with him the words I had prayed over their house before they owned it and joked that this was not what I meant when I asked the Lord to make our neighbors a blessing to us. Amir and I laughed at the irony together.

But I was greatly comforted that God had provided my friend as my doctor to navigate these scary parts of my journey. Amir advised me to wait before jumping into surgery based on all the factors involved, most notably that I was now nursing our new baby, Annika Faith. He scheduled a second MRI for six months later.

> God honors faith efforts and hears our prayers.

In the months of waiting between scans, Scott and I used our faith tools, including the newest practice of anointing with oil. I also read a scientific article about a type of frankincense called AKBA that was found to shrink meningiomas.[1] So, we got some of this, mixed it with olive oil, and then Scott used it to anoint me each night before bed. I knew God honors faith efforts and hears our prayers. I also hoped that whatever He had placed of His grace in the properties of the frankincense would make a difference. If not, I still felt deeply loved in being anointed by my husband, who sought my healing with me.

Six months later, at the reading of my next set of scans, which happened just before Amir's family moved to Israel, I learned that neither tumor had grown, and one had even shrunk. "How did this happen?" I asked. "Is it normal for them to shrink on their own?

Amir said, "No. Either they were mismeasured the first time, or the praying you are doing is working."

"Do you think that they were mismeasured?" I asked him.

Amir answered confidently and with a knowing smile, saying, "I took the measurements myself both times, so, no, they were not mismeasured."

Was God healing me through anointing prayer? Perhaps. But even so, God had already done far more for my soul than shrink the tumors and, as my subsequent MRIs would reveal, stop any new growth. God had handpicked our neighbors for this critical season of our lives and revealed them as timely conduits of tremendous assurance and blessing. The regular practice of anointing also brought Scott and me to a new level of tenderness and intimacy in our marriage, experiencing deep inner healing and relational growth. The powerful and multidimensional nature of anointing was becoming increasingly evident to us all.

THE HOLY SPIRIT'S MINISTRY

Anointing is the essence of the Holy Spirit's ministry on the earth. It is for healing, sanctifying, empowering, and distributing spiritual gifts to people. We see this imaged in Scripture as doves, seeds, and olive branches. When Noah sent out a dove from the ark after the time of the great flood, the dove returned with an olive branch in its beak, affirming the Lord's continued anointing upon the earth and His presence among people (Genesis 8:11). When John was baptizing Jesus, a dove came to rest upon Jesus' shoulder, as a sign of His heavenly Father's pleasure and the Holy Spirit's anointing for the launching of His public ministry. Matthew described the scene when Jesus came up from the water, saying, "At that moment heaven was opened, and he saw the Spirit of God descending like a dove and alighting on him. And a voice from heaven said, 'This is my Son, whom I love; with him I am well pleased'" (3:16–17).

As believers in Christ, we also receive anointings from the Spirit. When we first come to believe in Jesus as our Lord and Savior, the life-altering seed of the Holy Spirit is planted in our hearts. The Bible affirms that when the Holy Spirit takes up residence in the hearts of those who believe, it is a type of anointing. "He anointed us, set his seal of ownership on us, and put his Spirit in our hearts as a deposit, guaranteeing what is to come" (2 Corinthians 1:21b-22).

When we receive this seed of God's Spirit, a tree of life begins to grow in us and will, in time, reveal itself through the production of spiritual fruit. Galatians 5:22–33 delineates the kinds of fruit that come from this spiritual tree. The Spirit's fruit is "love, joy, peace, forbearance, kindness, goodness, faithfulness, gentleness and self-control." And even though we are all meant to bear every kind of spiritual fruit as we mature in Christ, we all receive a different measure of each anointing depending on the Spirit's allocation. We can see this in how one person may express God's character through exuberant joy but another more readily through patience or gentleness. Though we have received the same Spirit, Scripture teaches that the manifestations vary.

> There are different kinds of service, but the same Lord. There are different kinds of working, but in all of them and in everyone it is the same God at work. Now, to each one the manifestation of the Spirit is given for the common good. (1 Corinthians 12:5–7)

In addition to the anointings planted in us at birth or when we first come to believe, we also receive subsequent anointings along the way of life through prayer and impartation. Romans 11:29 reveals that our anointings are meant to remain with us. "God's gifts and his call are irrevocable."

But just as Jesus would receive fresh anointings in preparation for various stages in His earthly ministry, we are also meant to receive fresh anointings from the Spirit, so we have the power we need for each new assignment.

THE FRAGRANCE OF CHRIST

Anointings are not something we can create ourselves or choose for ourselves, nor are they something we can learn.

> As for you, the anointing you received from him remains in you, and you do not need anyone to teach you. But as his anointing teaches

you about all things and that anointing is real, not counterfeit—just as it has taught you, remain in him. (1 John 2:27)

Moreover, the spiritual anointings that we receive are determined by God and intended to be exercised for the common good and the edification of others.

Now to each one the manifestation of the Spirit is given for the common good. To one there is given through the Spirit a message of wisdom, to another a message of knowledge by means of the same Spirit, to another faith by the same Spirit, to another gifts of healing by that one Spirit, to another miraculous powers, to another prophecy, to another distinguishing between spirits, to another speaking in different kinds of tongues, and to still another the interpretation of tongues. All these are the work of one and the same Spirit, and he distributes them to each one, just as he determines.
(1 Corinthians 12:7–11)

Some of the gifts we receive from God come directly through prayer and the laying on of hands, but some of our gifts come by way of our lived experiences. All our experiences with God are like seeds planted in our souls, meant to grow up into maturity so they can be shared through us as testimonies of God's love.

Just as we see God's distinctive character traits imaged in the many different kinds of animals in creation, such as the bravery of a lion, the diligence of ants, and the sweetness found in a honeybee hive, we can also see many aspects of the Lord's character through the great variety of plants in creation. God endowed each garden plant with a different essence and usefulness, just as He endows each of us with different gifts and anointings meant to be used to build His kingdom on earth. The Word explains how the mysteries of cedarwood and hyssop were revealed to Solomon when he was filled with wisdom. Solomon ordered that his palace, the Hall of Justice, and the Lord's temple be constructed out of cedar because it was not only strong but also decay-resistant and pest-resistant. Its benefits have become widely known for improving mental, emotional, and respiratory function. Our God is not only spiritual; He is also practical.

Diffusing the Essences of Heaven

I was amazed when I read in Psalms how King David even named specific oils to describe what the presence of the Lord smelled like to him. "Your throne, O God, will last forever and ever. All your robes are fragrant with myrrh and aloes and cassia" (Psalm 45:6–8). Growing up, David would have taken in the aroma of the warm cinnamon-like scent of cassia oil each time he entered the Lord's sanctuary for worship. It is one of the most aromatic fragrances in the oil blend God had instructed His people to use in the holy anointing oil as far back as the Israelites' wilderness journey. I took the time and care to make up this blend of oils at home because I wanted to know what God smelled like to King David.

Revelation says that our prayers are like incense to God presented as an offering to Him in heaven. David prayed to the Lord, "May my prayer be set before you like incense" (Psalm 141:2). In the Song of Solomon 1:3, it is written, "Pleasing is the fragrance of your perfumes; your name is like perfume poured out."

We also see how Esther was anointed with oil for an entire year in preparation for becoming queen (Esther 2:12). She was massaged for six months with myrrh and then six additional months with a blend of other essences. These oils had spiritual implications as well, denoting wisdom, preparation, and empowerment. They were repeatedly massaged into Esther's body and given time to soak in before she would be called to go out and fulfill her calling to marry the king and, ultimately, to save the Jewish people. Because Esther had been orphaned as a child and raised by her cousin, I wonder if part of God's purpose in this extended anointing process was the deep inner healing she needed based on the losses she suffered in childhood. God wants to heal all of His children from the pains

> As we become more like Christ in character, we begin to diffuse the sweet-smelling aromas of God's kingdom.

and losses of our pasts and to prepare us fully for the good works He has ordained for us to do. Therefore, we, too, must be patient in the healing and anointing process. Some anointings require extended times of receiving, resting, and waiting before we are adequately prepared by God for the work ahead.

When we consider how oils come from different types of plants, we can better understand the life of Jesus as a type of the garden of Eden, possessing all the varieties of spiritual gifts. Wherever He went as He walked on the earth, Jesus' life diffused the essences of heaven. As we become more like Christ in character, we also begin to diffuse the sweet-smelling aromas of God's kingdom. "But thanks be to God, who always leads us in triumph in Christ, and through us reveals the fragrance of the knowledge of Him in every place" (2 Corinthians 2:14 NASB). Once we have taken in the essence of Christ, we are able to ANOINT others with the same anointing that we first received from Him. This is an essential part of our BECOMING like Christ as His disciples.

The different aspects of His Name that have become part of our lives become like unique oil blends housed in the vessels of our souls. If my husband's life were an oil blend, it would diffuse the fragrances of peace mixed with patience and order. Mine might give off the essence of joy and wonder. The fragrance blends emanating from our lives can also change from season to season based on what we have received from God and what is blooming in the gardens of our souls. Just as all plants in a garden do not flower simultaneously, different aspects of God's character mature in us at various times. Some people may come across as pure joy, especially in their younger years, but as they weather the trials of life and take on new aspects of the Divine Character, the aroma of their lives changes, becoming richer in complexity.

This process, called *theosis*, where God's character manifests to us, in us, and through us, is about BECOMING more like our Lord according to the divine aspects of His name as Yahweh, the One who causes us to become. BECOMING like Christ is something that happens incrementally and differently in every believer.

No matter the specific spiritual impartation of gifts and anointings, all are intended to lead us into greater participation in His divine nature and equip us to bring light, healing, and blessing to others. "For this very reason, make every effort to add to your faith goodness; and to goodness, knowledge; and to knowledge, self-control; and to self-control, perseverance; and to perseverance, godliness; and to godliness, mutual affection; and to mutual affection, love" (2 Peter 1:5–7).

Mercy Through Rejection

The way we represent Christ matters. We are also responsible for keeping sin from spoiling the fragrance of our lives. Solomon reminds us that the sweet-smelling aromas of God will become contaminated and spoiled when we allow the sins of our flesh to remain. "As dead flies give perfume a bad smell, so a little folly outweighs wisdom and honor" (Ecclesiastes 10:1).

Nevertheless, even pure oil that has been made ready for God's good use may still be met with adverse reactions from people.

> For we are to God the pleasing aroma of Christ among those who are being saved and those who are perishing. To the one we are an aroma that brings death; to the other, an aroma that brings life. And who is equal to such a task? (2 Corinthians 2:15–16)

Do not despair when this kind of rejection happens to you. Remember, Jesus was rejected, too, even by those who would come to believe in Him later on. It is also important that we take time to look back on how we, too, have rejected God's truth or parts of the Christian faith expressed through others. This will help us show mercy to those who may be rejecting us or parts of our message now.

I found this understanding helpful when considering how I had grown to love the very things I had rejected in the past. For many years, I was not fond of the smell of lavender, even though I had heard a lot about its calming and healing properties. I rejected the scent of lavender in the same way I refused to understand my own need for healing. My self-sufficiency kept me from knowing Christ as my Healer and God's people as vessels of healing. When I experienced the Lord and His people as vessels of healing, I began to appreciate the smell of lavender until, eventually, I loved it.

Understanding this allowed me to give mercy to others when I felt rejected by them. Instead of pressing into the feeling of being unloved or unworthy of acceptance in these times of strange rejection, I started to consider what it might be of Christ in me that they are not ready to receive just yet from Him.

> Often, the most painful parts of our stories give rise to our most significant purposes.

Every life experience invites us to partake in a new aspect of the divine character so that we have every anointing we need to accomplish the work we are called to.

> His divine power has given us everything we need for a godly life through our knowledge of him who called us by his own glory and goodness. Through these he has given us his very great and precious promises, so that through them you may participate in the divine nature. (2 Peter 1:3–4a)

Anointing represents the transitional practice where the gifts and love of God that have been given *to* us can become manifest *in* us and then eventually pass *through* us.

Even our painful experiences, entrusted to God, will, in time, grow up and produce leaves for healing, flowers for beauty, and fruit for nourishment. Often, the most painful parts of our stories give rise to our most significant purposes. Out of the losses of my own babies, my heart had become open to anointing Laura and her baby for healing because I longed to see her spared from the pain I had felt. "Praise be to . . . the God of all comfort, who comforts us in all our troubles, so that we can comfort those in any trouble with the same comfort we ourselves received from God" (2 Corinthians 1:3–4).

LOVE ABOVE ALL

The chief of all oils is olive, just as the chief of all virtues is love. Judges 9:8 puts these two together for me when it says, "The trees went out to anoint a king for themselves. They said to the olive tree, 'Be our king.'" Without a carrier oil, like olive oil, essential oils can irritate the skin. However, with it, the healing properties penetrate more deeply, and the effect is exponential. Like olive oil, love is a spectacular delivery agent for all aspects of wisdom and words of truth. The work that we do and the words that we say are intended to bring healing to others. But anything we do or say will fail if not administered in love. Only when we speak the truth in love are we drawn together and built up as one family in Christ (Ephesians 4:15).

Love is the greatest anointing of all. So, if you feel that sometimes all you have to give is love, be encouraged; it is the most essential ingredient. When all I had was plain olive oil in a Tupperware container, I learned the truth about the power of love's anointing when it is walked out in obedience by faith. As vessels of God, we must do all we can to deliver truth in genuine love. In Colossians 3:12–14, Paul explains the attributes with which we should be clothed and affirms love as the supreme of all virtues, saying, "Over all these virtues put on love, which binds them all together in perfect unity."

Consider how quickly people will reject the truth when it is delivered by someone with an arrogant or judgmental spirit rather than in a posture of love. Pride is frequently the fly in the holy ointment. How often do we hear people justify their rejection of the church or Christianity based on the unkindness they have felt from those wielding the words of Scripture?

> If I speak in the tongues of men or of angels, but do not have love, I am only a resounding gong or a clanging cymbal. If I have the gift of prophecy and can fathom all mysteries and all knowledge, and if I have a faith that can move mountains but do not have love, I am nothing. If I give all I possess to the poor and give over my body to hardship that I may boast but do not have love, I gain nothing. (1 Corinthians 13:1–3)

No spiritual gift is greater than the gift of love. No matter how powerful our anointings, spiritual our gifts, or brilliant the wisdom we have to share, if it is not delivered in love, it will not bring the healing God intends. How good and pleasant it is when God's people live together in unity. "It is like precious oil poured out" (Psalm 133:2a).

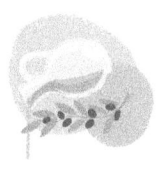

YOUR BECOMING STORY: ANOINT

Consider what seed anointings or sense of calling you may have had from a young age. In what area of your life did you sense God's power when you first came to believe? What additional gifts have you received through prayer or life experiences in God?

Have you ever felt that the Lord handpicked someone to be in your life because of how their giftings could answer your needs? Have you ever felt handpicked by the Lord and anointed to meet the needs of others?

Consider what you may have rejected in others that your soul has been unwilling to receive from God. Also, consider times you have experienced rejection and how it may be connected to the other person's rejection of the aroma of God emanating from your life. This way, you may be able to take the hurt less personally, have mercy, and pray for them.

Knowing what is in your soul's garden and being mindful of the plants that have become ready for sharing requires consideration and intentionality. What is growing in your life's garden? How have you shared what has come from it for the healing, blessing, and nourishment of others? Consider how you have sought to deliver God's truth. Has it been in the context of genuine love?

As you proceed with the exercise of anointing yourself or another person, remember this is a symbol of immersion into the likeness of Christ and BECOMING complete in His love by grace. Oil represents the pleasing aroma that rises to God when a soul is entrusted to Him by faith for healing, restoration, wisdom, and guidance. Anointing with oil is a simple, powerful, and practical exercise representing our choice to trust God with all our heart, mind, soul, and strength.

"To Anoint a King"

Like trees of the field,
We long for a king,
To bind up the wounds
Of our broken wings.

Restorer of breaches,
Power to the meek,
Father of orphans,
It's wisdom we seek.

Fulfill what concerns us,
Let kindness endure.
Give eyes to see rightly,
And confidence sure.

Defender of widows,
The stranger, the weak,
Pour forth Your spirit,
It's justice we seek.

Pray for us, Savior,
That we will become
Rooted and grounded
In unbiased love.

We ask for Your power,
To walk in Your ways.
We wait for You, Lord,
Oh, Ancient of Days.

Help hearts become tender,
Teach souls to do right,
To sit with the lowly,
Who wait in the night.

We'll dive beneath waves,
As they crash down upon.
When storms do abate,
We'll rise with the dawn.

Today, we will mourn,
With those who are sad,
And also rejoice,
With those who are glad.

There's no choice between us,
Yet, leaders we laud.
Help us remember,
We're one under God.[2]

10

CREATE

Work and Worship

It was late autumn, and the weather in St. Petersburg was getting colder, but I had warmed to the idea of completing my semester abroad despite all the challenges of living in Russia. A second Christian mission team arrived from Seattle, and I volunteered to serve as an interpreter for them in between my university studies. During one of their musical outreaches in an underground metro station, I noticed a young girl sitting on the filthy floor beside a mangy dog in a puddle of blood. The sight of her transfixed me.

I crouched down beside her and began speaking with her in Russian. Her name was Irina, and she was twelve years old. She invited me to call her "Ira" and then explained how she had found the wounded dog and bandaged his paw using material she ripped from the lining of her worn-out bomber jacket to stop the bleeding. She told me the stray had gotten his paw stuck in the metro's escalator.

We sat together for a while, sometimes talking and sometimes in silence. All the while, she petted the pup and listened to the music playing on the other side of the metro corridor. Eventually, she shared details about her life with me. Ira spoke as if her reality was "normal," but her lived experiences were heartbreaking. She had been living on the streets since running away from her orphanage to escape the abuse she had suffered there. She was wounded, tired, dirty, cold, hungry, and alone. Her words were piercing. I hardly heard the music or noticed when the dog quietly departed after receiving all it could from the little girl's hand. Ira indicated she had no one in her life to care for her and nowhere to go. I invited her to come to the hotel where I was staying with the mission team for a few days.

Before turning in for the night, Ira read to me from the handwritten journal she kept in her pocket. It told of her many troubles and the places where she had slept along her life's sad journey: in alleys, hallways, cold, filthy streets, and under bridges. I learned that the orphanage director would punish and humiliate her by stripping her naked and forcing her to stand in front of an open window to be seen by everyone who passed by. As she spoke, my heart felt like it was breaking into a thousand pieces.

> As she spoke, my heart felt like it was breaking into a thousand pieces.

The mission group took up a collection of items and presented them to Ira, including some new clothes and a warmer jacket. We discussed getting her some real help, which seemed to please her. Ira stayed close by my side, that is, until two days later when she slipped away silently before I woke. Perhaps she, too, had received all she could from my hand. Though Ira was gone, she has lived in my heart ever since. Had our meeting changed her life somehow? Perhaps only for as long as that new coat would fit, but it had certainly changed mine forever.

The exchange that took place between us made me a story-keeper of her burdens. Her heartbreaking memories, the way she had extended mercy to the injured dog, the stoic manner in which she shared her suffering, her slipping away, still as an orphan; all of it weighed heavily on my heart. Some of Ira's brokenness had been entrusted into my keeping, requiring me to lay all these pieces in front of the Lord in prayer. I needed Him to carry the weight with me—it would crush my soul to hold it on my own.

My encounter with Ira would prove to be a foreshadowing of things to come. Meeting others in their brokenness, bearing witness to their pain, and journeying with them in their healing would become critical parts of my ministry call and necessary for the creative work to come. I would REMEMBER my time with Ira as another living answer to the questions I had hung on my spiritual clothesline years before. Jesus had come to me through a hungry boy in Africa, a poor little girl in India, an elderly widow in Russia, and now as a homeless, orphaned child.

> Then the righteous will answer him, "Lord, when did we see you hungry and feed you, or thirsty and give you something to drink? When did we see you a stranger and invite you in, or needing clothes and clothe you? When did we see you sick or in prison and go to visit you?" The King will reply, "Truly I tell you, whatever you did for one of the least of these brothers and sisters of mine, you did for me." (Matthew 25:37–40)

These encounters taught me more about Christ, myself, and the work God desired in the world. "He has shown you, O mortal, what is good. And what does the Lord require of you? To act justly and to love mercy and to walk humbly with your God" (Micah 6:8).

Seeds of holy empathy were embedded in my soul, and passions grew in me that would shape the life-long unfolding of my creative calling. These formative experiences began to take me beyond my questions and into answers, from an intuitive understanding of pain to an experiential belief in redemption. In this process, I was BECOMING formed and transformed into a more usable vessel for doing and creating good around me.

GOD DESIRES OUR CREATIVITY

Because of the narrow lens through which I had long viewed the ideals of creativity and productivity, I never considered myself particularly creative. I was not adept at what I considered traditional creative endeavors, like painting, drawing, or inventing. Most of my work to that point had been in a volunteer capacity or for very little pay. So, when the Lord began to show me what He considered creative and productive, I realized that my thoughts were not well-aligned with His thoughts on the topic. I had wrongly connected productivity to financial gain and creativity to human affirmation. We were never meant to measure creativity or productivity by what we receive in return but by how we uniquely steward our gifts and talents for God's glory. And the rewards do not always "add up" by pragmatic standards. In fact, no one on earth has ever stewarded their creative work as perfectly as Jesus did, but being the perfect Creator *and Creative* did not stop His people from killing Him.

Having been made in God's image, we are the good work of the Creator, created to do good works like our Creator. Ephesians 2:10 addresses our call as generative beings, "For we are God's handiwork, created in Christ Jesus to do good works, which God prepared in advance for us to do."

Our Creativity and God's

There are, however, differences between our way of creating and God's. Several words in Scripture mean to CREATE. *Bara* in Hebrew means to make something out of nothing, to call "into being things that were not" (Romans 4:17). This is the creating only God can do. Psalm 8:3 gives an example of *bara* when describing how God set the stars in place.

Asah is the Hebrew word for remaking or re-creating. *Asah* is the kind of creating that people, animals, and plants can do. They make something new out of the raw materials entrusted to them. Ants building a home out of sand and dirt, bees making honey from nectar, trees bearing fruit, and people making bread from wheat or linen from flax are all examples of *asah* (Gen. 1:12; 3:21).

God also creates in this way of *asah* by remaking and repurposing things in His creation. God first interacted with humanity as their Creator, and He continues to interact with people as their Re-Creator. In Psalm 51:10, where God's servant asks Him to create a new, pure heart in him, the word *asah* is used, referring to the re-creating work that takes place in the fallen creation by the power of the Holy Spirit. The Holy Spirit is continually doing this re-creating work in the small details of our lives. This is why it is so essential for us, as living letters, not to finish God's sentences but to give room for His creative hand and even his editing hand when we have run ahead of Him.

Work and Worship

Avodah is a Hebrew word that carries the meaning of three words together: work, worship, and service. From God's perspective, they are one and the same. The separation of these concepts in Western culture has led us to see them as only integrated in "religious" work. We forget that our everyday work is supposed to be a form of worship. This tragic disconnect has made us less reliant on the Spirit, less powerful in our endeavors, and less satisfied in our work. The word worship comes from the Old English word *woerthship*, meaning to do something for what we deem worthy. When we integrate our understanding of work with our worship practices, our endeavors become more thoughtful and creative, and we become more mindful of how we can collaborate with the One who is worthy of all our heart, soul, mind, and strength (Mark 12:30).

The natural gifts and talents we have received speak to the endowed creativity of God. How we use these gifts speaks to our creativity. Like our individual voices and unique fingerprints, creativity is our personal expression of work and worship: it is what we do, say, and make. We all want to be needed and do needful things. The quest to experience significance, CREATE beauty, innovate, and fulfill some lasting purpose can occupy a lot of our focus and energy. In Scripture, expressing one's mind and heart is often mentioned as the words of one's mouth, the strength of one's body, or the work of one's hands (Psalm 90:17; 1 Peter 4:11). And while having a voice and fingers may not feel unique, the way we use them leaves distinctive marks on the people and things we encounter.

Just because someone has a beautiful face, natural athletic ability, problem-solving strengths, or the skills to draw, write, sing, play, or paint does not automatically mean they are creative by God's definition. What makes someone truly creative or innovative is determined by whether they are exercising their talents as God intends: to bring more goodness, beauty, truth, and life into the world.

> Even *I want-to want-to believe* is a mustard seed God can use to move mountains.

This multiplication of life-giving creativity happens by *theosis*, a process by which God's character traits are made manifest to us, then become manifest in us, and ultimately, are made manifest through us with maturing integrity. Integrity is the deepening integration of our beliefs and behaviors, attitudes and actions, and our work and worship so that what is going on inside us matches what is expressed through us authentically. God desires truth in our inward parts so that what comes from us is genuinely holy, even when our truth is nothing more than *I want-to want-to believe*. That is a "mustard seed" of faith God can use to move mountains.

God's Sacred Art

True creativity is always homemade; it is meant to spill out of us into expression as God is remaking and refilling us. A God-honoring creative process requires His truth to become true in us before it can become powerfully expressed through us. Even though Paul the apostle was already a scholar of the Jewish holy books, it was not until God created a new heart in him through his personal encounter with Jesus that he was transformed into a positive force for the kingdom and became one of the most prolific writers of Scripture. Just like Paul, we are God's sacred art, created to express more sacred art through work, worship, and service. I love how the Message version of Galatians 6:1, 4–5 encourages us, saying, "Live creatively, friends. Make a careful exploration of who you are and the work you have been given, and then sink yourself into that. Don't be impressed with yourself. Don't compare yourself with others. Each of you must take responsibility for doing the creative best you can with your own life."

CREATIVITY MISUNDERSTOOD AND MISUSED

There are plenty of gifted people that our culture considers highly creative but are practicing the opposite of creativity according to God's definition. The opposite of the word CREATE is to dismantle or destroy. To dismantle a person is to usurp their authority in position or calling, remove their work mantle, or tear down the walls surrounding the core of their life, making it harder to create. These dismantling activities are used to describe how the enemy of God's Spirit works. "The thief comes only to steal and kill and destroy; I have come that they may have life, and have it to the full" (John 10:10).

Scripture warns us to watch out for these damaging, impersonating practices, even within the body of Christ: "Watch out for false prophets. They come to you in sheep's clothing, but inwardly they are ferocious wolves. By their fruit you will recognize them" (Matthew 7:15–16). Those pretending to be what they are not or who steal the credit for another person's work, passing it off as their own, are not only acting disrespectfully but uncreatively. "Anyone who has been stealing must steal no longer, but must work, doing something useful with their own hands, that they may have something to share with those in need" (Ephesians 4:28).

When people try to take on a spiritual authority that God has not given them, it is like wearing clothes that do not fit or belong to them. It can be an indicator of a disassembled life. They may not have set out to dismantle another but have succumbed to the pressures to keep producing nonetheless. Sadly, the pressure to endlessly CREATE is a standard often set for individuals living in the public eye. But the Spirit calls us all to times of rest, and heeding this inner voice helps the soul maintain its integrity and gives room for others to shine.

Integrity indicates an assembled life and should be the mark of every God follower. "Whoever walks in integrity walks securely, but whoever takes crooked paths will be found out" (Proverbs 10:9). In contrast, the more that believers seek personal integration with the Spirit, the more integrated the church will become—a place where all the parts of Christ's body can be valued.

We don't have to look far to see how humans have misused God's gifts to design selfish schemes, manipulate others to garner influence for themselves, or stir up unrest. When leaders are not grounded and integrated, chaos ensues, affecting everyone under their authority and beyond. Some of the greatest evils in human history were envisioned and carried out by leaders whose creative gifts were driven by an ungodly spirit of greed, jealousy, malice, or lust for power.

Unfortunately, many of us can relate to these sad realities because they have played out in our own experiences, even in our churches. Nevertheless, the Scriptures remind us that our heavenly Father, who sees what is done in secret, will address all the wrongs done and reward all the good in due time (Matthew 6:4). God sees in the dark and is never fooled. "For there is nothing hidden that will not be disclosed, and nothing concealed that will not be known or brought out into the open" (Luke 8:17).

CREATIVE REDEMPTION

The Bible story of Joseph provides a tremendous example of how creative stewardship and the integration of a person's life story can lead to the redemption of pain. Despite being sold into slavery by his brothers, wrongfully imprisoned in Egypt, and forgotten, Joseph would eventually sit in a seat of honor and be empowered to devise innovative plans for the common good because of his perseverance in faith. When Joseph was eventually pulled from prison because of his reputation as a skilled dream interpreter, he miraculously stood before Pharoah to recount and interpret the Pharoah's dreams. His dream foretold seven years of plenty followed by seven years of famine.

Pharoah was convinced of Joseph's anointing from God and honored him by making him manager over much of his kingdom. During the seven years of plenty, Joseph stored up grain so it could be wisely distributed during the seven years of famine to feed the people (Genesis 41). Joseph's life affirms the verse in Proverbs 22:29, "Do you see someone skilled in their work? They will stand before kings; they will not stand before officials of low rank."

From the painful abandonment by his brothers and his imprisonment in Egypt to the honors and power bestowed upon him by Pharoah, Joseph entrusted it all to God. He was faithful to the Lord, using everything in his sphere of influence to bring about good and provision for all. Joseph's life is a beautiful example of the kind of worthy work described in Scripture. "Who then is the faithful and wise servant, whom the master has put in charge of the servants in his household to give them their food at the proper time?" (Matthew 24:45).

God's ways are always redemptive. He is notorious for exalting the humble who have been faithful and diligent in their work. Joseph's faithfulness to God, patience in suffering, and commitment to true creativity were rewarded with the redemption of his personal story and reconciliation with his family. God wants to bring redemption and reconciliation to all areas of our lives. To experience this, we must continue walking by faith, entrusting every difficulty to God, and working as Joseph did: "Keep your spiritual fervor, serving the Lord. Be joyful in hope, patient in affliction, faithful in prayer. Share with the Lord's people who are in need. Practice hospitality" (Romans 12:11–13).

A Many-Colored Mantle

Joseph is well-known for his coat made of many colors. When Scripture refers to a coat or a mantle, it is speaking about a person's work identity or position of authority, essentially what they become. A doctor's coat, a police uniform, or a painter's smock all represent different mantles. We still imply the reality of mantles when we ask children the question, "What do you want to be when you grow up?" Essentially, "What covering do you envision wearing one day?" My favorite response when asking someone about who they are and what they do was, "I'm a child of God, cleverly disguised as a businessman." This statement would shape my view of myself in every job I would have from that point on.

When Joseph was only a child, his father Jacob created for him a beautiful, multicolored coat (Genesis 37:3). Despite having his first mantle stolen from him, defiled, and torn by his jealous brothers when they sold him into slavery, and despite having his second mantle as overseer in Egypt ripped from him by Potiphar's lustful and lying wife, imaged by the robe she pulled off of him, Joseph kept his integrity. In time, we find that Joseph was restored to leadership and given a mantle of even greater authority so he could protect and preserve lives through the seven years of famine. Because God's truth was integrated into Joseph's soul, he mercifully used his knowledge and power to teach and comfort his brothers when they stood before him, genuinely ashamed of what they had done to him. Joseph said to his brothers, "Don't be afraid. Am I in the place of God? You intended to harm me, but God intended it for good to accomplish what is now being done, the saving of many lives" (Genesis 50:20). Joseph's mantle of many colors was indeed a foreshadowing of the many aspects of his life that would eventually become integrated into one multifaceted position of authority.

We all wear different mantles throughout our lives, depending on the season, environment, and role we are called to in work and service. Even though I am currently identified as a wife, mother, teacher, and writer, I have also worn the mantles of advocate, student, manager, missionary, and mentor. In God's mind, the mantles of our lives are far more layered and intricate than just our temporary jobs in one area of work or season of life.

I didn't fully realize it at the time, but God was teaching me about mantles through my encounter with Ira, the Russian orphan girl. Even if she didn't know it, the coat the missionaries gave her represented God's love and provision for her in that shared moment. Ira's care for the stray dog using the lining of her bomber jacket revealed how she was a kind steward using her mantle for the sake of a weaker creature.

> In a spiritual sense, we all wear cloaks representing the creative callings we've answered.

Our actions of giving and receiving compassion become like threads interwoven into our spiritual mantles. The impact of Ira's life on mine became a through-thread stitched into my mantle, calling me to walk in the fields of the fatherless. Her presence was a Divine Correspondence that made me want to become a living love letter with every mantle God would place upon me.

From a lifetime perspective, our mantles are more like patchwork coats. The threads are woven, and the swatches are sewn together from various aspects of our lives, including the past and present, the hurts and joys, identities old and new, and things lost and found. In a spiritual sense, we all wear cloaks representing the creative callings we've answered, the works we've done, the fragments we've entrusted, and the beliefs we've held that have led to our soul's integration. This long-term perspective provides a living and redemptive hope that our lives are continually expanding and growing more colorful as we persevere in faith. IMAGINE how God is saving different patches and weaving various colored threads from every coat we have ever worn for the coming revelation of our multicolored mantles.

BECOMING CREATIVE

It was not until I went to Russia that many things that had been tended in me since childhood finally reached a self-sufficient maturity and were highly useful for the common good. Just as with exercise and strength training, we do not know how much progress we have made until we are tested. Until my days in Russia, I had not perceived how God had been equipping and preparing me all along. My newly integrated and confident beliefs, along with my Russian language proficiency and tools of faith, proved valuable materials for doing good work in that season. Hebrews 13:21 promises that God will "equip you with everything good for doing his will" so He can "work in us what is pleasing to him, through Jesus Christ." When we find our lives bearing fruit, we should take the time to intentionally PRAISE the Lord.

After attending a Billy Graham Crusade in Moscow, I realized that many of the people I had befriended in Russia had come to know Jesus because of our friendships. While thanking the Lord for this fruit coming out of my life, I heard the inner whisper of the Spirit correct and inform me, saying that what I was experiencing was the fruit of my mother's ministry that was first poured into me. *Wow! I had not even considered how the salvation of my new friends was connected to my mother.* But God had. He never forgets all the components that make up any good work.

Straightaway, I ordered an international call to tell my mom how her investments in me were bearing fruit in this foreign land. She was so touched she cried. I also learned several valuable lessons. First was the importance of sharing with those who have poured into us. And second, I learned the importance of pouring into others who will bear fruit after us. The Message's wording of Galatians 6:6 beautifully affirms this: "Be very sure now, you who have been trained to a self-sufficient maturity, that you enter into a generous common life with those who have trained you, sharing all the good things you have and experience."

By using the resources we already have and the things we already know, we can creatively devise plans with God and share the good things with those who cross our paths. For years, my mother has run three creative ministries out of our home in the most natural way. She learned gardening from her mother and photography from her father, and she received recipes passed down from her grandparents. Out of these, she continually blesses people in her life. She takes pictures throughout the year and then gives them to those in her community in the form of Christmas tree ornaments during the holidays. She regularly takes flowers from her garden to anoint her neighbors' tables with beautiful bouquets. And when an elderly community member falls sick, she makes them custards using her family recipe. She has passed all these ministries down to her grandchildren, who have enjoyed making and delivering these gifts with her.

God does not ask everyone to cross oceans or start an international ministry. But He has asked us to cross the street, reach out in kindness to our neighbors, and do good to those around us. Creating beauty was never meant to involve the kind of human striving for notoriety or financial gain seen everywhere in our modern world. What we produce through busyness and selfish human ambition inevitably amounts to unhealthy exhaustion and disconnection from the Spirit. The Bible says, "Make it your ambition to lead a quiet life: You should mind your own business and work with your hands, just as we told you" (1 Thessalonians 4:11).

THE PLAN REDIRECTED

After graduating from Bucknell University, I had planned to go straight to graduate school. However, I felt a call to return to Russia and continue serving there in Christian ministry. My parents gave room for this curveball while holding on to the comfort that I would return after a year and get back on track with *the plan*.

I went to Russia, served another year, and grew deeper in my love for the Russian people, an understanding of their hardship, and my own need to continually seek the Lord for strength and wisdom. But as the time to come home drew closer, *the plan* was upended again. I took a train trip from Russia to Austria to attend an international missions conference. There, I met Pastor Brian Brodersen. Though he did not know me, he seemed to have insight into my life and calling. He challenged me to dedicate a few years to the intensive study of Scripture. He even offered to cover the expenses of attending Calvary Chapel Bible College.

"Thanks, but no thanks," I said. "I already finished college, and my time in Russia's just about done. I'll soon be heading back to the States to go to grad school," I told him. When I returned to Moscow, however, I found myself lying awake night after night, fighting a strong internal pull to say yes to this two-year study of God's Word and abandon *the plan* yet again.

Much to my parents' dismay, I postponed graduate school *again*, causing my deferral time for admittance to expire. God was calling me deeper into letting go of family expectations and higher into a state of willingness to be misunderstood. I have since come to see that being misunderstood and separated in this way is part of nearly every believer's journey of BECOMING the unique creative vessel God intends them to be. "And everyone who has left houses or brothers or sisters or father or mother or wife or children or fields for my sake will receive a hundred times as much and will inherit eternal life" (Matthew 19:29).

So, Bible college, it was. I used the set-apart time to dive deep into scriptural study while also working as a ninth-grade teacher at Calvary Chapel High School. Still, I worried this was merely a distraction from *the plan*. As these two years concluded, I received a letter from The American University in Washington, DC, offering me a full-ride scholarship to their master's program in Russian Studies. It had been nearly three years since I had even applied, and now they offered to cover all my expenses. It felt like something I couldn't refuse, as it allowed me to return to a version of the *plan* that promised the approval of those who saw my recent years in ministry as a distraction. So, with Bible college behind me, I moved to

DC to jump into grad school and seemingly get my life back on track. Still, I wondered how these divergent pathways could possibly lead me to a sensible career and prosperous life.

It was near the end of my first semester at graduate school that God's voice seemed to divert my "plan" yet again. One day—literally on the same day—I received three letters from three different people, all living in different countries, but all mentioning the same Bible verses from the book of Deuteronomy.

> Observe the commands of the Lord your God, walking in obedience to him and revering him. For the Lord your God is bringing you into a good land—a land with brooks, streams, and deep springs gushing out into the valleys and hills; a land with wheat and barley, vines and fig trees, pomegranates, olive oil and honey; a land where bread will not be scarce, and you will lack nothing. (Deuteronomy 8:6–9)

While sitting in my car in the dark and empty parking lot in front of Washington, DC's National Cathedral, I turned my head toward the sky and thanked the Lord for the Scriptures that were sent to me. They brought a mysterious and deep comfort as I wrestled with feeling divided and vulnerable, unsure about my future. I also asked the Lord if these Scriptures were truly meant to be a promise for me and if He was really bringing me into a "good land." It was hard to imagine such a future could be mine amidst all the confusion and winding pathways that had recently marked my life.

The Plan as an Idol

As I opened my heart to listen to the Spirit, images of the Israelite people worshiping the golden calf came to mind. *Why am I seeing this?* I wondered. *Is the Lord likening me to them?* I would realize that the answer was yes. God opened my spiritual eyes wide that day, showing me that my desire for human approval was in direct competition with my call to seek God's approval. I saw that I was clinging more tightly to the worldly security offered by higher education than looking to God as my safety. *The plan* was still at the center of my life.

That day, God invited me to turn away from these idols and set my face like a flint upon Him and "the race" He had marked out for me. My heart understood this as the way for me to become complete in Him and to fulfill the work and creative purposes He had for me, one assignment at a time. "Am I now trying to win the approval of human beings, or of God? Or am I trying to please people? If I were still trying to please people, I would not be a servant of Christ" (Galatians 1:10). I wept as I saw more clearly how my doublemindedness had been the cause of my soul's inner turmoil. I had been seeking both the approval of people and of God.

It wasn't that higher education or people's approval were bad things; it was the place I had given these things in my heart. "Whatever you do, work at it with all your heart, as working for the Lord and not for human masters, since you know that you will receive an inheritance from the Lord as a reward. It is the Lord Christ you are serving" (Colossians 3:23–24). The Holy Spirit was inviting all the parts of my soul to become integrated. This required returning my focus to the Lord by confessing my fear, people-pleasing, and idolatry. I resolved to put this bad pattern behind me. I could only become an integrated and peaceful soul by walking in my calling and abiding in the truth of Deuteronomy 6:5. "Love the LORD your God with all your heart and with all your soul and with all your strength." God was dealing with me on the inside so that when the good He intended to do through me came forth, I would know His grace was the power behind it.

> Obstacles and redirections are not the end, so keep moving.

After one semester, I left grad school and returned home to Pennsylvania feeling reduced. I spent the rest of that year helping sort some of my Mema's collected things. Unknown to me then, this season would be my last chance to glean from my grandmother's wisdom before her passing.

"Mema, how can I know God's will for my life?" I asked one afternoon in tears. "And how can I end up where I am supposed to if I am a sinner and sin messes everything up?"

Mema answered, "Finding God's will for your life is a lot like how a submarine's torpedo finds its target. When it encounters obstacles, it will find its way around. Even when it looks like it is going in the wrong direction, you don't need to worry. It will realign itself to the right path because it has already been locked onto its mark." She assured me that "as long as it keeps moving, it will eventually reach its intended destination."

Her words comforted me. I was desperate for assurance that I had not sabotaged my future with my oscillating ways. I took mental notes. Number one: choose the right target; number two: obstacles and redirections are not the end; and three: keep moving.

Until then, the paths of my life had felt disconnected. I couldn't imagine how the different storylines could combine into one cohesive narrative. I longed to find meaningful work, somewhere my heart would feel alive. God assured me that all the pathways of my life would come together in His time, just as Joseph's eventually did, but that it would take a little more waiting and trusting on my part. The mantle I would need was apparently still upon the Divine Weaver's loom. Like a wise contemplative once told me, "God writes straight with crooked lines." And as Scripture reminds us, "In their hearts humans plan their course, but the LORD establishes their steps" (Proverbs 16:9).

THE PATHWAY TO CAPITOL HILL

My passion for applying language and faith to human stories grew during this time at home. I often dreamt about developing creative solutions to societal problems. Yet, I still did not know how these competencies would be used. After six months in limbo organizing my Mema's things, I finally secured a temporary job as a translator for some Russian government officials visiting the US to learn more about international adoptions.

This eventually became part of my full-time work with an adoption agency that required me to travel back and forth to Russia. Over the next three years, I would visit dozens of Russian orphanages and meet with hundreds of older orphans. I saw how difficult it was to find adoptive families for older kids still waiting for families. Nevertheless, I truly believed that if people in the US could know some of these children as I was coming to know them, then they would not live out the rest of their childhoods in these lonely, unseen places.

When the Lord revealed I would soon be moving on from that job, my heart was troubled to think of leaving these precious kids behind. I knew the gut-wrenching statistics that spoke of the fate of the youth who would leave these institutions without finding families to protect and support them. So, on my final trip to Siberia, I visited some of the orphans I had befriended during previous trips and invited them to write letters about themselves that I could take home to share. I returned to the US with their stories and letters and passed them on to my colleagues, hoping the children's own words would help find them adoptive families.

Time would prove that this transition was God's Spirit leading me into a new assignment while also bringing together many desires, skills, and past experiences for His specific purposes. Ironically, this assignment would take place where my parents had long believed I was destined— Capitol Hill.

A Program at Risk

After several tragic news stories about Russian adoptions gone bad, some regions in Russia began to close to international adoptions, and the Russian federal government was considering a moratorium on them altogether. One of the first regions that threatened closure was Irkutsk, Siberia, where many of the older orphans I sought families for still lived. Thanks to my experience working with Russian government officials, I had come to understand the effectiveness of increasing human connectivity and intercultural communication to build more trust between our two countries. The Russian officials needed a robust human dialogue to get answers to their specific questions and concerns. But, at the time, in the US, adoptions were not handled at the federal level, even international ones, but rather at the level of individual states. In fact, international adoption was a relatively new phenomenon, especially from China and Russia, which came about after the fall of Communism in the USSR.

A multilateral treaty overseeing international adoptions would eventually be implemented in the US. Still, because it was not yet in place nor was the communication streamlined, foreign officials seeking answers from our federal government could not get satisfactory ones. Instead, they were often shuffled to local governments without the help of interpreters. It was an intercultural communication problem that was proving harmful to the most vulnerable population. It is hard enough for US citizens to navigate their own local bureaucracies, so for foreigners, it is near impossible.

My agency director sent me to DC to join a lobbying group scheduled to meet with US immigration officials, the State Department, and congressional offices to find a remedy to this problem. I was the only person who brought a prepared statement to the meetings. At first, I felt foolish, thinking I was still acting like a student instead of a legitimate career person, so I kept my document to myself. Many words were exchanged at the State Department meeting, but no practical solutions were reached. One of the Russian adoption agency directors I had just met spoke up and announced, "Kerry wrote a document to share," as she pointed to the papers I was hiding in my lap. I'm sure I turned red, then reluctantly handed them over.

Open Dialogue

At the next meeting in the congressional briefing room, I was thrust to the front and told to share what I had written. I was afraid, but I shared anyway. Once the briefing concluded and my heart rate returned to normal, a man introduced himself to me as Bill Dolbow, legislative assistant to Congressman Tom Bliley. Bliley was the Republican co-chair of the bipartisan caucus called the Congressional Coalition on Adoption (CCA). Mr. Dolbow said he wanted to work with me to implement my ideas. The first was an international letter-writing campaign seeking to open communication with the Russian Duma on the matter, to which over a hundred congressional members would eventually become signatories. This open dialogue proved crucial to Russian adoptions remaining open during those years. What astonished me was how God made a way for many of my ideas written on that original document to be implemented, not only with Russia but with several other countries. At the time, I could never have imagined this happening. But God knew; it was His plan, and His Spirit had been behind it all. "Not by power, nor by might, but by my Spirit,' says the LORD Almighty" (Zechariah 4:6).

Soon, God made it clear to my heart that I should move to Washington, DC, and seek work in this field on Capitol Hill. I obeyed and prepared to go, even though I was feeling called to do a job in DC that was not even posted yet! I continued to pray earnestly, hoping I had heard God correctly and I was not just upending my life again on a whim. When the job working for the caucus was finally posted, I submitted my résumé along with the eighty-eight other qualified applicants, who, unlike me, already had experience working on Capitol Hill.

I vividly remember the call I made to my dad's fraternity brother and football teammate from Bucknell, Bently Elliott, to ask if he would write me a recommendation for the job. Ben had been the director of speechwriting for President Ronald Reagan. I figured his support might be helpful. Much to my dismay, he responded to my request, saying, "Oh no, Kerry, I don't want someone like you to work somewhere like that. Politics has a way of changing people, and I don't want you to change."

I am pretty sure that by the time we got off the phone, Ben thought he had talked me out of applying. But when we hung up, I prayed over his concerns and mine. I was also not sure I could handle a place like DC, especially since I had little interest in politics. I was a registered voter but did not feel closely associated with either party. *Lord, maybe Ben's right. I don't even know if I'm supposed to be a Democrat or a Republican.* But the Lord's Spirit quickly answered me, saying, "Be Mine."

Ben's words of warning forced me to consider my ways. I set an intention to remain aligned with heaven in all my endeavors if I did get the job. Then, I called Ben back and tried to address his concerns.

"Mr. Elliott, if I promise not to change, will you reconsider writing me that recommendation?"

He realized I was serious and said, "I'd be happy to. And DC will be the better for having you in it, Kerry." Against difficult odds, I got the job. It seems this was part of the Divine Weaver's plan all along.

In this position, I would learn how critical it is for my workflow to be sourced from the Spirit, not from fear of man or human striving. I would need to use all my spiritual resources in the workplace of DC, especially my knowledge of God's Word. The mission field and Bible college had, in fact, not been divergent from God's plan after all, but instead, they had been critical training for keeping my soul intact in a place like Washington.

He Uses What He Chooses

In DC, where egos are enormous and party logos prominently displayed, God still can bring about His will using whomever or whatever He chooses. He is sovereign. Yet, this does not mean we can walk in the ways of the world and not end up broken and exhausted. If we, His sheep, are to remain safe, we need to be mindful of our Shepherd's guidance, especially in a place with so many wolves. The quest for power in Washington, DC, and the confusion of partisan politics makes it particularly challenging to remain rightly standing in one's work and creative endeavors. I committed myself to the truth expressed in Luke 12:30–31: "For all these things the nations of the world eagerly seek; but your Father knows that you need these things. But seek His kingdom, and these things will be added to you" (NASB).

It was in this season that I would marry Scott. God knew I needed a loving and supportive partner to help me through these battle years in DC. Scott had a lot of wisdom and often spoke about the soul's most significant distractions—power, fame, and wealth. We started calling these soul distractors "the three bears" because we recognized that the more they are pursued, the more likely those who run after them will be wounded or wholly devoured. If we do not beware of the three bears, we will build human kingdoms rather than God's and lose out on what our souls most desire from our work: to be genuinely successful, fulfill our life purposes, and receive lasting rewards. My passion and work had become one: to CREATE ways for the story-keepers of suffering to connect to the gate-keepers of power so that the keys to the courtrooms of wisdom and the storehouses of provision would be shared as God intends.

During those years, my work was driven by my belief in the power of human stories to affect positive change. I organized many events that would bring those with the power to affect change for children together with those who had the lived experiences to inform them. On my way to one of these events in the Senate Rotunda, where I would be speaking on older child adoption, I heard my name being called out in Russian. It was the diminutive form of my name, which few people ever called me. "*Kerrichka, Kerrichka,*" came the young voices. Standing in the center of the massive hall, I saw two familiar faces smiling at me through the two-story wooden doors.

Seeing these girls transported me back to where I had last been with them, in their orphanage in Irkutsk, Siberia. I could hardly believe my eyes. They were biological sisters, and two of the children I had asked to write letters for me to take home and share as a way to advocate for their adoption. I had deeply hoped they would find families one day, but I could never have imagined a moment like this, together in the US Capitol with them and their adoptive families. What a tremendous gift from a generous God to know how He had honored their hearts' desires and mine and infused all of our tiny seeds of faith with his abundant grace to bring about this layered miracle. Sometimes, we get to taste the fruits of our labor in a way that deeply satisfies our souls and empowers our will to keep on keeping on, even when it's hard. This experience spoke to me of Proverbs 27:18: "He who guards the fig tree will eat its fruit."

> I could hardly believe my eyes. I could never have imagined a moment like this.

COLLABORATING WITH GOD

Our creative work is intended to be a form of worship practiced by faith for the good of others. When we work creatively using the gifts we have been given and the positions we hold to multiply beauty and bless other people, we draw closer to the Lord, become more like Him in character, and find our place in the world. Our work should reveal the integration of our faith with the strength of our will. "But someone will say, 'You have faith; I have deeds.' Show me your faith without deeds, and I will show you my faith by my deeds" (James 2:18).

The years of working in the politically charged environment of DC revealed how easy it can be to put away the building materials of faith and prayer, exchanging them for human-grade materials like striving, manipulation, and withholding information to maintain power. There were days I was sure I would be squashed like a bug by the giants I faced all around me. But more times than I can remember, I watched God multiply my efforts, even the most minor things I did out of love. I felt like a daughter standing upon the feet of her heavenly Father as we danced together before some of the great power players of this world. God went out of His way to show me His sovereignty over my story, with all its twists and turns. God made sure to reveal in magnificent ways that *all* of the children whose handwritten stories I had carried home had found their way into the hands and hearts of couples called to adopt them. I will never forget these expressions of God's Fatherly love.

Three Prayers

Looking back and considering how my praying mother had long believed I was destined for Capitol Hill, I can now see that she was not wrong. Nevertheless, God had a higher way and alternative timing for this to come about so that when I would wear that mantle, it would be fuller, multicolored, and multidimensional—that it would not lack the integrity that only comes when intellectual knowledge is combined with the experiential understanding of caring for the poor.

God has a way of making our paths straight in the most creative and roundabout ways. "In all your ways submit to him, and he will make your paths straight" (Proverbs 3:6). If you have ever felt like a misguided torpedo, a noncreative leaving no lasting mark, or that your story doesn't matter in God's grander plan, I encourage you to ask the Lord to give you a glimpse of the garment He's weaving out of the threads from the various works of your life. Trust that as you continue to walk by faith, He will place upon you the mantle of authority intended for you and present the rewards of your labor according to His love.

Growing up, when I would dream about what I might become one day, I would pray three different prayers: I asked the Lord to make my life a living love letter that others could read and know Christ's love for them. I asked God to let me ride some of His big waves so I could experience the thrill of His power here on earth. And I also asked for a seat on the 50-yard line to His "glory show," even if I wasn't going to be a major player in the game.

I feel God has answered each of those prayers. Today, I find myself praying a new prayer for myself and for those seeking to become complete in Christ. I desire to see how all our lives together can become like one giant painted canvas that displays every color of God's kingdom, from the yellow of joy to the blue of peace and even the red of sacrifice, so that, in time, we will become radiant white, entirely complete in His spectrum of light, a perfect reflection of Jesus, the *noble, readied* Bride of Christ.

YOUR BECOMING STORY: CREATE

When you consider the different roles you have played, the work you have done, and the spiritual clothes of belief you have put on, IMAGINE what the coat of the many colors of your life might be shaping up to be. Consider what colors the different seasons of your life might represent. Which one represented the red of passion or sacrifice, the orange of being purified by fire, the green of growth, or the blue of creativity flowing freely from your soul? And what colors might your life still be lacking?

How have you misunderstood or misused creativity in your life? How have you wrongly dismissed yourself as lacking creativity? How might you have dismissed another for seemingly not wearing a mantle you understood? Consider how you might bring greater good, beauty, and life to the world using the raw materials you have been given. This can begin by writing down the experiences, knowledge, and gifts that have been unique to your story—even (and sometimes especially) the ones that have brought pain or confusion. How might God be asking you to use the raw materials of your life, your experiences, gifts, and faith to answer a call on your life?

"Coloring Souls"

Our words leave marks on others' souls,
We paint in wisdom or stain like fools.
Ask yourself what hues you leave, and
What you're teaching to believe.

Pushing down or helping fly?
Acts that scar or beautify?
Shades of kindness, hope, and joy
Words to build and not destroy?

Because our wounds turn into weapons,
And bring harm from self-protection,
We must repent and turn from anger
To not become a source of danger.

It's time to choose your palette well,
For one day soon, your work will tell,
How you spoke in secret spaces,
What you wrote on others' faces.

Do you inspire hope or fear,
Addressing pain from yesteryear?
Sorrow's tears will help the healing,
And give room for others' feelings.

Your choice to pick tones dull or bright,
To weave with threads of love and light.
God brings the rain and hangs the colors
For us to use to love each other.[1]

11

ASSEMBLE

Integrating Parts and People

After twenty years of living away, I moved back to my hometown of Danville, Pennsylvania, in 2008. I was anxious about starting over, building new relationships, and reconnecting to old ones. Scott suggested I host a Bible study in our home, saying, "People will self-select out of a Bible study, and you won't be offending people in the same way as forgetting to invite them to a party." It turns out that this was a beautiful way to begin an assembly, placing the Lord at the center from the start.

BONDING AGENTS

The first new person I met in town was Jen Swartzentruber. She had also been praying about organizing a Bible study. I took this as confirmation from God to open my home so we could begin it together. Several of the relationships I made through that study became part of our family's core community. I met Laura Corbeil, the woman whom I would one day anoint for the healing of her baby and through whom I would come to experience God's character as the Divine Healer.

I also met Dr. Erica McElroy, who would become a dear friend and vital member of the work God would bring about over the next decade. At the time, I could not have known the beauty I would see, the glory I would witness, or the love I would feel by saying yes to assembling and being willing to step out to form new relationships. We only see in part, but God sees the whole (1 Corinthians 13:9–10). Every day is an exercise in trusting God enough to let Him work out His plan as we walk by faith (Ephesians 2:10). At the end of our first study, I asked Erica about her passions and interests, apart from her work as a wife, mother, and ER doctor.

"I've always wanted to do international medicine," she said. Her response amazed me, considering a recent prayer of mine. I had been dreaming about having our local hospital, Geisinger Medical Center, collaborate with Scott's work at Show Hope to bring care to orphans with special medical needs in China. But, up to that point, all my attempts to bring this about failed. *Maybe Erica's meant to take up this mantle*, I thought. So, I shared with her the vision God had given me for it on my last trip to China.

"Hmm, well, since I speak Spanish and not Mandarin, I always thought I'd do this in a Spanish-speaking country. But I'm open to whatever God has for me," Erica explained.

My basement soon became a storage center for donated medical supplies. Erica and Scott began taking surgical teams to China. Dr. Amir Kershenovich, a pediatric neurosurgeon and our next-door neighbor, also participated in some of these medical trips. With all that was happening, I could see how God had been assembling many things over many years to bring this work into being. Still, I remained curious about one thing. When God first impressed this idea on my heart, I assumed I would eventually go with the teams to China. But by the time the dream had come to pass, I had been blessed with two healthy baby girls. First came Leah Joy and then, less than two years later, Annika Faith. It was clear that I was far more needed at home. Still, I participated on the edges of this assembly as an encourager, prayer warrior, volunteer fundraiser, and bonding agent. God showed me that my part was to help bring others together for this work and then play a more invisible role.

The Lord was faithful to bring the image of Elmer's Glue to mind as a depiction of my ministry role and as an encouragement to me in that season when my responsibilities of nursing our baby and homeschooling our older children kept me more homebound and less seen. When Elmer's Glue is applied, the glue can be easily seen, as it is white and opaque, but when its work of securing the bonds is completed, the glue becomes clear, transparent, and nearly invisible. God reminded me that this was the very essence of Jesus' ministry here on earth. Having made His divinity visible to us in the form of Jesus, God came down and lived among us to reconcile us to Himself. And when He had finished His work, He returned to the unseen realms. And though He is unseen to our physical eyes, the transparent bonds He forged still hold.

Thinking of Jesus as a bonding agent helped me know that God knows, sees, and will never forget the reconciling work that we do. Those with the wisdom, understanding, and spiritual eyes to see are not only able to honor the bonds forged by Jesus, but they also appreciate the bonds forged by other people in obedience to Him. Above all, God will never forget anyone who does this unseen work. "All this is from God who reconciled us to himself through Christ and gave us the ministry of reconciliation" (2 Corinthians 5:18).

> When we are unseen, it is not a punishment; it is an invitation to know our Savior more.

God was showing me that He had called me to play the role of "Elmer" in the early days of this medical work in China. When we are unseen, it is not a punishment; it is an invitation to know our Savior more and to learn the importance of flexibility and playing new roles in His body. It was also an honor for me to become a mom to more children. Staying home was about provision for my children, who needed me physically present.

After a couple of years, Erica and her husband, Matt, answered the call to adopt a child from China. When their son Benjamin came home, Erica realized she needed to let go of her role in leading these medical mission trips and fulfill the duties that this new role of being an adoptive mom now required. But just as God does not forget any of His children, God did not forget Erica and her desire to do international medicine in a Spanish-speaking country. In time, God would lead Erica to open Casa

Materna, a midwifery clinic in Guatemala, founded to stem the tide of maternal and infant deaths in that region. This clinic is where a little boy named Thiago would be born several years later, marking a divine call for us to reassemble for a new kingdom assignment.

ASSEMBLY REQUIRED

To hear a symphony orchestra in harmonized performance, or see the synchronized movements of birds in flight, or taste the collaborative work from a honeybee hive is to witness a kind of glory that only comes through an assembly. Musical notes become songs, living cells form living beings, stones become homes, and people find belonging through assembling. The incredible power, efficiency, and varietal beauty found in coordinated unity cannot be achieved by any one thing alone.

Assembling is something more intentional and coordinated than gathering. You can gather puzzle pieces into one big pile, but assembling them requires making connections in particular ways to reveal a bigger picture.

I am a natural gatherer, just like my father. I was brought up to believe there is always room for more. "The more, the merrier; just add a little water to the soup." Adherence to this family philosophy led to me having a huge wedding. And it was at my wedding that God showed me the difference between a gathering and an assembly. The ceremony was a gathering of several hundred guests who had come together to witness the assembling of Scott and me. Planning the seating chart for the reception is an example of assembling, requiring more mindfulness than gathering. I wanted the guests seated based on relationships and shared interests. The seating chart proved quite challenging for me, having so many people from faraway places and different walks of life.

For instance, I chose to seat a new friend, Sarah Gesiriech, a legislative policy expert working for President George W. Bush, with a couple of teenage girls who had been adopted from Russia. Their lives were vastly different. But remembering that Sarah was an adoptee and had nieces adopted from Russia, I put them at the same table, hoping for an exciting conversation.

As I had hoped, the Russian adoption connection did come up during the dinner. Not only this, but God would reveal that His providence was at work in their table assembly in far more extraordinary ways than I could have ever asked or imagined. It turns out that these teen girls were not only from the same region in Siberia as Sarah's nieces, but they were from the same town, the same orphanage, and even had grown up in the same "family" group in the institution. These girls had been raised like older sisters to Sarah's nieces in the orphanage. Apparently, her nieces had even mentioned them by name when they came to the US, praying that they would someday find adoptive families of their own. These discoveries left everyone at the table dumbfounded.

God was using the occasion of my wedding to close some circles for these little girls, answering their prayers and giving them a chance to see His faithfulness in the here and now. In learning about what had taken place among these guests at my wedding reception, I was astonished afresh by how the Creator of the Universe still deeply cares and is mindful of the needs of every single person on earth. "What is man that you are mindful of him, or the son of man that you care for him?" (Psalm 8:3–4 ESV).

This miraculous experience also taught me the difference between a human-orchestrated gathering and a divine assembly. Through it, I became more acquainted with the Lord as a Master Mosaicist who fits fragmented parts together to bring greater wholeness into being and reveal His love. Colossians 1:19–20 from *The Message* reads:

> So spacious is he, so expansive, that everything of God finds its proper place in him without crowding. Not only that, but all the broken and dislocated pieces of the universe—people and things, animals and atoms—get properly fixed and fit together in vibrant harmonies.

Living Puzzle Pieces

Tikkun olam is a Hebrew term that refers to how man and God work together to "repair the world." It is usually mentioned in the context of healing and assembling. Having joined the Lord in His work of assembling,

I could now see how I had gotten to play a small part in the grander healing and reconciling ministry of *tikkun olam*.

Like living puzzle pieces, we become shaped through our experiences in a way that makes us ready to be fitted together at the right time with the other pieces in God's grander puzzle of the universe. Just as puzzle pieces are individually shaped and joined together as one piece fills the space that another piece lacks, I now understood that this is how God works with His people. The placement of each member of a human assembly matters to God. And although some parts may seem to have more prominent roles, each has equal value to a picture's wholeness. If you've ever spent time assembling a puzzle, you know that every piece matters to its completion.

> Every assignment of God is ultimately a team project, whether we realize it or not.

We have all had the experience of something essential to an endeavor going missing. We often do not recognize its value until it is not there. It is also this way with people. Surely, we have all felt like the forgotten piece at some point or seen how the importance of one member is disregarded until their absence proves detrimental to the group.

Every assignment of God is ultimately a team project, whether we realize it or not. Spiritually speaking, the Lord is not big on solo careers. It is foolish to think our successes have come about independently from others. The biblical record of the life of Judah's King Uzziah is a tragic account of what can happen when ego leads someone to consider themselves or their abilities more crucial to the assembly than that of its other members. After God gave him tremendous success, King Uzziah forgot the importance of other people's contributions to the work. His success fueled his ego, and his pride led him to overstep the boundaries God had placed between his work and the work of his fellows.

Essentially, Uzziah did not stay in his lane. When King Uzziah walked into the temple and started doing the priests' job, God struck him with a disease that would last the rest of his life. This story reveals how displeasing it is to God when the work of others is dishonored or disregarded (2 Chronicles 26). "Do nothing out of selfish ambition or vain conceit. Rather, in humility, value others above yourselves, not looking to your own interests but each of you to the interests of others" (Philippians 2:3–4).

THE POWER OF ASSEMBLY

By practicing to ASSEMBLE, we learn about our unique gifts and callings and how to honor other people's skills and anointings. God intentionally created us to be different. We do not need what we already have, but that which we have not. Flowers need pollinators such as bees and hummingbirds. Without flowers, the hummingbird cannot feed, and bees cannot make honey; without pollinators, flowers cannot bear fruit. As we consider what we are, we should also consider what we are not and, therefore, need. By doing this, we will more naturally honor the Lord by respecting the roles of those who are different from us in our assemblies.

The work of Christ not only made a way for the Holy Spirit to unite the people of God but also to keep them from trespassing over the lines separating where one person's work ends and another's begins. Being unified with others does not mean we have the right to impose ourselves on them, usurp their roles, or micromanage the work God has given to them. If we think, *I can do that person's job better than they can*, it is likely we have forgotten that what comes naturally to us is only by the grace of God. It is far better to give encouragement and room for another person's development than to step in and arrogantly take over their rightful role, thinking we are more equipped. Plus, it often results in failure and loss of relationships.

OUR CHANGING ASSEMBLIES

When God wants to do something new in our lives, He will often change the composition of our communities. From childhood friendships to those in adulthood, from one job to another or one town to the next, God moves us along, brings new people into our stories, and removes others for

His purposes. We ought to remember that, in every change, God always has our best interest in mind and will give us the grace we need to overcome the fear associated with these changes. Many of our experiences of belonging are temporary in this life. Eventually, every earthly community is made smaller through loss or death or more extensive through marriage, birth, or friendship. It is natural to set up our belonging to a group as an idol or identity. It is also easy to get so tied to a specific role in a group that we cling to it and don't give room for healthy change. For these reasons, God will bring change into our lives and communities, reminding us that we belong to Him first.

The Lord is also notorious for giving us just enough grace to fulfill a particular calling for a limited time in a specific assembly, like on a sports team, a class project, or under one job title. God's Word promises His grace will be sufficient, but it is worth noting that "sufficient" means "just enough." Transitioning from one assembly into another will likely require letting go of an old identity before a new one can fully come into being. When the grace to remain begins to wane, this may be God's signal that it's time to let go.

> There is a time for everything and a season for every activity under the heavens: . . . a time to plant and a time to uproot . . . a time to tear down and a time to build . . . a time to scatter stones and gather them, a time to embrace and a time to refrain from embracing . . . to tear and to mend, to be silent and to speak. (Ecclesiastes 3:1–7)

Changes in our community and our roles can serve as catalysts to experiencing new aspects of God's character. But sometimes, these transitions require us to pass our mantles to those who have shown themselves faithful and able to take on the work. Carrying multiple mantles of authority can overburden us and keep us from moving freely into our new callings. Perhaps we should consider yet another layer of the Spirit's wisdom regarding the passing of our mantles of authority through the words spoken by John the Baptist: "He who has two coats, let him give one coat to him who has none" (Luke 3:11).

ASSEMBLE

MAKING *ALIYAH*

About seven years after moving in next door, our friends, Hila and Amir, decided it was time to move back to Israel. They were embarking on what is known as "Aliyah," which means "the ascent" and refers to the return of Jews to the land of Israel. Hila had grown up in Israel; her parents had made Aliyah from South America. Amir grew up in Mexico and was the first in his family to be making Aliyah. Both Hila and Amir spoke fluent English, and of course, Spanish and Hebrew were their heart languages based on where they grew up. And though we could not have predicted when we first became friends, it would be this great variety of languages, plus the many different talents, relationships, and experiences, that would make it possible for us to accomplish the work we would later be called to do together in Israel.

Before their departure, Amir and his family stayed with us for a few days. On one of those evenings together, I asked what they wanted to take back with them to Israel from their time here in the States. Amir said he and Hila had already discussed this very thing. "We want to take back a spirit of charity that we learned here, specifically from your family and Erica's." Amir referenced how influential his trips to China with Scott were and how Hila's trip to Guatemala with Erica had been so important. The rest of the evening, we discussed their hopes of setting up a charitable organization in Israel to help poor children from other nations who needed surgery.

On Amir's final evening with us, Erica came to visit and mentioned to us that a baby boy named Thiago had just been born at the midwifery clinic in Guatemala with an encephalocele, a skull defect causing his brain to protrude onto his face. She explained that no medical facility or surgical team in his home country could perform the surgeries he needed.

> It would take a great deal of providence to bring such a surgery together in such a short time.

"Perhaps this will be our first patient," Amir said, explaining that this kind of surgery would ideally be performed when the child is around one year of age. "And if we do this, you both must come to Israel," Amir told Erica and me.

I remember thinking it would take a great deal of providence to bring such a surgery together in such a short time through a foundation that did not yet exist. Amir had not even started his job, nor did he yet live in Israel. Still, we prayed together and committed it all to the Lord.

Within six months, a donor from Mexico came forward to fund Thiago's surgery. Hila and Amir had launched their new organization called KIBS—Kids International Brain and Spinal Cord Surgery. Amir had become the head of the pediatric neurosurgical unit at Schneider's Children's Medical Center in Israel. He was also granted permission to use the facility and receive help from the other doctors on staff to do the surgery. So, Erica organized her travel to escort Thiago and his parents from Guatemala to Israel. I bought a plane ticket to meet them in Tel Aviv.

Thiago's surgery would be the primary purpose of our trip to Israel. As a non-medical person, I felt like the trip's least essential member. Nevertheless, the Lord made it clear I was to go, and I felt very wanted by the other members of the team.

Common Language

The fact that Erica, Hila, and Amir all spoke Spanish made this family's transition from Guatemala far more comfortable. Amir invited Erica and me to put on hospital scrubs and join him in the operating room for Thiago's surgeries.

I can't believe it. I never told anyone except Scott that I had dreamt of this, I thought in amazement. I had even confessed my jealousy when Scott had been given the incredible opportunity to watch Amir operate in China because I had so wanted to experience something like that. And being present in the operating room proved an even greater marvel than I could have imagined. To see the way my dear friend Amir and his colleagues operated so meticulously and caringly on this beautiful baby boy was beyond my wildest dreams.

Amir said that he had never had so many surgeons volunteer to work on one patient before. The charitable nature of the case had brought them all together, Arab, Jew, and Christian alike. The common language spoken among the doctors in the operating room was Hebrew, but among the nurses, it was Russian. Still, it was the shared language of "truth in love" that was spoken throughout the surgery, as each person was fulfilling their unique role in this joint task.

> Speaking the truth in love, we will grow to become in every respect the mature body of him who is the head, that is, Christ. From him the whole body, joined and held together by every supporting ligament, grows and builds itself up in love, as each part does its work. (Ephesians 4:15–16)

I witnessed the perfect balance of art, science, and math, as God had ordained this assembly for His multilayered purposes and by His higher heavenly ways. When I realized I could understand the nurses speaking Russian, I was reminded that I was meant to be present. I was also beginning to realize that God has new and beautiful things to reveal to us every day. We just need the spiritual eyes to perceive them. On this particular day, God was choosing to highlight the miraculous nature of a holy assembly where every member is committed to doing their part generously, joyfully, and humbly and to consider the work of others just as necessary as their own.

Walking in the Blessing

After nearly seven hours into the eight-hour surgery, when Amir had completed his part and turned the rest of the work over to the maxillofacial and plastic surgeons, he invited Erica and me to come with him to meet the director of the hospital. Amir told us how instrumental we had been in his foundation getting started and the importance of this first surgical case to its future work. But, because Erica had promised Thiago's parents she would stay until the end of the surgery, I agreed to represent us both at the meeting with Amir's boss.

"It would be my honor," I told Amir. But as a non-medical observer, I worried I would give myself away as a nonessential member of this extraordinary team. However, not far into the conversation, God would show me that I was not insignificant at all. He had pre-ordained steps for me to walk in for the blessing of my friend Amir.

After shaking hands with the hospital's CEO, I asked him how he had come to live and work in Israel. He shared how he had made Aliyah from his home country of Lithuania. I responded to his words excitedly, telling him, "My father's family line is from Lithuania; Jews, from Kaunas."

"Kaunas?! I'm from Kaunas!" he said, with his face now wearing an enormous grin.

He continued, "I was recently awarded the keys to the city of Kaunas; it's our city's highest honor." Undoubtedly, God wanted this proud part of his life to be brought to the forefront straightaway. Like the confluence of the two rivers that feed the city of Kaunas, which means beautiful, God had brought us together as a beautiful display of His providence. By the time our meeting with Amir's boss had ended, pure joy had taken the place of his exhaustion from surgery.

As we left the meeting and walked down the hallway, Amir expressed gratitude for my helpful interactions with his boss and the Russian OR nurses. I found this ironic, almost comical, as I compared my role to his and joked, "It wasn't like I was performing brain surgery or something." Nonetheless, my brilliant friend, who had just performed a complicated skull and brain surgery, was sincerely thanking me for my relational contributions. My interactions with his colleagues had touched on several of his hopes in that season of his life. Because Amir had been called to an entirely new land, new community, and new assembly, he needed to quickly build trust with his coworkers to perform life-saving surgeries on children; thus, he longed for cohesion. Thiago's surgery had brought a hoped-for cohesion that would bear more fruit in these relationships over time.

THE WHEELWORK

When considering the various assemblies of our lives, I find it helpful to picture each of my life assemblies as its own wheel. I envision the names of the members of the assembly listed around the rim of its wheel. The spokes represent the pathways upon which the assembly members move as they work together. The wheel's hub represents the central purpose around which all have gathered for a particular work. Just as the spokes of a wheel get closer to one another as they move toward the wheel's hub, the assembled members grow closer together as they work toward a common purpose.

Every assembly gathers around something, a central point that keeps its members connected and aligned. Ask any child what is most important to their parents, and you will likely discover the hubs of their family wheels. Whether it's a person, a common interest, a gift, an event, or a competency, it is critical to remember that none of these things can ever prove themselves capable of bearing the heavy burden of being the family's central focus in an ongoing manner.

When our wheel's hub is faulty, or if all its members are not "bought-in" on the common purpose, a peripheral agenda can easily usurp the vision and cause the wheel to break. In these cases, the wheelwork begins to fall apart; the members become disassembled, and the work ceases and may never be accomplished. But when God's purpose for a group is kept at the center, and its members remain committed to it until the job is complete, true peace and a sense of belonging can continue to reside among its members, and the project can prosper.

If the wheels of our work do fall apart, God may call for them to be restored or rebuilt rightly. We see this when God called for the rebuilding of Jerusalem after its destruction. He first called the people to rebuild the wheel's hub, the temple, representing the worship place of the Lord's Holy Presence. This gave the Israelites a common focal point for worshiping the Lord as their central purpose. After the temple was rebuilt, the Lord called Nehemiah to rebuild Jerusalem's rim and spokes, represented by the city's walls and gates.

The Wheels of Gilgal and Golgotha

Based on how the wheels of work and worship are mentioned in the Old Testament, we also see that wheels often signify God's spiritual operations in the world and the movements that come through His assembled people. Interestingly, Gilgal, which means wheel in Hebrew, was not only the name of the location where the Israelites began their work in the promised land and the place where God rolled away the reproach of their sins, but it was also where they would reassemble before each new endeavor God called them to do (Joshua 5:9).

Even the location of Jesus's crucifixion at Golgotha is a reference to Gilgal as the ultimate wheel.[1] The word Golgotha can be understood in Hebrew not only as "the place of the skull" but also as "going to the wheel" or even where "one cycle ends, and a new one begins." Just like Gilgal was a place for the Israelites to gather for work and worship, the cross is where Christian believers are meant to ASSEMBLE in a spiritual sense for the work of God's kingdom on earth. We cannot fully fathom the power that is possible when the body of Christ comes together in the Spirit realm. The modern-day places of the wheelwork of worship are wherever believers come together to accomplish God's purposes; it is wherever the Holy Spirit is moving in the assembly. "When two or three gather in my name, there I am with them" (Matthew 18:20).

The word wheel(s) mentioned in Scripture should evoke our understanding of the active movement of the Holy Spirit, both in heaven and on earth. "When the cherubim stopped, the wheels stopped. When they flew upward, the wheels rose up, for the spirit of the living beings was in the wheels." (Ezekiel 10:17 NLT). In Daniel 7:9, we read that "thrones were set in place, and the Ancient of Days took his seat. . . . His throne was flaming with fire, and its wheels were all ablaze."

God has called us to do this wheelwork and provided us with *how* to do it. The twelve faith practices from *The Way of Becoming* were mined directly from Scripture. Hence, they are a gift from God for us to know how to operate upon these biblical wheels of work and worship. Engaging in these practices invokes the movements and operations of the Holy Spirit in and through our lives. In reference to the ancient wheelworks of worship, we refer to the movements we experience in our own BECOMING stories as Cycles of Grace.

In addition to providing *the how* the Lord also gives us *the what* and *the why* of His ultimate purposes and vision for His children. Like in the days of Nehemiah when Jerusalem was rebuilt, we are being called to another kind of building project today. But this will not be a city built by human hands, but rather a spiritual one built by the power of God operating through His people by their actions of faith and made out of living stone.

> I saw the Holy City, the new Jerusalem, coming down out of heaven from God, prepared as a bride beautifully dressed for her husband. And I heard a loud voice from the throne saying, "Look! God's dwelling place is now among the people, and he will dwell with them. They will be his people, and God himself will be with them and be their God. 'He will wipe every tear from their eyes. There will be no more death' or mourning or crying or pain, for the old order of things has passed away. . . . To the thirsty I will give water without cost from the spring of the water of life. Those who are victorious will inherit all this, and I will be their God and they will be my children."
> (Revelation 21:2–4, 6b–7)

Each of the assemblies God calls us to in this life is somehow part of the preparation for this more significant work. God has promised to complete the transformational work in each of us so that all of us can become one united, satisfied people, to dwell with Him and with one another forever. We should remember that in doing the work to which we have each been called in our little corners of the world, we are also participating in this more extensive work. It is the ultimate wheel where all the spiritual wheelworks are assembled together.

SWEET BELONGING

Once Thiago was stable and on a clear path to recovery, God reassembled a group of us around a new purpose. The healing of Thiago was the hub of the first wheel, and exploring the land of Israel would be the second. God was seeing to it that our hearts' desire to experience the Bible come alive in the land of milk and honey and walk the Jerusalem footprint would be met. Always having in the back of my mind how the physical Jerusalem speaks as a type and foreshadowing of the more perfect spiritual New Jerusalem, we had much to glean from our pilgrimage here.

Jeff Cuozzo, an old friend of both Scott and mine, came from England to be our guide. With the addition of Jeff and his unique understanding and connections to the Holy Land, we reassembled for a new assignment to explore the wonders of Israel. When I realized that Thiago's name was a translation of the name Jacob, like the Jacob of the Bible whose name God changed to *Israel*, I realized God was speaking to me about the dual purposes of our trip. Not only had the Lord wished to heal Thiago and put this purpose at the center of our first assembly, but He also desired to answer many of my spiritual questions and longings by placing *Israel* at the center of our next one. Upon this new wheel, we would move about in this land of promise and grow increasingly joyful by the wonderment of it all. God had already revealed Himself to me in Israel as the Divine Healer, God of Wonders, and the Great Assembler, but now He would reveal Himself as even more.

After we had a chance to tour and see many sites in the land, I joked about how we had not seen any honey at all for sale in this supposed "land of milk and honey." I had been hoping to bring some honey home as gifts. And it seems God had known this hope of mine and perhaps even heard my joke as an ASK. Just as we started moving on to our next site-seeing location, we happened upon a vendor selling only jars of honey with sections of the honeycomb floating within. He had not been there when we arrived, but here he was as we departed. We could not believe it; it felt providential!

When we returned to where we were staying, on the shores of the Sea of Galilee, I researched the honey we had just purchased on the Golan Heights. The timing of the vendor's appearance was strangely perfect, which made me even more curious about it and its meaning. I would soon come to find out that honey from this location is considered the most potent on earth because it is produced by border-crossing bees. This location was not far from the very high Mount Hermon, where Syria, Israel, and Lebanon come together and where many believe the transfiguration of Jesus took place (Mark 9). Unaware of these man-made borders, that is, country boundaries, the bees naturally mix the nectar from all the different flowers unique to each country, thus making it so potent. I realized that God was speaking to me about the work we had done by crossing international borders and bringing our gifts together.

As our purposes in Israel were coming to completion, we began to see just how all that we had accomplished by God's grace had required the passage of a great deal of time, trusting and waiting, as well as the creative contributions of us all, so that this divine assembly could produce something as sweet as honey for our souls. Like the tying of a bow, God revealed an extraordinary thing about the place where we had found this honey, called the Golan Heights. Golan means an entire circuit, a closed circle, or a completed revolution. Not only had God brought us together from distant lands to be part of a sacred assembly, but together, we had Cycled in Grace.

BLESSINGS OF ASSEMBLY

We were created for relationships. Even though human relationships can be messy and the work they require is ongoing, it is through assembling with others that the most beautiful works and sweetest things in creation are produced. We can experience the fullness of God if we are willing to walk humbly by faith and remain curious enough to glean from others while respecting their unique roles. Although there are no perfect human assemblies, God has supplied us with glorious and near-perfect examples in His creation that reveal the main principles of a divine assembly.

We can learn a lot about the principles of assembling by observing nature. The schooling patterns of fish and the flight patterns of birds provide a beautiful picture of what is possible in coordinated movement. When thousands of starlings collectively transform in flight from one shape to another as a harmonized whole, it's called a murmuration. This flying phenomenon is utterly mesmerizing and reveals the main principles found in any divine assembly, which are *unification*, *differentiation*, and *coordination* with one's neighbors. In other words, stay together, stay in your lane, and stay flexible.

Scientists used to think starlings had telepathic abilities, allowing them to coordinate their movements in this way. However, additional research has revealed that their power has nothing to do with telepathy and everything to do with each one being mindful of its neighbors.[2] The studies found that because each bird pays close attention to the movements of its six or seven immediate neighbors, the whole assembly continues moving in perfect cohesion. Individual birds do not need to be aware of a single leader nor be able to view the other side of the murmuration. The stunningly fast responses of each creature to the movements of their neighbors are what produce the synchronized perfection witnessed by those on the ground. It would only take a few starlings to respond slowly to the signals of their neighbors in flight for the murmuration's cohesion to lapse or even be lost altogether. This aerial phenomenon provides an excellent framework for human assembling, reminding us to be mindful of our neighbors—those closest to us.

Perhaps that is also why Scripture instructs us to consider and apply the lessons taught by fish and birds.

> "But ask the animals, and they will teach you, or the birds in the sky, and they will tell you . . . or let the fish in the sea inform you. Which of all these does not know that the hand of the Lord has done this?" (Job 12:7, 9)

Just as with the starlings, coordination is essential for us to ASSEMBLE. Not only does it require flexibility, but also mutual respect and trust in God's timing and purposes.

Building the Honeycomb

We see how these principles of a well-ordered assembly are displayed through the collective work of a honeybee hive and its production of overflowing golden abundance. Even though each honeybee produces a mere teaspoon of honey in its entire lifetime, the unity and coordination of the colony are what bring about its sweet abundance. Each bee plays the part for which it was created, and the collective whole makes the honey flow.

God's promise to bring His people into the land flowing with milk and honey is about the blessings of assembling together. Milk can only come forth after the joining together of male and female and the birthing of offspring, and honey comes only after assembling an entire community dedicated to their individual tasks of building and creative production.

The construction of the honeycomb, with its geometrical perfection, speaks directly to the principles of assembly: *unification, differentiation,* and *coordination,* whereas the honey itself speaks to the blessings of abiding in all faith practices, including the practice to ASSEMBLE. Therefore, there can be no honey without the colony first doing the coordinated and united work of building the honeycomb. The construction of a honeycomb requires the coordinated unity of the bees. The making of their individual circular cells, separated by waxy borders, speaks to the differentiation in their work.[3]

> Our assemblies produce the good God intends.

The heat and surface tension brought to bear on the cell's waxy borders by its six neighboring cells is what transforms the comb from a collection of circles into the hexagonal geometrical masterpiece for which the honeycomb is known. What is required of each honeybee is to prepare its vessel for holding the honey, doing just what God has already empowered it to do. So, too, are we called to work at what God has already empowered us to do. As we continue to Cycle in Grace personally, while those in our assemblies also cycle—doing the wheelwork—then as each assembly continues in this way adjacent to one another, like many bees spinning beside another, we CREATE a honey-like abundance, too. Doing the human version of this wheelwork, while our neighbors do the same, we will all grow together so our assemblies can produce the good that God intends.

Just like with the bees and their honey, abundance can only come through us if we act as a coordinated and united body made up of differentiated parts. God is ever rebuilding us individually, assembling the different parts of our unique stories so that we can come together regularly with others to do the collaborative building work of His kingdom. In time, we are revealed as integrated people able to share our unique stories, which comprise the *all* story of God.

From Genesis to Revelation, the Lord calls His people to ASSEMBLE for His divine purposes. He calls them forth, whistles them in, and empowers them to come together based on their needs and anointings. "I will whistle for them and gather them in, for I have redeemed them" (Zechariah 10:8 ESV). This is exactly what He did for us in Israel.

When God calls an individual into a collective, the reason may seem singular or even random to the one being called. But, in time, God's purposes are revealed as multifaceted and highly coordinated. His ways of assembly are beyond our understanding. "'For my thoughts are not your thoughts, neither are your ways my ways,' declares the LORD. 'As the heavens are higher than the earth, so my ways are higher than your ways and my thoughts than your thoughts'" (Isaiah 55:8–9).

Our God is a God of the long view, but humans are short-sighted by nature. He sees the whole story from beginning to end, but we only see it in part. In faithfulness, nothing is wasted. Therefore, it is only when a work is finished that we marvel at how His providential hand had been weaving many threads to bring about the glory in assembly. "But when completeness comes, what is in part disappears" (1 Corinthians 13:10).

Nevertheless, when we find ourselves in the messy middle places of life, where our understandings are limited, let us consciously practice assembling together. Because in the assembly, the lonely find belonging, the hungry are filled, the thirsty are quenched, and we all receive a foretaste of His unimaginable beauty, power, and love. "Let us not neglect our meeting together, as some people do, but encourage one another, especially now that the day of his return is drawing near" (Hebrews 10:25 NLT).

> When our understandings are limited, let us consciously practice assembling together.

YOUR BECOMING STORY: ASSEMBLE

Consider your assemblies, past and present. What was their purpose (hub), who was in them (spokes), how did you operate together (wheelwork), and what was accomplished or produced (honey)? How did the principles of *unification*, *differentiation*, and *coordination* play a part in each success? What went well, and what would you do differently in light of these principles? Which assembly principle comes most naturally to you? Are you more naturally gifted as a gatherer—drawn to togetherness, or as a differentiator—keeping boundaries, or as a coordinator—remaining flexible to the movements of those around you? Consider the people closest to you in light of these principles of assembly. How are you better together as a result?

Consider also how the absence of a part, person, or idea from an assembly proved detrimental to you or a group. Have you ever felt like the forgotten piece? How might God be asking you to come together with other believers for His kingdom work in this season of your life? What might God be asking you to do by faith so that the broken-down walls of your life can be rebuilt?

Ask God to show you how to experience more excellent order, blessing, and joy in your future assemblies. Also, if you have ever wondered if your small contributions matter, I invite you to consider that a single bee can only create a single teaspoon of honey in its lifetime. Only through an assembly are its contributions magnified and the sweet glory made in abundance.

"Longing for the Promised Land"

Where, O Lord, is that
Land of Your Promise,
The one flowing with milk
And with honey?

Broken and distant,
Covered in fragments,
We buzz like honeybees,
But make nothing.

We ache to belong,
And partake of the good,
Not only to blossom,
But bear fruit.

We give of our wombs,
Yet labor in vain,
Our creative
Endeavors upended.

Forty years in the desert,
'Tis idols and fear.
Lord, teach us
To cycle in grace.

To BECOME as You are,
We return to Your Name,
And bask in the light
Of Your face.

Roll away the reproach,
We've carried along.
Pour oil down upon us at Gilgal.

When we're filled up again,
We'll go out from this place,
To bind up the hearts
Of the wounded.

We'll join Your assembly,
With joy of heart.
In honeypots and wine vats,
We'll present you.[4]

12

ABIDE

Sacred Rhythms and Cycles of Grace

Nothing is more exhilarating than having God's power flow through us. Nothing this world can offer compares to it. Once we have tasted the fruit of God's goodness and witnessed His glory up close and personal, our hearts long for it to continue. The Scriptures teach that abiding leads to more fruit-bearing, a fullness of joy, and receiving answers to our prayers (John 15:5–11). Therefore, understanding what it means to ABIDE is very important.

Abiding, however, can be a challenging concept to understand and even more difficult to practice. By definition, ABIDE means to stay, remain, live, continue, rest, or dwell. Yet these words seem counter to ideals central to faith, like moving, walking, becoming, and transforming. How are we supposed to stay and move at the same time? How do we dwell and walk simultaneously?

I have decided that abiding is best understood using oxymoronic phrases like remain dynamic, stay moving, keep walking, and continue transforming. Basically, "pat your head and rub your tummy."

GOD'S GLORY SHOW

I have seen the glory of abiding realized through the natural wonder of Murchison Falls. Located in Uganda, Africa, near the source of the Nile

River, Murchison Falls has much to teach us about how our souls can ABIDE in the resplendent glory of God's free-flowing grace. It is also an image that can help us understand why the life of Christ tends to flow more powerfully through some than others.

The Nile River's width varies significantly as it makes its way up the African continent, extremely wide at some points and exceptionally narrow at others. In the broader places, it flows slowly, even lake-like in its stillness. I had pictured the Nile this way growing up based on the story of baby Moses gently floating in a basket among the bulrushes where Pharoah's daughter found him (Exodus 2:5–10). This, however, was not my experience in adulthood when I had the chance to whitewater raft it. The Nile is no lazy river! At some points, it is extraordinarily powerful. Its rapids are some of the wildest in the world!

The water's power reaches its apex at Murchison Falls, the Nile's narrowest point. Because the Nile's waters span several miles across at some points, funneling such a large volume of water through a 24-foot-wide opening creates the magnificent display of power that *is* Murchison Falls. Here, the water comes alive, shooting in all directions: erupting like a geyser, down-pouring as a waterfall, and rushing onward as a mighty river.

It is clear from this image that the smaller the conduit through which the water flows, the more powerful and alive the water becomes. This kind of power, refreshment, and glory, imaged through Murchison Falls, can be reflected through our stories, as well. However, this requires staying small and abiding close to our Source.

After Saul's miraculous encounter with the risen Christ on the road to Damascus, he is referred to as Paul, meaning small. Being called small in this context would prove to be a prophetic word, foretelling the extraordinary power of how the waters of God's Word would flow through him. Paul, the apostle, would become one of the most prolific writers of the most-read books in human history. He is responsible for scribing more books of the New Testament than anyone else. Paul's life became like Murchison Falls.

As I stood above the waterfalls, I noticed that the natural gateway through which the water flowed was flanked by two enormous rock walls. These rock walls play a crucial role in creating the extravagant water show of Murchison Falls. I perceived these two rock walls as images of our stones of belief in God, the Father, and God, the Son. Together, they form the narrow gate through which every soul must pass to experience the Spirit's cleansing and abundance and through which God's power flows (John 9:9–10). "Enter through the narrow gate . . . small is the gate and narrow the road that leads to life. . . ." (Matthew 7:13–14).

If we become small enough and remain open enough, knowing God holds us securely enough, our lives can become part of the glory show of God. By abiding by these ways of faith, we become conduits of the Spirit's powerful flow of grace.

BECOMING THE NILE

In considering the uniqueness of the Nile, I began to see the river itself as an extended metaphor for our BECOMING journeys in Christ. Not only is the Nile the world's longest and most comprehensive fresh-water delivery system, spanning nearly the entire African continent, but it is also one of the few rivers that flows south to north and travels through thousands of miles of desert.[1] This is fitting in light of how our BECOMING journeys in Christ require us to move against the natural flow of the world, pass through desert places, and dispense the waters of life as we go along.

Just as the Nile's journey begins in Uganda, with its waters sourced from Lake Victoria, meaning victory, our new life flows out from our belief in Christ's victory over sin and death. Egypt is where the Nile's journey concludes, and it is also the place from which the Israelites were rescued after their seventy years in captivity. The Nile expresses the call on every transformed believer to bring the freshwaters of the gospel back to the places where they were once held captive. In light of this and the potential call on my life to go back and minister in the areas where I had been broken and from which I had been freed, I struggled to believe God would ask this of me. *Why would He send me back to the same unsafe places where He rescued me?* I wondered.

Go in Shalom

God called Moses to go back to Egypt after he had completed his own wilderness journey so that he could lead others out of *their* captivity and show them the way in the desert. This was the message of the Nile and God's message to me. Just like when Moses asked his father-in-law, Jethro, for permission to return to his brothers in Egypt and Jethro told Moses to go in *shalom*, which means in the wholeness you have become, God was calling me to return to the places of my breaking, not as I was but as I had become (Ex. 4:18).

When we consider the word shalom, ideas of being made complete or having our peace restored should come to mind. Shalom is a process of adding and subtracting whatever is necessary to become whole and holy.[2]

Shalom is a beautifully layered, pictographic Hebrew word that references the journey we must all take in God. That journey begins at the place of our breaking (*shin*), meaning cut to pieces or tooth, and is imaged by the letter "s" in shalom. Next, we all must be led by the Good Shepherd (*lamed*), meaning shepherd's staff, imaged by the letter "l" in shalom—to the point at which our disconnected parts become reconnected (*vav*), meaning nail or tent peg, and imaged by the silent letter "v" in shalom. Having been reconciled and made ready to flow with the waters of God's Word, our lives are able to deliver the flow of grace, ministered in the hard places (*mem*), meaning water or chaos, and imaged by the final letter "m" in shalom.[3] In short, we get broken, but God makes us whole; we are filled up to be poured out.

Just as Moses' wilderness journey had changed him, mine had changed me. God was not sending me back in the same state of brokenness but more whole in Him. The irony of ironies is that the Lord would affirm this call for me to enter back into places of my former pain by sending my daughter Annika and me on a trip to the actual land of Egypt! This would be my first trip back to the African continent since experiencing my first miscarriage in Uganda twenty years earlier.

It would also be the first international teaching of the BECOMING tools. While in Cairo, we visited the garbage slums where Mama Maggie's

Foundation, Stephen's Children, ministers to the poor living around *Mokattam* Mountain, which fittingly means Fragment Mountain.

I could hardly believe that God had taken me back to the continent of my breaking, nor that I would be sharing the tools of my healing with leaders who minister to the poor and needy in a place called fragments. Yet, I was not going back dressed in the same old garments of sorrow, but instead in new, more becoming vestments of confident beliefs, and able to flow in my gifts as a teacher of God's Word. I marveled, thinking this had to be the most elaborate show-and-tell I had ever experienced with God.

> The call on our lives is to become rivers of living water that bring refreshment and life back to the places of our former captivity.

The call on our lives is to become rivers of living water that deliver refreshing hope to the places of our former captivity. In this, we become part of the fulfillment of the promise given to those who cry out to the Lord for help. "I will open up rivers for them on the high plateaus. I will give them fountains of water in the valleys. I will fill the desert with pools of water. Rivers fed by springs will flow across the parched ground" (Isaiah 41:18 NLT).

LIFE RHYTHMS

God gives us instructions for engaging in the proper rhythms of abiding. These sacred rhythms are found all throughout creation. The earth's orbital patterns teach us about abiding by daily, weekly, seasonal, and annual rhythms. This can be seen by how it spins on its axis, creating day and night, rotates around the sun, giving rise to the seasons, and even how its revolutions mark the years. Just as the world spins upon the celestial wheels in relation to the sun, our lives are meant to move in relation to God.

As the moon reflects the sun's light, we are meant to reflect Christ's light so that those in darkness can know the Source of all light. I used this analogy of the sun and the moon to teach my children the importance of looking to God and not other people or themselves as their Source. And

I am glad I did because when I found myself struggling with my own limitations, my son, Cole, reminded me about this truth, saying, "Mom, it seems unfair to compare a star and a rock. It's like demanding a rock give off enough light and warmth to make the flowers grow."

The need to be restored, refilled, reassembled, resupplied, renovated, renewed, rescued, or revived indicates that it is time to return to God for these things. These needs are not indicators that we have done something wrong or sinful, but instead that we need more. As believers, we should retreat into God for rest, healing, washing, and wisdom to receive provision and prepare for the days ahead. We must consider the need for a night's rest after a day of work, a day's rest after a week of work, and even a season of sabbatical to replenish our souls after long periods of busyness. "For I have satiated the weary soul, and I have replenished every sorrowful soul," says the Lord (Jeremiah 31:25 KJV).

Experiencing times of emptiness, desolation, or exhaustion does not mean we have stopped abiding. It means we need to get filled up before we can pour out again. It can be pride, fear, or even greed that keeps us from resting from our labors. But sometimes, it is simply that we misunderstand God's ways of abiding. We should stop thinking of ourselves as self-fueling creatures. Despising our need to return for more is like hating a car for needing to be filled up, charged, or serviced.

JESUS ABIDED

Jesus modeled the way of abiding through His humility in relation to His heavenly Father. Jesus said, "Very truly I tell you, the Son can do nothing by himself; he can do only what he sees his Father doing, because whatever the Father does the Son also does" (John 5:19). Jesus chose intentional times to get away from the crowds to be alone and communicate with His Father; He even left His disciples regularly to be alone with His heavenly Father in prayer. "Very early in the morning, while it was still dark, Jesus got up, left the house, and went off to a solitary place, where he prayed" (Mark 1:35).

Jesus abided in healthy rhythms. He was mindful of the times and seasons and the proper balance of work and rest, coming and going, retreating and representing. As followers of Christ, we are meant to engage in similar rhythms. "Whoever claims to live in him must live as Jesus did" (1 John 2:6). When Jesus called His disciples, He said, "Follow me." Following the footsteps of Jesus means abiding by going where He goes, walking as He walks, and following where He leads. Jesus said, "Learn from me, for I am gentle and humble in heart, and you will find rest for your souls" (Matthew 11:29). Even the Son of God abided by the rhythms ordained from the beginning, and these are the same rhythms ordained for us today.

MILK AND BREAD PUDDING

During a particularly busy season of my life, when I was spending most of my time mothering our two young children, I was invited to speak at a charity event on adoption and orphan care. I agreed to do it, thinking I could simply pull relevant teachings out from some of my old writings. I sensed I could do it without a lot of preparation, but I was less confident I could find someone that Maya, my highly attached nursing infant, would allow to hold her.

On the day of the event in Nashville, as the time for my talk drew closer, everything seemed to fall apart. Maya would not stop crying. As her "stranger danger" went into full force, my confidence turned to fear and my calm to panic. She let out blood-curdling screams each time I tried to put her into someone else's arms. With only fifteen minutes before I had to teach, I put Maya in a baby wrap and disappeared into a closet-sized bathroom nearby. I slid down the wall in my fancy clothes, put my feet up against the toilet, and nursed her on that bathroom floor. I felt defeated before I had even started. I cried while I nursed her.

My mind raced with questions. *What is happening? Lord, what are You trying to say? Why won't You let someone else hold her, even just this once? You are the Lord over everything, everyone, and every detail, even the sleep and cries of my child. Won't You help me?*

It seemed impossible to do this event now, considering how distressed my baby was and what a jumbled mess my mind had become. I tried to hold on to the truth of 1 Thessalonians 5:24, "The one who calls you is faithful, and he will do it." I knew God had called me to this, but it was becoming increasingly challenging to keep believing He would do it. I had found myself back in the valley of need. "Lord, I do believe; help me overcome my unbelief" (Mark 9:24).

El Shaddai

The name of God as El Shaddai popped into my mind. I knew Him already as Almighty God and that He could do anything. But it seems the Spirit was trying to show me something more. Only recently did I learn that the root of El Shaddai is *shad*, which can mean breast. Therefore, *shad* speaks to the all-sufficient role that a nursing mother plays in the life of her infant child. As I sat nursing Maya on the bathroom floor, I could suddenly see God's love in my mothering and my mothering in God's love. I was Maya's sole source of comfort, care, cover, drink, food, and movement, and God wanted to be all these things for me and for every woman there. When my self-sufficiency turned to panic, God used my baby's needs to separate me from the crowd and compel me to seek Him alone in prayer.

During those fifteen minutes on that bathroom floor, through our Divine Dialogue, God cleared my mind, calmed my heart, and my baby fell fast asleep. I walked to the front of the room with Maya still wrapped and sleeping on my chest and then succinctly delivered my newly edited message. Maya had become a living "show and tell," expressing the Lord's points vividly and creatively. Though I kept much of my original message about God being the Father to the fatherless, it was changed by the new ingredients God had added. I shared the importance of knowing our human frame and remaining dependent and connected to the heart of El Shaddai, apart from whom we cannot stand, walk, work, live, or bear fruit.

The Lord's Spirit can indeed be like a tender, nurturing heavenly mother who holds us close, comforts us in distress, and provides for our needs. The name El Shaddai calls us to REMEMBER the Spirit as our All-Sufficiency, knowing that God always remembers us. "Can a woman forget her nursing child and have no compassion on the son of her womb? Even these may forget, but I will not forget you. Behold, I have inscribed you on the palms of my hands; your walls are continually before me" (Isaiah 49:15–16 ESV).

Warm and Nourishing

The Lord wants His Word presented in a timely, loving, and nourishing way. Therefore, whether we're offering something entirely new, made from scratch, or recycling old gems, every impartation of God's grace through us requires faith and a willingness to listen and receive new things daily.

Preparing our testimonies to share about the goodness of God, using treasures of old and treasures of new from our life stories, is a lot like making bread pudding. We can use the leftover pieces of bread if we mix them with fresh milk, oil, and honey and serve it warmly. Similarly, God does not always require us to make the spiritual bread we will share from scratch, especially during our more complex or extra busy seasons. Still, we need to draw out fresh ingredients from His Word, like milk, oil, and honey, so that our offerings are not dry or stale but instead warm, tasty-sweet, and nourishing. The fragments of dry bread from yesterday's meal often makes the very best bread pudding. "Every scribe who has been trained for the kingdom of heaven is like a master of a house, who brings out of his treasure what is new and what is old" (Matthew 13:52 ESV).

MANNA FROM HEAVEN

In the Bible, manna from heaven refers to the fresh and sweet-tasting bread sent from above for the Israelites to eat during their desert journeys (Exodus 16). Because the Israelites were nomadic during this wilderness period, they needed God to sustain them between their rescue from Egypt and their entrance into Canaan. An important thing to know about this manna from heaven is that it was only good for one day. The manna became inedible on the second day to show the importance of seeking daily provision and wisdom from God. "He humbled you, causing you to hunger and then feeding you with manna, which neither you nor your fathers had known, to teach you that man does not live on bread alone but on every word that comes from the mouth of the LORD" (Deuteronomy 8:3).

Receiving fresh manna is part of abiding, not only for our consumption but also to share with others. The Lord showed me through my little one how continuing to ASK for new treasures and fresh manna, or in her case, crying for mother's milk, was part of the practice of abiding. No wonder Jesus taught us to pray, "Give us this day our daily bread" (Matthew 6:11 KJV). When we continue to seek His presence expectantly, we find even our past prayers getting answered.

God also used the manna to teach how to ABIDE by the Sabbath. Though the wandering Israelites depended on new provisions from the Lord each day, they were told not to expect fresh manna on the seventh day because none would fall on the Sabbath. "Bear in mind that the LORD has given you the Sabbath; that is why on the sixth day he gives you bread for two days. Everyone is to stay where they are on the seventh day; no one is to go out" (Exodus 16:29).

God even called the Israelites to let the land rest for one year after it had been worked for six (Exodus 23:10–11). We do not blame or shame the land after being harvested and left empty or think it is a failure on the tree's part when its fruit has been picked. Certainly not! Harvesting the fruit of the tree or the grain of the land indicates their perseverance in abiding to the end of a cycle. Likewise, our need for rest is not something strange happening to us. Instead, it is a kind of heavenly dinner bell ringing to invite us back to God's supper table to enjoy the fruit of our labor and a time of loving fellowship. We are not to blame nor be ashamed when times of emptiness and weariness follow long periods of work.

Sadly, in our modern culture, we wonder what is wrong with workers who suddenly cannot produce after long periods of productivity. Their choice to rest or take time for healing after suffering loss may be the most authentic sign of their abiding by proper faith rhythms and Cycles of Grace. Instead of honoring the tree, the vine, the land, or the man from which the goodness came forth, we wonder why there isn't new fruit today. We were also meant to ABIDE by the rules set forth by God in creation and to apply the rhythms of planting and harvest, work and rest, day and night, to our lives so that we can remain aware of our ongoing need for God.

WALKING THE ANCIENT PATHS

I've considered Enoch a kind of life mentor because of how his life story has long captivated my imagination. I wanted to be like him because of the miraculous conclusion to his earthly story; I hoped this could be the finale of mine, too, one day.

When I consider the words in Jeremiah 6:16 about walking the "ancient paths" and finding "the good way," Enoch comes straight to mind. "Stand at the crossroads and look; ask for the ancient paths, ask where the good way is, and walk in it, and you will find rest for your souls." Few paths are more ancient than the ones Enoch walked. He lived even before the time of the great flood. His story is about pleasing God by practicing abiding.

When Enoch's story is first mentioned in Genesis 5:18–24, it seems both peculiar and wonderful. "Enoch walked faithfully with God; then he was no more, for God took him away." Yes, it says, "And then he was no more." This seems confusing because it's hard to believe that Enoch just ceased to be. But what is being conveyed is something slightly different, even higher, than that. Enoch simply ceased to be in this world. He was here one day and gone the next. The New Testament gives us a little more information. "By faith, Enoch was taken from this life so that he did not experience death." It also says, "he could not be found because God had taken him away. For before he was taken, he was commended as one who pleased God" (Hebrews 11:5).

Thanks to a simple kindergarten story, Enoch has been my favorite Bible character since childhood. Enoch's name means discernment, and in hearing his story, we will see how he lived up to his name by abiding with the Lord, growing in discernment as they walked together daily. Here is his story as it now resides in my heart:

> Every morning, after Enoch woke, he would go out and meet with God to take a walk. As they walked, they talked about many things. Enoch asked many questions, and God answered them all by unfolding beautiful mysteries hidden in His creation. They laughed a lot as they walked along together.

But sometimes, the way they went was challenging for Enoch, especially when he was younger, and the path unfamiliar. But God always helped him and showed him the best way to go so he could succeed. Over time, Enoch grew stronger and learned to trust the Lord as his Shepherd and Friend. Each night, Enoch would return to his home. But every new morning, he and the Lord would meet up again and take another walk together. This pattern continued for many years.

But one day, as they walked and talked, Enoch became so enraptured in their conversation that he did not realize how far away he had walked from his home, and it was getting very late. At this point in the journey, the Lord looked at His beloved friend Enoch and tenderly said, "We're closer to My house than we are to yours; why don't you just come home with Me?" Enoch did just that, and they walked on together to the Lord's dwelling place.

THE SPOUSE OF OUR SOULS

Scripture often speaks of God's people who ABIDE with Him as His bride. It also talks about how Christ's Spirit comes to dwell in the houses of our souls when we come to BELIEVE. These concepts made me consider Proverbs 21:9, which talks about a husband moving to the edge of his own rooftop rather than abiding in his own home with a quarrelsome wife, as being about the relationship between Christ and His people.

Just because the Lord has come to live in the homes of our souls does not mean we are reaping the many potential benefits of the relationship. Even though God promises that His Spirit will never abandon us, no matter how contentious we act toward Him, it is hard to perceive His presence, hear His voice, and receive His grace when we have pushed Him to the far corners. This is often the reason His comfort and power feel far away.

James 4:8 confirms that our actions affect our sense of proximity to God's Spirit. "Come near to God, and he will come near to you." We know that any fruitful union requires coming together regularly in an intimate way. Jesus said, "I am the vine; you are the branches. Whoever abides in me and I in him, he it is that bears much fruit, for apart from me, you can do nothing" (John 15:5 ESV). God invites us to retreat into His presence, where the Tree of Life is found and glean from His wisdom and enjoy fruitfulness in Him. "The fruit of the Spirit is love, joy, peace, forbearance, kindness, goodness, faithfulness, gentleness and self-control" (Galatians 5:22-23).

RETREAT AND REPRESENT

As children of God, we are called to regular times of retreat so we can be made ready to go out when we are called to represent His love to the world. We must learn to hear and respond to His call. To retreat means to be pulled back or dragged from the extremities of life to manage, deal, negotiate, or find a cure. By quieting ourselves and getting alone with the Lord, we experience the renewing of our minds, the restoration of our strength, and the realignment of our hearts. We also find our anxiety being replaced with peace and our sadness with joy. We even gain a higher perspective of our realities, receive the healing we need, and glean from God's wisdom. Once we have received from these storehouses of His grace, we can go out to represent Him well.

Even Solomon, when he became king and was asked by God to make any request, Solomon asked to understand the rhythms of "coming in" and "going out." "Now, LORD my God, You have made Your servant king in place of my father David, yet I am like a little boy; I do not know how to go out or come in. . . . So give Your servant an understanding heart to judge Your people to discern between good and evil" (1 Kings 3:7, 9a NASB).

Because the Lord's presence dwells in us, "coming in" does not necessarily mean we must attend an organized church retreat, though it can. But it does mean quieting the world's noise so we can hear His gentle whisper (1 Kings 19:12). It is especially important when we are battle-weary or need a fresh perspective. The Scriptures use this language of "going out" and "coming in" to indicate battles we face and provisions we need to receive for the journey ahead.

THE WAY OF BECOMING

ABIDING IN CHANGING SEASONS

After leaving my work in Washington, DC, I entered a new season of being a stay-at-home mom, where my work in child welfare would become far less prominent and homeschooling and household chores increasingly took center stage. I had been praying I would know when the time had come for me to leave my job. I did not want to embarrass myself by holding on too long, as I had seen other leaders do. The Lord was faithful in telling me when it was time to transition. Still, it felt sudden.

Living in a small village in the Pocono Mountains, away from almost everyone I knew, I began questioning my decision. Entering obscurity, wondering if I'd be forgotten, and hardly knowing the new place I was moving to. I sought the Lord for comfort.

In response, I heard the Spirit of God whisper to my spirit, "I know where you live," which amused me *and* brought me comfort.

I was often alone with my two children in this "hidden" season, as I only knew one family in the town. Scott spent much of that season traveling on a series of Christian music tours and going back and forth to Nashville and China for his work with Show Hope.

> God would soon show me that He was just as present in the laundry room as in the legislature.

My life had boiled down to nursing babies, making simple meals, doing laundry, reciting the ABCs, and taking walks in the woods. It was a small and simple existence compared to my complicated, hectic life inside the Washington Beltway. I went from hours of commuting in bumper-to-bumper traffic to only leaving my house once a week to grocery shop down the mountain. I had gone from changing policies to changing diapers. But God would soon show me that He was just as present in the laundry room as in the legislature.

During a typical day, after finally getting my two little ones down for a nap, I began my laundry routine. While doing the mundane work of washing clothes, I suddenly felt taken back in my mind, reliving old memories as if they were happening right then. It felt akin to the way the smell of a wood fire can take us back to the days of our youth at summer camp or smelling the fragrance worn by a loved one and realizing their nearness. This feeling took me to a moment when Romania's Prime Minister, Adrian Năstase, took my hand and expressed his pleasure in our visit to Romania to discuss the welfare of orphaned children.

Presently, in my laundry room, I was feeling what I had felt in Romania as the "king" regarded me and showed his pleasure in my work. But the King who had entered my laundry room was not an earthly king, but instead my Lord, the King of all kings. I sensed His admiring eyes looking at me and showing His pleasure in the good work I was doing. There, in the laundry room, my King was abiding with me, and I was abiding with Him.

After that, I started referring to God as Lord of the Laundry Room, which made me wonder, *Is this a thing?* Not many days later, I was reading the book of Malachi, and the Lord brought Malachi 3:2 before my eyes. It referred to God as the "Launderer's Soap."

Hmmm, I guess it is a thing, I thought. And that *thing* was God washing away my wrongful thinking about my situation so that I would value abiding with Him over every other way of living.

In Zechariah 4:10, we are reminded not to "despise the days of small things." In Mark 10:14, Jesus explains that He values children as highly as the "important" men of any day and time. He said, "Let the children come to me, and do not hinder them, for the kingdom of God belongs to such as these." When we take the time to ask the Lord to reveal His evaluation of our work and relationships, we will likely be surprised by how upside-down the world's values of work, rest, beauty, and usefulness are compared to God's. And as we ABIDE in sacred rhythms of work and rest, going out and coming in, and being seen and being unseen, we begin to more easily detect the aroma of His presence and grow in discernment of our callings.

THE HUMMINGBIRD

"Mom, Mom, you have to come. There's a bird stuck in our garage!" yelled my girls as they came running into the house. They had found a hummingbird that kept flying into the wall above the open garage door.

Maybe if I open the second door, it will fly out, I hoped. Sadly, the bird continued to fly into the wall above the two open garage doors.

This is the dumbest bird I've ever seen, I decided. *Hummingbirds are supposed to be smart. I'm going inside. I can't watch this lovely creature bring about its own demise.*

As I walked back inside, it dawned on me that the hummingbird was meant for me, like some warning or invitation. Then, the thought occurred to me: *Could God really be telling me that it's time to go out and fly? Am I going to hurt myself if I stay inside like this foolish bird?* Fear came over me at the idea that this might be the case. I didn't want to believe it. But from somewhere deep inside, my heart came before the Lord: *I'm not ready; I don't want to fly because people will shoot me out of the sky.*

A Birdie on the "Pooter"

I had grown afraid. Even though I had experienced a tremendous amount of healing since my long season of overlapping hurricanes, I feared leaving my place of safety. But for some time, God had been showing me that the time for "going out" was approaching. He was calling me to share with others what He had taught me. Dismissing these nudges felt safer; *I don't need to teach or be heard by others;* my internal rhetoric was trying to convince me that my feelings sounded like humility. But much of it was actually fear dressed up as humility.

The Lord used this experience to catalyze a deep dive into the significance and symbolism of hummingbirds. After several more "incidences," I would come to view the hummingbirds as representing the spirit of believers who have experienced the Lord's healing and become transformed. Just as the hummingbird needs food and flowers need to be pollinated, we all need other people. We are intended to experience and receive the beautiful gifts of God that come forth from one another. I was being invited to deliver what I had been given, teach what I had been taught, and enjoy the beauty and gifts others brought. Thinking of myself as a hummingbird reminded me of how Scott would often say, "Everyone is like a beautiful flower to you, Kerry."

While out for a walk with my teenage son, Cole, nearing the time to teach a retreat, fear, and doubt started rising up in me again as I thought about going out. So, I asked Cole if he would pray for me. He did, and my heart became calmer and a little more open. When we returned from our walk and entered our beach condo on the sixth floor, we encountered the strangest thing. Lying on top of my laptop was a dead hummingbird, with its beak pointed straight at the sticker on my computer, which read, "God is within her; she will not fall" (Psalm 46:5).

What in the world! I was amazed and wondered how this dead hummingbird could possibly have ended up on my computer. It remained a mystery until later that evening when two-year-old Annika said, "I put a birdie on your pooter, Mommy."

After my debrief with little Annika, I learned that the hummingbird had flown in through a tiny opening in the balcony door and flew headfirst into the top of the condo wall. It then slid down the wall, and from there, Annika picked it up and put it on my computer.

Clearly, the Lord was inviting me to contemplate the messages of the hummingbird more deeply. I kept the bird.

Blown by Doubt

This dead hummingbird became an incredible image of the harmful effects that doubt can have on the work of the Spirit in our lives. The Word says, "But when you ask, you must believe and not doubt, because the one who doubts is like a wave of the seas, blown and tossed by the wind" (James 1:6). Through this little creature, God revealed the tremendous harm my fear would have if I did not repent of my choice to hold on to doubt. I had seen far too many miracles to justify clinging to fear and doubt.

> Doubt is the demise of our spirits' rising.

When we are called to go out, we must follow where God leads and trust that He goes with us. Doubt is the demise of our spirits' rising. God was asking me to BELIEVE like King David, who knew the Lord's presence surrounded Him as he went forth in the world, "You hem me in behind and before, and you lay your hand upon me" (Psalm 139:5).

However, after a time of retreat, in which we have grown comfortable in receiving and feeling safe, it can be scary to reenter the places where we have gotten depleted or even hurt. But we should not fear because we are never the same when we go out from His presence as when we first came in. We have been fortified, enlightened, and prepared to be sent out on assignment. Paul prayed that "the eyes of your heart may be enlightened in order that you may know the hope to which he has called you" (Ephesians 1:18a).

While diligently researching hummingbirds, I noticed some uncanny connections between the traits and actions of a hummingbird and the twelve faith practices of BECOMING: BELIEVE, REMEMBER, ASK, IMAGINE, TRUST, REDEEM, STAND, PRAISE, ANOINT, CREATE, ASSEMBLE, and ABIDE. I would come to view the hummingbird as a living parable representing an abiding soul, a risen spirit of a person made to fly, defining a life operating in the ways of God.

The Parable of the Hummingbird

As the smallest bird in all creation, the hummingbird represents the awe-inspiring and transcendent power that can flow through something extraordinarily tiny. As one of the fastest-moving creatures, it requires continual food to survive, making it the picture of utter dependency. Its resting state, known as torpor, is an image of the Sabbath and provides a fabulous example of this aspect of the spiritual rhythms of abiding. The hummingbird represents the practice of remembering because it is the only bird that can fly backward.

When a hummingbird hovers in front of a flower to engage in the interdependent work of receiving its nourishment from the nectar while pollinating the flower, the bird appears to be floating effortlessly in the air. This reciprocal work speaks of the peace and rest that can be realized by assembling together. The hummingbird is a marvelous and beautiful image of abiding, representing movement in stillness and stillness in movement. Similar to our way of asking in prayer using a spiritual clothesline, this tiny bird is known to build its nest on clotheslines, entrusting what is most precious to the hanging process.

The greatest danger to the hummingbird is the spider's web. Yet, the hummingbird needs the webbing produced by its natural enemy, the spider, to construct its nest for its young. The elasticity of the webbing is what allows the nest to cradle the chicks while expanding as they grow. What a perfect picture of redemption.

The hummingbird is also the only bird that feeds in the middle of a heavy storm because it requires constant provision for its survival. It will go out even in the eye of a hurricane, using its feet to anchor to a branch. In this way, it can keep standing and gathering the necessary provisions to make it to the other side of the storm.

As prolific pollinators, hummingbirds have an extraordinary ability to CREATE more beauty, especially among some of the deepest, hardest-to-reach, and most brightly colored flowers. They are undoubtedly some of the most magnificently colored creatures in the world, with their feathers perfectly constructed as light reflectors, just as God calls us to reflect His light.

But how its wings operate makes it a true marvel, with the fastest wingbeat of any bird on earth and possessing the quickest heartbeat as well. Hummingbirds can fly forward, backward, sideways, straight up, and even hover for long periods of time. Most astonishing is how their wingtips trace a horizontal figure eight, speaking of continually abiding by faith according to the ancient Cycles of Grace. As its wings spin in these two connected circles, the bird rises to go out and pollinate beauty, creating more abundance in the world. I am confident that the hum of the hummingbird's wings must be perceived by heaven as praises to God.

Preserved

Over a year later, I was retelling the story of finding this dead hummingbird to my cousin Jody and shared what I had learned through my research and reflection. I offered to show her the beautiful hummingbird I had kept in my desk drawer for further study.

"Here it is," I said, pulling out the dead bird from a red plastic cup I had kept inside my drawer.

"WHAT?! GROSS!" she exclaimed. "You're joking? You can't just keep a dead animal in a drawer! It has got to reek!"

"Nope, it doesn't smell at all!" I assured her while bringing it closer to her on the couch.

To Jody's great astonishment, not only did the hummingbird not have a foul odor, but it was also perfectly preserved in shape and color. The iridescent radiance of its feathers was undiminished.

"This does not make sense!" Jody exclaimed. "Dead animals decay and smell horrible! Kerry, you understand that this doesn't make sense, right?! It's been dead for a year, and its feathers are still shimmering. Now, CONTEMPLATE THAT!" Jody added emphatically, breaking into laughter.

"How about you do it?" I responded. "Clearly, *your* heart wants to know this," I said half-jokingly.

We soon discovered that an entire bottle of myrrh had spilled in the drawer just below where the hummingbird had been laid to rest. I couldn't help but consider how the myrrh, which obviously played a role in the bird's preservation, speaks to the anointed life and death of Jesus. We found through a bit of research that of all the earth's creatures, hummingbirds have the least amount of flesh for their size. Reading the word "flesh" caught my attention as I made the scriptural connection between the word flesh and the sinful part of our lives, I thought about how the flesh of a creature makes it smell bad after death. And how the absence speaks to its pristine preservation.

Theories about how Daniel of the Bible had been preserved in the lions' den resurfaced. My mind mused that *If Daniel had smelled like flesh or fear to those lions, they would have devoured him for sure.* These thoughts and this hummingbird image helped me see how the anointing of God's Spirit had covered Daniel's fear, like the fragrance of myrrh, and kept him safe, even among lions. Similarly, the near absence of flesh in the hummingbird and the diffusion of the spilled myrrh had kept the fragrance of life rather than death upon this creature. The shimmering feathers had remained bright because their colors do not come from any inner substance or dye but from the way God formed them as finely chiseled reflectors of light. This is why the colors of a hummingbird's feathers remain intact even after death.

Jody and I found the most perfect Scripture as we contemplated the dead creature together. "Whoever sows to please their flesh, from the flesh will reap destruction; whoever sows to please the Spirit, from the Spirit will reap eternal life" (Galatians 6:8). The many messages of God we were observing through the life and death of the hummingbirds were inviting us to consider our way of life and what might remain and resound after our own deaths. It all had much to do with the importance of living according to the Spirit and not according to the flesh, at least if we want our lives to be kept safe, reflect God's glorious colors of light, and leave behind a sweet-smelling fragrance wherever we go.

Ready to Fly

The parabolic life of the hummingbird seems to be a complete teaching on the way of worship, giving us a beautiful living picture of how the human spirit can ABIDE in God's presence according to the twelve BECOMING practices of faith. Like the hummingbird, we are not to go out confident in our flesh but trusting in the Spirit. Having spent time in the Lord's presence, we are changed, anointed, and made ready to fly as reflections of His light and revelations of His love.

To overcome my fear of "going out," God showed me that my soul was now wearing new garments of well-fitting beliefs. My eyes had become open to see myself and others more clearly and to love more purely. While in prayer, I agreed with God, saying, "I will go if You'll go with me." The Spirit reminded me of His omnipresence, saying, "I am IN you." My heart praised the Lord, and my fear and doubt disappeared. I had become convinced that PRAISE is the best way to fight fear and overcome doubt. This image of the hummingbird showed me that I do not need to be afraid of being shot out of the sky like some game bird flying high. Hummingbirds are tiny, quick-moving pollinators that minister in the fertile soil of life's valleys, making what is already beautiful even more abundant. God was inviting me through the parable of the hummingbird to follow Him as He led me out to pollinate the beauty found in other living beings.

THE WAY OF BECOMING

THE INHALE OF LISTENING PRAYER

Even though the times and seasons of work and rest, moving and standing, coming and going, asking and imagining, giving and receiving, and cultivating and waiting are all significant, their timing can be challenging to discern. Discerning the Spirit's presence and hearing the Lord's voice requires living in the sacred rhythms of abiding.

After coming through quite a long season of suffering and then being blessed with daughters Leah Joy and Annika Faith, I felt at long last as if I was coming up for a bit of air. Even though having these two babies in two years and doubling our brood to four was a blessing and an answer to prayer, it did wear me out at times. Nursing our babies, keeping our home, and homeschooling our older kids kept nearly every moment occupied. Apparently, Scott could see my weariness because he came to me and suggested I take a weekend away for a private retreat. He indicated he could take a few days off so I could have this time for respite. I agreed, hoping I might be able to finally do some writing.

I returned to the same monastic community on Cape Cod and its Church of the Transfiguration, where I had seen the vision of my daughter, Isabella, standing upon a freshly cut golden field that told of a coming harvest. I was given a beautiful spot on the property in a lighthouse on the bay, where other writers had created beautiful works in the past. But despite my hopes of being able to write freely, I only experienced writer's block. Eventually, I gave up forcing my will and asked the Lord to show me His.

Looking out at the frozen bay, still with my pen in hand and my notebook on the table, I sought the Lord, "I will listen and write if You will speak to me." I listened, my Lord spoke, and I scribed the notions His Spirit poured into my heart:

"Listening Prayer"

I am like the ocean, a tempest of great power.
Be careful with your ways,
I am not something to take lightly.

ABIDE

It is I who sets the limits.
It is I who says to the sea, "To here and no farther."

Do you see the tree in the winter?
Although you see death—barren and useless,
Beneath and inside, what is happening is necessary,
It is all part of My plan.

In season, it will prove that this rest
and time of protection was necessary.
Why do you rush, child?
Wait! Wait patiently for Me.

I have always guided you.
Why would I not guide you still?
I am here with you. Do you not perceive Me?
I am all around you!

Even in the disappointments—
This is My providence.
This is My hand.

In the distance, you hear the rolling waves,
Yet before you is the frozen, quiet ground.
Rest and wait patiently.
Do not be anxious. For I am with you!

Trust what you hear of Me in the distance.
Trust what you hear in your inner man.
I am at work—always at work on your behalf,
On behalf of all My children.

I desire unity.
To love one another.
To forgive as I have forgiven.

Do not waste time on petty differences or jealousies.
Comparing yourselves to each other is only foolishness,
And will waste precious time.
Look up! Look up, My child. Know My love!

You are wounded.
My children are wounded greatly in this life.
I am Healer. I know your pains intimately.
I was wounded for you.

Come to Me. Fellowship with Me—
There is a fellowship of the suffering—
Open your eyes. Be open to My love for you.
In it, you will find your healing!

The years of seeking Me,
the choice to love and forgive
instead of holding on to hurts,
has heightened your senses to spiritual things.

Listen carefully, My child.
I have much I want to teach My children.
Love is the end of all things,
Love beyond your human ability to understand.

My Son has made a way for you to hear Me
and to see Me with your spiritual eyes.
I am in everything.
Trust and do not be anxious!

I did not realize it then, but God had brought me to this place so that I could inhale His holy breath through listening prayer. The Spirit had brought me for a time of quiet retreat. This deep inhale was preparation for the coming season, only known to Him. All too soon, the Lord would call me to write, CREATE, and go out to teach *The Way of Becoming*. But today, I was being called to be present with Him as He was present with me. My Lord and I had come to simply ABIDE together.

In God's time, the words to write would flow freely, coming forth as a long PRAISE song of ascent, a testimony to His faithfulness, and an encouragement to those who will come after me. "Let this be written for a future generation, that a people not yet created may praise the LORD" (Psalm 102:18). Just as with the many mountains we will all climb in our lives, this one began in the valley of need and brokenness but concluded on a higher plane of wonderment and PRAISE. God had gently led my soul to the point of rising so I would know His love for me and have the courage to minister truth, healing, and hope to others. Only those who have sought God's presence and received from His grace can go forth in an integrated manner, ready to impart the wisdom and wonders of His kingdom to others. This is the way to BECOME a finely edited living letter, a refined poem, and Divine Correspondence revealing God's love.

My prayer is that you will take up the ways and wings of a hummingbird as you go out singing praises to your Savior and multiplying beauty in the world around you; that you would see the fragmented parts you have entrusted to God become transfigured into pearls; and that your mourning heart would begin to dance as you travel along the ancient and ascending paths of life in the Spirit. May your heart be filled with wonder, your eyes with light, your wounds with oil, your hands with strength, your mind with wisdom, your home with love, your table with abundance, and your lips with praises to the Lord your God because you are His beloved.

> May your heart be filled with wonder and your lips with praises because you are His beloved.

YOUR BECOMING STORY: ABIDE

What is your experience with the God who gives you rest? How has God brought abundance into your spiritual life? What is your experience of having spent time in the presence of God that others notice the afterglow of His glory remaining upon you? What new manna have you received from the Lord lately? What treasures of old and treasure of new might God be inviting you to bring forth from your life as a representation of His love and creativity through you?

Consider where you have not been mindful of abiding by proper rhythms. Have you felt shame or blamed by others or even yourself for taking time for needed rest? Consider how understanding ordained spiritual rhythms might enlighten your way forward in abiding.

"The Wisdom of Wonder"

Wisdom, be our sister;
Understanding, be our kin.
Birds and fish, please minister,
O Sea Cross, do weigh-in.

It's fear we've given into;
It's pain we hold too dear.
Lord, teach us to release it,
That our lenses become clear.

For self and wealth, we all have striven,
Misusing eyes and hands once given.
Our flesh sees little hindrance,
As if sin has no consequence.

But when the battle comes along,
Our wits unfound and souls alone,
Confused like men of Midian,
We wake and turn and kill our kin!

We search for God in humanity,
Yet, close our ears to eternity,
And fall like babes from sheltering nests,
And block Your voice that bids us rest.

Seeing much, we perceive so little,
When focused on the carnal realm.
How fear seeps in is very subtle
When misjudgment's at the helm.

Illuminate our eyes, O Lord,
To perceive the truer things,
The wonders of Your kingdom,
Of which the songbird sings.

May we like branches waving,
Lift up our holy hands,
And call upon Your savings,
To see victory in our lands!

After all has been considered,
And all has been endured,
It's the wonder of the hummingbird,
That makes my heart bestirred.

The beauty that her presence brings,
The sacred motion of her wings,
The way she drinks of beauty's nectar,
She is our souls' most needed lecture.

THE WAY OF BECOMING

Taste and see that the Lord is good,
Her life speaks clear what all ours should.
For in receiving, we gain to give,
In awe, we learn the way to live.

Now, with our focus more repentant,
We set our view on grace in movement.
The way of faith in every trait,
She's imagination's splendor mate.

She makes her nests on drying lines,
A prayer to ask, a wondrous sign.
For these on wings and those with fins,
Bring sacred songs to clothing pins.

These words, like garments cover shame,
Preaching all to stop the blame,
For fear and pride and misplaced gaze,
Has put us here in a cloudy haze.

Every creature knows its Author,
Yet man rebels against one Father.
Lord, let us hear reproof in thunder,
And praise Your love in every wonder.[4]

THE ART OF PRACTICING

The twelve BECOMING practices operate much like different music pieces that we can learn by heart and call upon from memory through the Spirit's timely promptings. They become well-worn pathways in our faith journeys. By making the daily decision to practice the tools in small ways regularly, we are choosing to seek the Lord's presence continually.

For you, this might mean remembering God's blessings in the last twenty-four hours, asking Him your questions and requests as they come to mind, or entrusting small hurts as they happen. It may mean identifying what stole your inner peace and confessing your trespasses in real-time so your peace can be restored. Perhaps it means searching the Scriptures for a verse to stand in through your current season. It could entail going out for a nature walk in search of living parables hidden in God's creation or simply praising God before closing your eyes each night. It's not so important how or when you practice your faith, but only that you do it according to the rhythms that draw you nearer to your Savior.

SOUL SORTING

God designed us to experience His goodness through one another, and we certainly cannot fulfill our life callings entirely by ourselves. We need each other to become the finely hewn, living stones we are meant to be. We are also meant to be built together into one spiritual house for the Lord's glory. "As you come to him, the living Stone—rejected by humans but chosen by God and precious to him—you also, like living stones, are being built into a spiritual house to be a holy priesthood, offering spiritual sacrifices acceptable to God through Jesus" (1 Peter 2:4–5).

God is always willing to give us the grace we need. We access that grace by continuing to practice our faith. These twelve faith practices we use for personal reconciliation and spiritual formation are meant to be applied not only to our individual lives but also to our relationships. God illustrated how all these faith tools can be used together through a beautiful interaction with my dear friend Kathy Zakarian. She and I met in college and learned to trust one another during those years. In adulthood, after Kathy earned her doctorate in psychology, our relationship grew, and we became mentors to one another using our different competencies.

One day, Kathy called and asked if she could come over to pray together. She had just experienced an unexpected and profound breach in one of her relationships that sent her spiraling in fear.

As I prepared for her arrival, the Lord gave me a vision of a pile of tiny things in front of her on the table, each a symbol of a different tool we had been practicing together. Imagining this brought to mind a comment from a recent BECOMING retreat:

"It felt like I came here and dumped out my soul like a messy purse, but I am leaving with my soul sorted. I'm not stuck anymore; I can move forward."

God was inviting Kathy and me to do this soul-sorting work together, to apply the tools and practices of BECOMING to her relationship and messy situation so she could move forward.

Before Kathy arrived, I went to the basement, gathered supplies, and laid them on the table. There were stones, clothespins, gold nuggets, glass fragments, a seashell, and two puzzle pieces. Upon her arrival, I handed her a new notebook and a pen. Then, I began asking questions that would lead us into the faith work of sorting out her soul in God.

For each stone in the pile, I asked her to name an experience she could remember where God had blessed her through this particular relationship she was struggling with now. For each broken fragment, I encouraged her to identify hurts inflicted by the difficult incident, things triggered, or that resurfaced from her past so she could entrust it all to the Lord for healing and reassembling. She traced the broken pieces in the notebook and labeled them. The clothespin reminded her to ask questions and write down her requests for God to hang on her spiritual clothesline. For each golden nugget, she confessed her own sin, which she recognized was trying to get a foothold in her wounded heart but would have impeded the flow of God's grace if allowed to remain. As for the puzzle pieces, I asked her to think about how she had come together with this person in the past most successfully so she could consider how they might come together again in search of reconciliation.

Finally, we considered together what aspect of God's divine character we could see reflected in the wonder of the tiny seashell in her pile. It was a lightning whelk with its many crooked lines running parallel from the tip of the shell to its wide circular top. Here, all the lines seemed to merge and form a beautiful golden spiral. I asked her to consider how seeing these lines assembled might give her hope that God can work together all the parts of this trying situation for her good. Kathy was filling up her tiny notebook and growing more peaceful as we went.

We were both in awe of how God instructed us on how to use all our faith tools in this integrated way before reengaging in a wounded relationship. We also marveled at how we had been called to do this soul-sorting exercise together and perceive His higher way of assembling. Once all had been identified, we prayed together. Kathy entrusted every need as a prayer request, every fragment as a promise of future wholeness, every sin for forgiveness, and every hope for redemption. In the days that followed, whenever Kathy would begin spiraling in fear again, she would return to her notebook. And each time, a wave of peace would wash over her. Months later, Kathy phoned to say, "Our Soul-Sorting Session was the best crisis counseling I've ever had."

Reconcile with God, Then Others

Reconciliation with other people requires us to bring our faith work into fellowship. Still, the work of faith must begin with us. The healthier the individual members, the healthier the whole. Community revival always begins as personal revival. This is why we are called to apply the tools first to our vertical relationship with God, submitting our needs to Him so He can reveal Himself to us. Second, we are to use them as Kathy and I did—to sort out the struggles we are facing within ourselves because of events we've experienced that need to be submitted to the Holy Spirit. This way, our souls can be realigned to God's mind and heart first. Once we have engaged in the vertical work of reconciliation with God and the internal work between our souls and spirits, we should apply these tools to our horizontal relationships. Even though this is the third and last step, it is certainly not the least. Our relationships with other people are significant to God. They also refine and improve our condition: "As iron sharpens iron, so one person sharpens another" (Proverbs 27:17). Let us seek to become rightly aligned with God and reestablish our inner peace before reengaging in relationships in conflict.

Consider a strained relationship that God might be inviting you to submit to Him using *The Way of Becoming* to sort your soul. Whether your *neediness of the now* involves a struggling relationship or some other area of your life, I invite you to consider some of the questions I asked Kathy that day.

Just as remembering God's goodness helps us reengage more easily with Him, recalling the goodness we've experienced through others allows us to reengage with them. We ask questions of others to learn more about them, just as we learn more about God by asking Him questions in prayer. Similar to our relationship with God, human relationships also require times of confession, repentance, and healing. Just as we must seek forgiveness from God, we must make amends with the people we've sinned against. Sharing our needs, sorrows, and creative gifts with others is also essential to healthy relationships. These practices are meant to be applied to every kind of reconciliation: with God, within oneself (soul and spirit), and with other people.

Daily Becoming

On the following pages, you will find a *Soul-Sorting* exercise called *Daily Becoming*. It provides a structured way to use the twelve tools in an integrated fashion. This exercise is meant to serve as a navigational tool that points you heavenward no matter your circumstance—whether you're in the valley of need, treading water in a season of waiting, a fiery trial, or feeling swept into a hurricane. This guided exercise is designed to be completed in just a few minutes using simple self-reflective questions that help you ascertain the condition of your heart and soul. The questions will help you name your need, ask your questions, identify God's seeds of promise, and then rest in the waiting and hopeful anticipation, knowing that you have entrusted it all to the Lord and that He will fight your battles and provide the wisdom and provision you need.

DAILY BECOMING

NEEDINESS OF THE NOW	DATE

Name your focus area of need.

BELIEVE — Name something you already confidently believe about God, and what you are struggling to believe about Him, His Word, or His character.

REMEMBER — Name a stone of remembrance, a time God showed His faithfulness to you in the past.

ASK — Name your questions and requests of God.

IMAGINE — Name the seeds of hope you are noticing in nature, Scripture, people, or your inner spirit.

TRUST — Name the fragments—fears, brokenness, or unreconciled parts—that need to be released and entrusted to God.

REDEEM — Name any unconfessed sins (of commission or omission) that may be impeding your sense of God's presence.

STAND — Name a Scripture verse or promise of God you can stand on during the time of waiting or amid the storm.

PRAISE — Praise God for the good He has done and praise Him by faith for what you have asked of Him.

ANOINT — Name ways of sharing your spiritual gifts, anointings, or experiences for the healing, comfort, or blessing of others.

CREATE — Name ways of stewarding your time, talents, and resources creatively for the common good.

ASSEMBLE — Name ways you could come together to share your competencies with others and to glean from theirs so your work is multiplied.

ABIDE — Name ways you can practice abiding in healthy rhythms of work and rest, of "coming in" and "going out."

DAILY BECOMING

NEEDINESS OF THE NOW   DATE

BELIEVE

REMEMBER

ASK

IMAGINE

TRUST

REDEEM

STAND

PRAISE

ANOINT

CREATE

ASSEMBLE

ABIDE

After years of practicing my faith in this way, I saw how the twelve practices not only built upon one another, providing a spiritual staircase out of brokenness and into abundance, but also how they formed scaffolding for the building up and restoring of a belief system.

Understanding that these faith practices were meant to operate in an integrated and ongoing fashion led me to see them much like the inner wheelwork of a clock, where the gears move individually and corporately in an ongoing fashion. Our lives usually require multiple tools and faith practices based on the circumstances we face at any given time, with some areas experiencing desolation and others experiencing more growth and abundance. This further confirmed the framework of the BECOMING wheelwork and its Cycles of Grace.

CYCLES OF GRACE

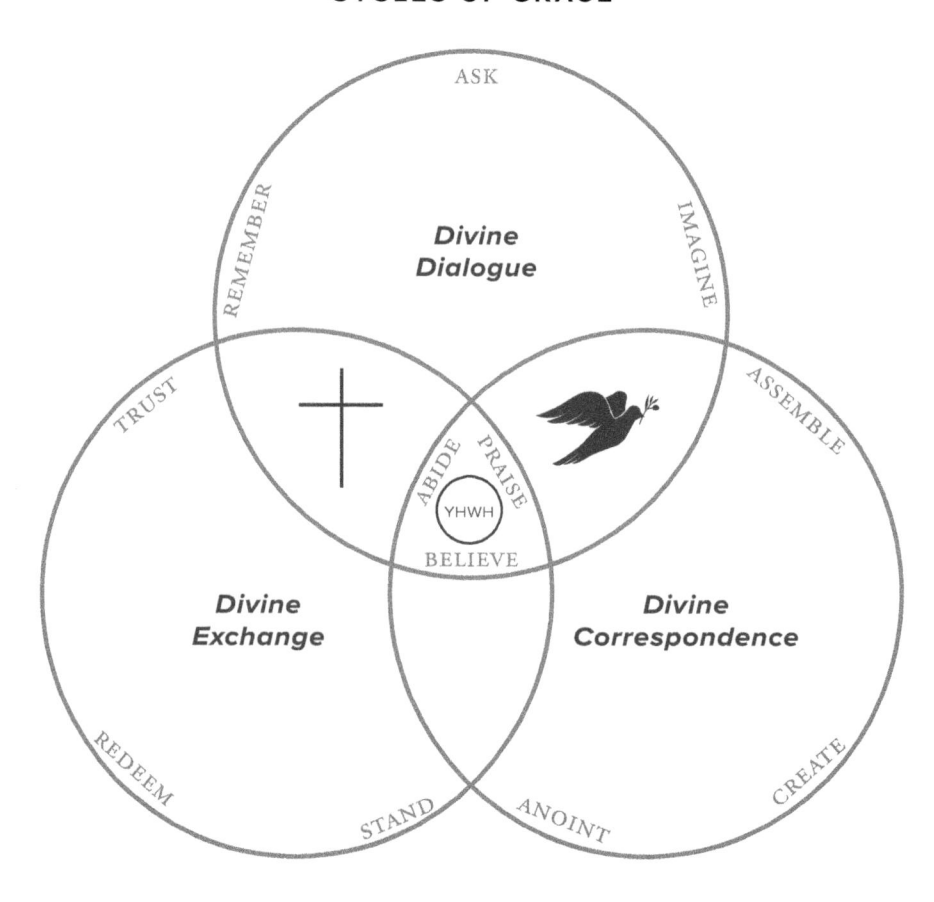

With its three overlapping circles, the Cycles of Grace diagram provides a picture of the ongoing movements involved in walking in this way by faith and the integration and reconciliation it offers on three levels: with God, within ourselves, and with other people. These three wheels, designated here as the Divine Dialogue, Divine Exchange, and Divine Correspondence, help communicate the daily rotations, seasonal cycles, and yearly revolutions of our BECOMING in God.

The twelve practices are divided into three groups of four based on their primary usage in reconciliation. The practices of BELIEVE, REMEMBER, ASK, and IMAGINE are part of the wheel of the Divine Dialogue because they address the mind's connection with the ways of the Father; humans have had access to these four tools from the beginning of their creation. TRUST, REDEEM STAND, and PRAISE make up the wheel of the Divine Exchange and primarily address matters of the heart. The Divine Exchange speaks to the progressive reconciliation of a person's soul and God's redemptive Spirit that was only made possible by the life and death of Jesus. The practices of ANOINT, CREATE, ASSEMBLE, and ABIDE make up the wheel of the Divine Correspondence and speak to a believer's work of faith operating by the power of the Holy Spirit and according to their unique gifts and callings. We use these faith practices to do the good works God has set out for us—bringing healing to others, creating beauty, finding belonging in assembly, and fulfilling their unique purposes in the world.

I pray you will experience the joy of BECOMING more peaceful, whole, and courageous as God transforms you daily. Though there will always be soul work involved in faith, the more you do, the more natural it becomes. To dive deeper into your personal story in God and continue along *The Way of Becoming*, visit https://www.kerryhasenbalg.com. To partner with our foundation in its discipleship, soul care, or advocacy work, visit https://www.becomingfoundation.org.

The best is yet to (be)come!

AFTERWORD

When I first sensed a call to write down my stories, I questioned the Lord: *Why would I write my stories if mine are no more important than anyone else's?* God's Spirit replied to mine, "Write *My* story through you."

I wrote these books in a valley time, but a valley of a different kind. My life assemblies were being shifted and sifted while passing through the "Covid years." Scott and I were also grieving the losses of both of his parents, his oldest brother, Norman, and my uncles, Frank, Tommy, and David. The timing deepened my soul and my writings, as I wrote both for posterity and out of my own neediness before God. My longing to see beyond our cloudy circumstances compelled me to employ all the faith tools I was writing about. My freshly activated faith and real tears authenticated every idea, prayer, and plea. The work required many deep dives into Scripture. I am grateful it did because having the waters of God's Word continually wash over me replenished and rejuvenated my dry and weary soul. Every fragment revealed in this season led me to the cross of Christ, and here, I would access the wisdom I needed to write.

As I recalled my *Ebenezer* stones, I found myself recording them not only as stories to teach the twelve tools but also as stepping stones to cross the raging waters before me. My integrated beliefs held firm, and the "stress wood" I had developed kept me standing. This continual seeking resulted in a steady stream of ASKS coming down from my "clothesline." This kept me cycling in grace and rising in PRAISE upon the *Way of Becoming*. Today, I am out of that pit and climbing higher in hope. I sense the light of the Son of God as I anticipate His coming. In truth, the deprivation did help me appreciate the beautiful parts and people already present in my story. Life is a journey of many mountains and valleys. But if we continue to walk by faith, we never go it alone! May we, like Enoch, feel the joy of drawing closer to God's house than we are to ours and hearing our Savior invite us to "just come home" with Him.

ACKNOWLEDGMENTS

I want to thank my editors, Deb Keiser, Pam Pugh, and Bethany Haley, whose names fittingly mean honeybee, honey, and house of figs, for your roles in helping this work cross out of the wilderness and into the "promised land." I am grateful to Mark Ford, Samantha Frolich, Brandi Davis, and Georgie Patt for your creative designs in the book. To my many friends, family members, and fellow *becomers* who have been reading, giving feedback, listening to my heart, and helping me sort my thoughts around this work, I am forever grateful. Just as it takes the hard work of many bees to make the honey flow and many notes for a song to be composed, your prayers and encouragement have been both the song and the sustenance that have strengthened me along the way since 2008 and helped *The Way of Becoming* BECOME ready for sharing.

    I am profoundly and eternally grateful to my parents for their love and unceasing support and for teaching me that "nothing is lost to a child of God." I bless my siblings, grandparents, mentors, friends, and family, who wept with us in our grief and rejoiced with us in our joys. Your quiet acts of faith greatly influenced my journey and helped me create this generational praise song of ascent. To my children, Cole, Maya, Leah, and Annika, I bless you for your unceasing prayers, many sacrifices, and pure-hearted celebration in these years of writing. Seeing my ASKS hung on your "clotheslines" made me weep. To my cousin Jody Olympia, my daily sojourner in this word-sorting world—though you claim to be no more than the taxi driver who caught "the baby" on the way to the hospital—I struggle to believe this would have seen the light of day without you and Scott. And to my beloved Scott, my greatest encourager and closest friend, you believed in me and this book long before I did. You are the pillar that has held us up and kept all the Blue House people united and flourishing. In our 25 years of marriage, we have been and will continue to be together, BECOMING one.

I pray the Lord rewards every one of you for your contributions, known and unknown, by answering your ASKS "hung on the line" and in a way that makes your heart declare, "God is really real!"

To Jesus, who is *The Way*, and to *Yahweh*, who is the Becoming One and the One who causes us to become, I present this humble work written with materials You first created and entrusted to me. May this story of Your grace, love, and beauty be good news to every soul seeking to *become*.

NOTES

INTRODUCTION

1. Flavius Josephus, *The Complete Works of Josephus*, "Antiquities of the Jews, Preface." Translated by William Whiston. Cambridge. 1737.
2. The Hebrew Tetragrammaton of the Lord's Name as Yahweh יהוה (YHWY) is rooted in the verb "to be." In its first biblical appearance at the burning bush, Moses asks for God's Name and God speaks the word אֶהְיֶה (*'Ehyeh*), which is a form of הָיָה (*hayah*), 'to be'; and grammatically means "I am" and "I will be." The longer answer God gave Moses of, *'ehyeh 'ăšer 'ehyeh*, brings clarity to the Name (YHWH) as something of the future tense, and is translated, "I *will be* what I *will be*," "I will be *who* I will be," "I *will become* what I will become," "I *will bring into being,*" or "I *will cause to become*'" (Exodus 3:14–15). God is presenting Himself as essential as VERB in all three forms: the "to be" verbs, action verbs: and helping verbs. This speaks to the process of "theosis," where His Divine Character becomes manifest to us, then, in us, and finally, through us.

CHAPTER 1: BELIEVE

1. "The Meaning and History of the Name Georgios," Venere, June 9, 2024, https://venere.it/en/the-meaning-and-history-of-the-name-georgios/.

CHAPTER 2: REMEMBER

1. "Chinese Pastor Sentenced to Death," *Voice of the Martyrs*, January 1, 2002, Koinonia House, January 8, 2002.
2. Shih, "Jiang Zemin Obituary: The Former Chinese Leader Ushered His Country Into the World Economy."
3. Rosenthal, "China Sentences Man on Reduced Charges for Importing Bibles."
4. Vocabulary.com Dictionary, s.v. "beget," accessed January 08, 2025, https://www.vocabulary.com/dictionary/beget.

CHAPTER 3: ASK

1. Oswald Chambers, *My Utmost for His Highest*, Classic Edition, 1935.
2. Cay Andersen and Judy Sorensen, quote from live retreat, Community of Jesus, Orleans, MA
3. Kerry Hasenbalg, "Cycles of Grace," Kerry Hasenbalg, February 12, 2021, https://kerryhasenbalg.com/2020/03/22/cycles-of-grace-a-poem/.

CHAPTER 4: IMAGINE

1. "Strong's Hebrew: 5769. עוֹלָם (olam)—Eternity, everlasting, forever, perpetual, ancient, world."
2. Mitchell First, "What Is the Meaning of the Word 'Olam'?," The Jewish Link, January 4, 2018, https://jewishlink.news/what-is-the-meaning-of-the-word-olam/.
3. Mark Cartwright, "Tyrian Purple," *World History Encyclopedia*, July 21, 2016, https://www.worldhistory.org/Tyrian_Purple/.
4. "In Israel, a 3,000-Year-Old Purple Factory," March 5, 2024, https://www.nytimes.com/2024/03/05/science/archaeology-tyrian-purple-murex.html.
5. Kerry Hasenbalg, "On Earth as in Heaven," Kerry Hasenbalg, July 17, 2020. https://kerryhasenbalg.com/2020/07/17/as-above-so-below/. Retitled Echoes of Eternity.

CHAPTER 5: TRUST

1. Jonathon Van Maren and Jonathon Van Maren, "In History's Bloodiest Persecution of Christians, the Russian Communists Murder Millions," The Bridgehead, June 1, 2023, https://thebridgehead.ca/2018/05/01/in-historys-bloodiest-persecution-of-christians-the-russian-communists-murder-millions/.
2. Natasha Frost, "How the USSR Turned Houses of Worship into Museums of Atheism." *Atlas Obscura*, May 7, 2018, https://www.atlasobscura.com/articles/soviet-antireligious-museums-of-atheism.
3. Kerry Hasenbalg, *The Companion Guide to Your BECOMING: Transform* (Blue House Books, 2021), 53.

CHAPTER 6: REDEEM

1. Becoming Collective, Kerry Hasenbalg, "Divine Exchange" (feat. Melodee DeVevo). 2021, Spotify.

CHAPTER 7: STAND

1. "Abducted: The Lord's Resistance Army and Forced Conscription in Northern Uganda," Harvard Humanitarian Initiative, n.d., https://hhi.harvard.edu/publications/abducted-lords-resistance-army-and-forced-conscription-northern.

Notes

2. Celestine Lakin, *A Voice in the Darkness: Memoir of a Rwandan Genocide Survivor* (Wheeler & James, 2018).
3. Steven Curtis Chapman, "You are Being Loved," *This Moment,* Sparrow Records. 2007, Spotify.
4. Steven Curtis Chapman, "Close to Your Heart (feat. Matt Redman)," *Safe in the Arms,* Sparrow Records, 2010, Spotify.
5. David Pascoe, "Safe Harbor—How to Protect Your Boats From Storms," National Marine Hurricane Preparation Symposium, 2008.
6. Pascoe, "Safe Harbor."
7. Pascoe, "Safe Harbor."
8. Pascoe, "Safe Harbor."
9. Pascoe, "Safe Harbor."
10. Aidan McCullen, "Organisational Stress Wood: Struggle Builds Resilience," *The Innovation Show,* June 30, 2022. https://theinnovationshow.io/organisational-stress-wood-struggle-builds-resilience/.
11. Kerry Hasenbalg and Melodee DeVevo, "I Will Stand" (feat. Melodee DeVevo), Becoming Collective, 2024, Spotify.

CHAPTER 8: PRAISE

1. Bill Perkins, "The Breath of YHW,H" Compass International. https://compass.org/the-breath-of-yhwh.
2. James A. Diamond, "YHWH: The God That Is vs. the God That Becomes," TheTorah.com, 2014, https://www.thetorah.com/article/yhwh-the-god-that-is-vs-the-god-that-becomes.
3. "Spirit | Etymology of Spirit." Etymolonline, *Online Etymology Dictionary,* https://www.etymonline.com/word/spirit.
4. Etymolonline, *Online Etymology Dictionary,* https://www.etymonline.com/word/spire.
5. "Strong's Hebrew: 3034. יָדָה (Yadah) -- to Give Thanks, to Praise, to Confess."
6. "Strong's Hebrew: 1263. בָּרוּךְ (Baruk) -- Baruch."
7. "Strong's Hebrew: 8426. תּוֹדָה (Todah) -- Thanksgiving, Praise, Confession," n.d
8. "Strong's Hebrew: 2167. זָמַר (Zamar) -- to Sing, to Make Music, to Praise."
9. "Strong's Hebrew: 3769. כָּרַר (Karar) -- To dance, whirl, or spin"
10. "Strong's Hebrew: 1984. הָלַל (Halal) -- to Praise, to Boast, to Shine, to Celebrate, to Glory."
11. Pamela Rosewell Moore, *The Five Silent Years of Corrie Ten Boom* (Zondervan, 1986), 92.

12. John Donne, "For Whom the Bell Tolls," Your Daily Poem, https://www yourdailypoem.com/listpoem.jsp?poem_id=2118.
13. Abarim Publications, "Zuph | the Amazing Name Zuph: Meaning and Etymology."
14. Bible Hub, "Strong's Hebrew: 8414. תֹּהוּ (Tohu) -- Formlessness, Emptiness, Confusion, Chaos, Nothingness."
15. Abarim Publications, "Elihu | the Amazing Name Elihu: Meaning and Etymology."
16. Abarim Publications, "Jeroham | the Amazing Name Jeroham: Meaning and Etymology."
17. Abarim Publications, "Elkanah | the Amazing Name Elkanah: Meaning and Etymology."
18. Abarim Publications, "Hananiah | the Amazing Name Hananiah: Meaning and Etymology."
19. Abarim Publications, "Elihu | the Amazing Name Elihu: Meaning and Etymology," n.d.
20. Abarim Publications, "Samuel | the Amazing Name Samuel: Meaning and Etymology."
21. Abarim Publications, "Ramathaim-Zophim | the Amazing Name Ramathaim-Zophim: Meaning and Etymology."
22. "Bethel Meaning - Bible Definition and References."
23. Abarim Publications, "Gilgal | the Amazing Name Gilgal: Meaning and Etymology."
24. Abarim Publications, "Mizpah | the Amazing Name Mizpah: Meaning and Etymology."
25. Kerry Hasenbalg, "Praise in the Low Notes," Kerry Hasenbalg, January 2, 2023, https://kerryhasenbalg.com/2023/01/02/praise-in-the-low-notes/.

CHAPTER 9: ANOINT

1. Yong Seok Park, Joung H. Lee, Jyoti A. Harwalkar, Judy Bondar, Hasan Safayhi, and Mladen Golubic, "Acetyl-11-Keto-ß-Boswellic Acid (Akba) Is Cytotoxic for Meningioma Cells and Inhibits Phosphorylation of the Extracellular-Signal Regulated Kinase 1 and 2." *Advances in Experimental Medicine and Biology*, January 1, 2002, 387–93. https://doi.org/10.1007/978-1-4615-0193-0_60.
2. Kerry Hasenbalg, "To Anoint a King," Kerry Hasenbalg, August 16, 2019, https://kerryhasenbalg.com/2023/01/02/praise-in-the-low-notes/.

Notes

CHAPTER 10: CREATE

1. Kerry Hasenbalg, "Coloring Souls: Integrate," in *The Companion Guide to Your BECOMING* (Blue House Books, 2018), 56.

CHAPTER 11: ASSEMBLE

1. Gail Landgraf, "GILGAL TO GOLGOTHA," The IN SEASON Lifestyle, September 8, 2022, https://theinseasonlifestyle.com/gilgal-to-golgotha/.
2. John Donovan, "The Secrets and Science Behind Starling Murmuration," *HowStuffWorks*, March 30, 2021, https://animals.howstuffworks.com/birds/starling-murmurations.htm.
3. B. L. Karihaloo, K. Zhang, and J. Wang, "Honeybee Combs: How the Circular Cells Transform Into Rounded Hexagons," *Journal of the Royal Society Interface* 10, no. 86 (July 18, 2013): 20130299, https://doi.org/10.1098/rsif.2013.0299.
4. Kerry Hasenbalg, "Longing for the Promised Land," Kerry Hasenbalg, May 8, 2020, https://kerryhasenbalg.com/2020/05/08/longing-for-the-promised-land/.

CHAPTER 12: ABIDE

1. Wikipedia contributors, "Nile," Wikipedia, November 2, 2024, https://en.wikipedia.org/wiki/Nile.
2. "Shalom, 'Peace,' Strong's H7965," A Little Perspective, January 1, 2001, https://alittleperspective.com/shalom-peace-strongs-h7965/.
3. Trent, "Shabbat Shalom," Hebrew Word Pics, January 9, 2022, https://www.hebrewwordpics.com/explain-shabbat-shalom/.
4. Kerry Hasenbalg, "Wisdom of Wonder: Integrate," in *The Companion Guide to Your BECOMING* (Blue House Books, 2018), 50.

www.ingramcontent.com/pod-product-compliance
Ingram Content Group UK Ltd.
Pitfield, Milton Keynes, MK11 3LW, UK
UKHW020937170325
5021UKWH00039B/421

9 781736 546956